RAMBLINGS WITH RUTH

to Joan,

May blessings
Love, Joy, Peace

Sam Schmitthenner

11-19-2009

Ramblings with Ruth

Sam Schmitthenner

Quiet Waters Publications
Bolivar, Missouri
2004

For information contact:
    Quiet Waters Publications
    P.O. Box 34, Bolivar MO 65613-0034.
    E-mail: QWP@usa.net.
For prices and order information visit:
    http://www.quietwaterspub.com

ISBN 1-931475-22-9
Library of Congress Control Number: 2003115017

CONTENTS

Foreword 9

Acknowledgments 11

Chapter 1
The End and the Beginning 15

Chapter 2
A Pleasant Ramble Around Priest's Walk, Delight in
Dancing, and Meeting Fear in the Fog......................27

Chapter 3
Clambering around Pillar Rocks and Hiking toward
Vembadi Peak...39

Chapter 4
Walks Around Pella, Bella Sylva, and Gettysburg...................49

Chapter 5
Walking with Ruth Again at Lake Geneva,
Chambersburg, and Bella Sylva................................65

Chapter 6
Married Ramblings at Bella Sylva, Karthaus, and
Gettysburg 77

Chapter 7
Ramblings in India around Peddapuram and Kodaikanal.....83

Chapter 8
Family Walks During our Yeleswaram Years 93

Chapter 9
Visiting Basrah, Children's First Bella Sylva Ramblings,
and Hartford..111

Chapter 10
Adventures around Narasaraopet and Kotapakonda,
Enjoying Priest's Walk Again, Kondaveedu, and Kodai
Hiking Club...115

Chapter 11
Hunting, Walking and Working with Ruth in the
Nallamalais, Narasaraopet, Palnad, and Krishna Valley.......137

Chapter 12
Ramblings in Switzerland, Germany, and once again to
Mehoopany Creek..151

Chapter 13
Walking by the Canal at Bhimavaram, Kodai Vacation
Hikes, from Berijam to Vembadi Peak, and Safaris.............155

Chapter 14
A Water Ramble on Colleru Lakes, a New Home in
Guntur, and Kodai Graduation 167

Chapter 15
Journeys through East Asia, Maui, Tucson to
Pennsylvania. Then back to India and Vadarevu on the
Bay of Bengal..175

Chapter 16
Cruising Down to Tope, and Meeting the Deity of
Vellagavi 181

Chapter 17
A Ramble of Praise to Kondaveedu and Serious Hikes to
Kukkal and Vanderavoo 191

Chapter 18
Walking With Those who Suffered in villages hit by
Cyclone, Meeting Mother Teresa and Leaving India............203

Chapter 19
Back in the States: Hana, Bella Sylva, New Jersey, and
New England..211

Chapter 20
Allegheny Walks and Climbs Around Claysburg 217

Chapter 21
Retirement Rambles around Pennsdale, Bella Sylva, and
Tucson..237

Chapter 22
Walking through Divine Providence—Where All Nature
Sings—and Savoring Heavenly Hana 251

Chapter 23
Joyful Celebration and Last Gentle Rambles.........................269

Chapter 24
The Story of Ruth Who Would Not Leave Us 275

Chapter 25
Ruth's Walk Into Glory 281

Epilogue
My Memorial Pilgrimage to Share Grief, Hope, and
Purpose...285

FOREWORD

DR. PAUL WIEBE FORMER STUDENT AND PRINCIPAL OF
KODAIKANAL INTERNATIONAL SCHOOL

To ramble is to walk at leisure, to follow a course with many turns, to roam for pleasure, to walk without a definite objective in mind. And *Ramblings with Ruth* is all of these.

We walk in the pages that follow across hillsides and valleys, into temples and bazaars of Tamilnadu and Andhra Pradesh, India, along scenic valley and forest trails in the backwoods of Pennsylvania. We enjoy images of the truly spectacular alongside images of the commonplace. We amble into places with names like Peddapuram, Narasaraopet, and Gundlabrahmeswaram in India, and into places with names like Pella, Tucson, Hana Maui and Claysburg in America.

We glimpse in the pages below the trials and great satisfactions of missionary learning and service in India through first hand accounts of travels as well as administrative dilemmas, blunders as well as successes, responses in the aftermath of great storms as well as encounters with persons like Mother Teresa. We glimpse in what we read what it means to "do justice, love mercy and walk humbly" in settings of wonderful beauty and varying persisting religious faith and practice.

But as we meander with Sam and Ruth - particularly as we walk with them through the joys of their teenage years in boarding school in South India, their questions of each other later on, their courtship, their joys and squabbles in marriage and the rearing of children, and, finally, Ruth's passage first into the "the valley of the shadow of death," then—as Sam tells it, "her walk into glory"—we gain deep understandings also of how two lives are shaped, then come together in the practical realities as well as the lasting mysteries of a truly meaningful marriage.

How many "rambles" make up a lifetime? A marriage? How many and which bits and pieces of life must be put alongside each other before lasting forms emerge?

Answers on these questions must vary of course, for no individual and no relationship is like any other.

But questions and answers at such levels, fascinating as they are, are less interesting than understandings of that which endures. And in his *Ramblings* Sam brings us back to this understanding as well.

Cups of tea were important in ritual as well as refreshment for Sam and Ruth along the way. So were songs and stories. So were friendships and family, the supports of communities, Sam's and Ruth's willingness to look beyond themselves, their willingness always to learn from the natural world as they returned time and again to familiar places. Important also were the meanings given to life in God's holy scriptures, particularly how these teach of the "endurance" always of faith, hope and love.

Sam's ramblings with Ruth have ended, now that she's gone. Were they ever there?

Yes indeed! And so they remain, and will always remain. In stories. And in a collection of stories. And in the lessons these stories together teach us all of what life can be about, in spirit and in truth.

ACKNOWLEDGMENTS

I have been a storyteller for most of my life, but never attempted to write my stories down. In 1997 I went to India after the death of my wife, Ruth, to revisit the places where we had lived and worked. While staying at Kodaikanal, where we had first met in school, I went on several favorite hikes and wrote down my memories of hiking to those places with Ruth. Dr. Paul Wiebe, the principal of Kodaikanal International School, and old friends and staff members Bob Granner and Betty Swavely (who had been a class mate of Ruth and me in high school), read these stories, made suggestions and greatly encouraged me to continue writing. Now and then I would pen another story or chapter in a lined note book. My hosts, Jerty and Rocky Nichol were most gracious making me feel at home during this period of grieving. How thankful I am for my Kodaikanal friends!

A very special thanks goes to Joyce De Bruin Dunham who was Ruth's roommate during high school in Kodaikanal and in Central College, Pella, Iowa. Joyce kept a daily diary of those years and had details, dates, weather, and stories from Ruth's side of our times together. Joyce was most helpful and generous in sharing this information with me.

After a break of a few months, during which time I courted and married Barbara Kolumban, I took up the task again in earnest. By 1999 I had finished the first draft. This was edited and typed up by my wife Barbara's sister, Jean Bentzel. Then I went to India again for six months. In Kodaikanal a professional writer, Philip Gross, read through the book and helped me rewrite the first chapter, solve problems of sequence, and suggested other changes. He was most helpful.

Returning to Gettysburg I acquired and learned how to use a new computer and then rewrote most of the chapters, adding some new ones. My proofreader, Roberta Trent, was most helpful and pointed out discrepancies and duplications and helped with sequence and grammar.

My test readers were my friends Dr. Paul Wiebe, recently retired principal of Kodaikanal School, Dr. Robert Frickenburg of the University of Wisconsin who helped me with historic materials and tried to find a publisher for me. Both of them being old "India hands" and Kodaikanal School alumni appreciated my book and have been most encouraging. Needing readers who had no grounding in Indian experience or background I was pleased to find Becky Brown, a Librarian and Marie Crouse, members of our church, who read through the book and asked for clarifications of terms and matters which I had taken for granted. I needed and was most grateful for their input. Robert Blezard, professional writer and editor read through the first part of my manuscript and spent an afternoon giving me much guidance about effective writing. I wish I had met and received instruction and guidance from him before I ever began this project.

One day while talking to my neighbor, John Fletcher, about my experiences with Mother Teresa, he insisted I should include that story in the book, even though I said "the book is finished." How thankful I am to him for making this a more meaningful book

I am grateful to Dr. Paul Wiebe for graciously agreeing to write the forward to the book. My children Bill, Hans, and Chris have read the book, helped me with their personal memories of events, editing and straightened me out on family matters. Peter, my youngest, helped me proof read the whole work after revision and with some of the historical data. My friend Dr. Ben Johnson, Kodai alumnus, a physics teacher who after retirement taught in Kodai School, helped me with pictures and maps, as did my son Peter. John Boyer, geographer and cartographer of Virginia Tech carefully put the maps in the final form. I am thankful to Dr. Vadrevu Krishna Prasad, a Telugu professor at Ohio State University for helping me with botanical names of trees in India, and to Pippa Mukerjee for helping me with names of flowers in Kodaikanal.

Finding a publisher took almost as long as did the writing of this book. To my joy I was guided by some friends to Quiet Waters Publications, Bolivar, Missouri. Stephen Trobisch received and read the entire work and then wrote the letter of acceptance I had been waiting for. He has guided me to make yet another revision, but in a way that was encouraging, wise, and helpful.

The cover picture of Mt. Perumal with Kodaikanal Lake in the foreground was taken in 1978 by Vaughn Ver Steegt of Janesville, Iowa, when he came to minister to the youth of the Lutheran Churches in India and the students of Kodaikanal School with the Lutheran Youth Encounter Team called "Rainbow of Promise." This picture has recently become very popular and is the symbol picture for a Kodaikanal School Alumni Reunion web site. I am most grateful to Vaughn for permission to use this photo. We have always had a copy hanging in our home and one adorns the Ver Steegt home in Iowa.

Thinking of all these helpful people and loved ones I realize I could never have done this alone and I thank God for my friends and their many ways of helping me to be more creative, expressive, and fruitful. For me there is no doubt that "It takes a village" to produce a book.

Finally, I am most grateful to my present wife Barbara who for the five years of our marriage has been putting up with me writing this book about my life with my first wife, Ruth. Not many women could tolerate that! Barbara has been assured by my elder brother, Jerry, that my next work should certainly be "Blessings with Barbara." She is a constant blessing to me and to all who know her. I call her "B.B." meaning Beloved Barbara.

CHAPTER 1

THE END AND THE BEGINNING

Bella Sylva Cemetery graces a knoll on a high ridge in the Endless Mountains of northeast Pennsylvania, four miles from the village of Lopez, in Sullivan County. Wild cherry trees, blueberry shrubs, and Juneberry bushes border this small country cemetery. In the evening deer come to graze on the abundant native grass and wild flowers of this hallowed ground marked with crosses. A large carved cherry wood sign by the road names this old place of burial. It is here that Ruth and I had decided many years previously to be buried in this beautiful and quiet spot near my ancestral home, under a shared stone that would express our mutual faith, life work, and history.

On May 31, 1996, I arrived at the Bella Sylva cemetery for the burial of my beloved wife, Ruth. As I glanced around and saw so many of the family and Bella Sylva neighbors gathered, my eyes filled with tears of joy and love. We took our time greeting and hugging each other and quietly shared memories of Ruth, expressing what she had meant to us.

With me were my oldest son Bill, daughter Christine, and Ruth's mother, Christina. Busy placing pine and spruce branches as symbols of everlasting life into the grave were our grandsons, Joseph and Davy, with their parents, our son Hans and his wife Joan, and our grand-daughter, Hillary, with her dad, our youngest child, Peter and his wife, Pam. Their enthusiasm and focus helped them to understand and share in the meaning of what was happening. Needing to take part in this activity with them, I called out, "Hey Joey, Davy, Hillary, save some of the pines and all of the wild flowers to put on top of the casket after it is lowered into the grave."

"OK grandpa, we will!" they said.

"Sam, you and Ruth have been such a large part of my life. What a blessing to have had a big sister like her!" said Chuck, Ruth's brother, as I approached him and his mother, Christina. This triggered memories of the many visits our family had experienced with them in Basrah, Iraq, and later in Tucson, Arizona, where Ruth's parents had retired. I remembered family times with Chuck and his wife Char and their children in Bombay, Kodaikanal, and Madurai in India, as well as happy visits with them during the years they had lived in Providence, Rhode Island and Rochester, New York. Chuck was more than a brother-in-law. His close friendship, his scholarly knowledge of Indian history, culture and lore, and his loving care of our children—as 'Uncle Chuck' and 'Aunt Char' provided a home while our children they were in college—had bonded us together. His presence at the graveside brought me comfort and peace and even more than the usual joy he always radiated.

Christina, Chuck's mother, calmly took everything in her stride. At age 96 she was accustomed to dealing with the death of loved ones. Her three brothers and two of her sisters had passed away, and her husband, George, had died in January 1990. She had lived with Ruth and me right up until the end, giving much comfort and help during the final months of struggle. Now, with deep faith, she faced the sorrow of losing her only daughter. Yet she watched her great grandchildren with delight as they readied the grave for Ruth's burial.

My sister, Molly, my brothers, Jerry and Fritz and their wives and children came to hug me. Having them all together here I was reminded of the adventures we had shared as children in our homes at Peddapuram, Yeleswaram, and Kodaikanal, India. As adults we had been with each other for special events and vacations at Bella Sylva, our mountain home just two miles away. I remembered many hiking trips that Ruth and I had taken in all those places; we called them *rambles*.

As I hugged Shurlee, Jerry's wife, I was shaken. "Shurlee, your being here means more to me than anything else. It's like having dozens of my best friends here," I whispered as I hugged her. Shurlee had been suffering from cancer for a long time and I knew she soon would be joining Ruth. What a tremendous effort she and Jerry had made to be with me at this service of burial!

* * *

"I called to the Lord in my distress and the Lord answered me setting me free ... Open for me the gates of righteousness; I will enter them ..." With these words from Psalm 118, Pastor George Doran began the simple and brief Lutheran liturgy for burial. This hope-filled service gives strong witness to how Christ gives triumph over death. After prayers and scripture my sons and nephews, the pallbearers, let the coffin down into the evergreen-lined grave with ropes. Together we said the Apostles' Creed, ending with the affirmation of faith, "I believe in the resurrection of the body and the life everlasting."

Then Pastor George pronounced the committal, "In sure and certain hope of the resurrection to eternal life through our Lord Jesus Christ we commend to almighty God our sister, Ruth, and we commit her body to the ground, earth to earth, ashes to ashes, and dust to dust."

After joining in the Lord's Prayer and receiving the blessing, my grandchildren and others threw the remaining evergreen boughs onto the casket and scattered wildflowers on top. Following an old German practice, still faithfully observed by Lutheran churches in India, I tossed three handfuls of dirt into the grave, saying, "In the name of the Father, and of the Son and of the Holy Spirit." Others then followed sharing in this act of farewell and closure. Even though I felt blessed with joy and belief that Ruth was with the Lord she had served faithfully, I was filled with a sense of loss. I had loved this wonderful woman for 54 years.

The wildflowers covering the casket brought a further flood of memories. Ruth and I had delighted in gathering and viewing wild-flowers on our rambles during our high school days in Kodaikanal, India, and then in many places throughout our life together. Wild roses in Gundar Valley; lavender rock orchids from rocky hillsides near Kodai with which I made corsages and bouquets for her; red rhododendrons from Upper Bear Shola Stream decorating our High School Valentine's dance; the high grasslands of Kodaikanal blooming with Easter lilies, bluebells, Scotch broom and butter-cups; the desert blooming after spring rains in Arizona, when we visited Christina and George; and the flowering Juneberry and white, violet, and yellow violets in the spring at Bella Sylva—had filled us with joy and wonder. On our many rambles in beautiful and diverse places, flowers had been part of the experience that had brought us happiness as our love blossomed.

Men took turns shoveling dirt into the grave until it was filled. Tears flowed as I watched the dirt fall on pine branches and flowers, the earth mingling with beauty to begin reclaiming the pines, the flowers, the casket and Ruth's body.

Standing at Bella Sylva cemetery, I recalled our first ramble together to Pambar Falls in Kodaikanal, though it had happened in 1942, fifty-four years before. I first became smitten with Ruth when we were in tenth grade at Kodaikanal School in the hills of South India. Until then she was just one of the pesky girls of our class. She had a ready beaming smile, laughed a lot, and enjoyed a good story. In grade school we had named her "Goofy."

Ruth and I had started together in second grade in 1935 and we graduated together in 1944. Kodai School—located in the Palni Hills of Tamilnadu, South India—had been established for missionary children in 1901 by Margaret Eddy, a missionary of the American Board of Missions. In Kodaikanal, about 7000 feet above sea level and with one of the best climates in the world, children could receive a quality American education. Mrs. Eddy had set high standards and established great traditions for the school. Eventually, eleven other mission boards joined the American Board of Missions of the Congregational Church to administer, fund, recruit well-trained teachers, and send their children to this school. Kodaikanal School became a pioneer ecumenical adventure that led to closer understanding and cooperation, and demonstrated how various mission denominations could work together, not only for the good of their children, but also for an effective witness to their oneness in Christ. The 150 missionary children at Kodai School came there from all over India, Burma (Myanmar), Ceylon (Sri Lanka), Thailand, and the Middle East.

Ruth was the oldest child of Christina Scholten and George Gosselink, missionaries of the Reformed Church in America, stationed in Basrah, Iraq. Every year in January she and other Arabian Mission kids journeyed to India by boat. The voyage from Basrah to Bombay by the British India Line mail boat often took ten days, stopping along the way at Kuwait, Bahrain, and Muscat, Oman where other children from the Arabian Mission bound for Kodai would join them. From Bombay to Kodaikanal, via Madras, took another three days by train and bus. Ruth's parents and younger brothers, Jim and Chuck, would usually come for their vacation from Basrah sometime in July, rent a cottage near the school for 6 weeks, and take her out of boarding. Each mission had from three to twelve cottages for vacationing families in this hill station. As July was the hottest summer month in Iraq, it was a good time for the Gosselinks to be in the cool Kodai hills. In late August Ruth's parents would put her back into boarding and return to Iraq. Ruth would return to Basrah for the long vacation which lasted from mid-October until mid-January. Her brother Jim joined her at Kodai School in 1938 and Chuck in 1942.

My parents, August Frederick Schmitthenner and Marian Eyster, were missionaries in Peddapuram and subsequently in Yeleswaram—named as Eleswaram on many maps—in East Godavari District of Andhra Pradesh, India. Recruited in 1921 as single missionaries to serve the Andhra Evangelical Lutheran Church, they met aboard ship after embarking from Liverpool. After language study they were married in November 1922. My oldest brother Jerry was born in September 1923; Fritz was born in April 1926. I came along in February 1928.

When we were of school age my brothers and I would travel from Rajahmundry Station to Kodaikanal by train with a dozen or more Kodai kids. Fritz and Julia Coleman, the older high school youth of our mission, were our chaperones. Mother always made a huge pound cake for our train journey, admonishing Jerry that it was to last for two days. Jerry was reliable, but not when it came to cake. We would finish it the first evening, then spend the next day trying out all kinds of Indian snack food, which Kodai kids still refer to as I.J.—Indian junk. I enjoyed going to boarding school because my brothers and all my best friends were there.

As high school began I respected Ruth as a pianist who practiced long hours and often played for church services. She was a good student, but also very direct. If she disagreed with a teacher she'd say so and give reasons.

Once, Mr. Musil, our Latin teacher, had become very angry when Ruth disagreed with the way he had criticized her translation of a sentence. A short, agitated, thin person with a quick temper, Mr. Musil had been living under considerable stress. While visiting India from his native Czechoslovakia, he had been stranded by the outbreak of World War II. Our principal, Mr. Carl W. Phelps had found him languishing in an internment camp and had managed to recruit him to be a teacher for Kodaikanal School. This involved getting permission from the British authorities on the condition that he could not leave the school grounds. Every evening Mr. Musil would pace around the perimeter of the school property like a tiger in a cage. The whole class was aghast when Ruth calmly challenged him. He stood over her desk scolding her. Then, as we held our breath she asked another probing question that so infuriated him he seemed ready to strike her. Some of the class couldn't bear to look, so they turned left to take in the view from our second story classroom. Rows of windows with teak wood framework painted dark green gave us a picture view of the boy's dorm— Boy's Block—below, a magnificent old eucalyptus tree, from which a rope swing was hanging, a glimpse of the lake below and hills to the West. But the calm beauty of the scene was spoiled by the shrill angry voice of our teacher, the linguist who knew 10 languages, who could not abide the disrespect of this rude, questioning girl. Mercifully, an upperclassman at that moment rang the old school bell just outside our classroom, on the veranda overlooking the quadrangle. The period was over; Ruth was saved by the bell. Mr. Musil stalked out of the class with an almost purple face. The girls gathered around Ruth amazed to see that she was unruffled. In the back of the classroom, some of us boys got together to make a pact that we would protect Ruth and beat up Mr. Musil if he ever tried to hit her. Little did I realize then that Ruth's critical mind, complete frankness, and probing questions would sometimes prick my ego and also strain my patience to the breaking point.

One day, at the beginning of our sophomore year, the high school was rehearsing for the Spring Concert. We always had features from different nations in our programs. From the wings of the stage looking past the bunched up navy blue curtains, I watched Ruth and her friends dancing the Irish Jig, wearing knee-length shamrock-green outfits. They danced beautifully. Something about Ruth, her joy and energy in dancing, her build, and hazel eyes, and the twirling of the green skirt awakened new and powerful feelings in me. Wow!

Shortly thereafter I asked her to walk with me around the lake. She calmly looked at me with her hazel eyes, smiled, and said, "Yes!" On Sunday nights, after Vespers Service, carefully chaperoned walks around Kodai Lake had been a tradition that made it possible for Kodai kids to date and get to know each other better. That's the way most Kodai romances started. On this lovely walk of about three miles, Principal "Papa" Phelps kept us moving right along zigzagging back and forth with his five-cell flashlight, making sure there was no hugging, kissing, or falling behind. We could hold hands, or the girl, when invited to, would hold the elbow of her date. That was a big deal! The boy would come back to the dorm and announce, "Tonight, we hooked up!"

In July 1942 Ruth's mother, Christina, came to Kodai from Basrah, and took Ruth, Jim, and Chuck out of boarding. Christina was good to me. The first time I brought Ruth home from a Saturday evening social, she invited me in and offered me a cup of coffee with Basrah dates, the finest in the world. I had never touched coffee before—being the shortest in the class I wanted nothing to stunt my growth. That night, however, I drank two cups so that I could have more time with Ruth. The effect that the coffee had on my bladder later that night was startling, something I hadn't experienced before.

One Saturday morning I asked Ruth, in the presence of her mother, if she would go with me to the top of *Pambar* (Snake) Falls, quite a jungly ramble, just two miles from Kodai Town. I assured them that I'd done it many times with my brother Fritz, and that we could do it safely. Ruth said yes. Her mother said, "All right." She trusted us. Anyway, she knew and trusted Ruth and her natural reserve.

We packed a lunch and off we went. Stopping at the school, I got forty feet of rope and changed shoes. On the way to Pambar Falls we walked past St. Peter's Anglican Church, up St. Mary's Road, to Fern Cliff, one of our Lutheran mission cottages, where my family had stayed every summer from 1939 to 1944. From there we took in the view of the plains 6000 feet below. It was a clear, crisp, breezy day. We walked past the monastery, where Fritz and I used to steal pears, through an avenue of huge eucalyptus trees, past St. Mary's Church, and the La Providence Franciscan Monastery, and finally down to Levinge Stream.

We followed the stream down to the first waterfall. One side of the waterfall was dry, so we climbed down backwards. Knowing the way, I descended first and helped Ruth with her footholds. We passed magnificent old boulders that had split off from the cliffs. Some of the huge rocks were covered with moss, leaf mold, ferns, vines, and flowers of many kinds. One vine had thick waxy latex-filled leaves with pink and red flowers that smelled like cinnamon. There were wild begonias, orchids, red trumpet flowers, and "jack-in-the-pulpits." Even great trees grew on some of the rocks, sending roots down around the boulders to find soil and water. I said, "Ruth, this is God's rock garden, with plants more abundant and beautiful than any gardener could raise." She liked that.

Black monkeys began to call, "uhg-ha, uhg-ha, uhg-ha," working up to a high crescendo, and the Malabar whistling schoolboy thrush whistled its tunes, which I tried to imitate. Magnificent butterflies were everywhere, and nine small blue butterflies were happily crowded together on a jackal turd. Delicate small flowers grew in the seepage-soaked moss at the stream's edge.

We came to a ledge by the side of a waterfall where we would need the rope. I said, "Ruth, we can go back now, the way we came, or use this rope and go all the way to the big falls and then home from the falls by way of Priest's Walk. It's a twelve foot drop to the next ledge, and very slippery." It looked wet and slimy and the ravine was pretty awesome below. Ruth had enjoyed the adventure to this point, and had been trusting and such a good sport.

"We'll go all the way to the falls," she said, "it's been great so far!"

I put the rope over a tree branch, tied the two ends together, and said, "Wait 'till I get to the bottom, then I'll hold the rope and help you." I climbed down and steadied the rope for her, and down she came. As I helped her she came naturally into my arms. It was the right time to keep her there for a long hug and a kiss, our first! I could tell that she enjoyed that. Then I untied the rope and jerked it off the branch since we'd probably need it later.

Down we went deep into the ravine. What beautiful old trees we passed! Because of the cliffs and ledges, no one has been able to cut these ancient great trees in this lush *shola* (rain forest). The rapids, potholes, sparkling small falls, many varieties of fern, magnificent trees, rock gardens; and rock ledges made this a splendid adventure.

Finally we came out on the ledge called The Jump Off. The more than 600-foot falls initially go down at an angle in several deep crevasses. We sat close together in the noonday sun, drinking in the view of *Periakulam* town on the plains directly below the falls. Eagle's Cliff dominated the southwest side of the falls, and to our left was the Coolie Ghat zigzagging down from Fisher's Seat—the last ridge in Kodai—to the mango orchards near Tope, 6000 feet below us.

The word *ghat* has several meanings. It can mean steps ascending from a river or a holy bathing place by a Hindu temple. It can also mean a range of mountains, like the Eastern Ghats and Western Ghats which border both sides of the Deccan Plateau in South India. A mountain road that ascends the escarpment with many twists and turns is called a *ghat* road. The Coolie Ghat is the old steep nine-mile trail by which the first residents came to Kodaikanal by pony or on foot, or by being carried by four porters in a blanket tied to poles. All building materials and supplies were carried by the human head load, pony, or pack oxen to Kodai up the Coolie Ghat until the Law's Ghat Road was opened in the 1920s. Now that 29 mile motor road going down the side of the mountain is simply called The Ghat Road by Kodai residents.

As Ruth and I sat watching the water flow over the edge of the falls, enjoying the spray dampened wind blowing up the cliffs and the panoramic view, I thought, "What a place, and what a person to be with!" We hugged and kissed for a while. There we were, the two of us alone like Adam and Eve, in the midst of God's rock garden. But we were not naked, and the serpent did not appear. How innocent we were! We were privileged to have a relationship based on affection and trust: the trust of our parents and trust in each other.

"Hey, I'm hungry. Let's eat," said Ruth in her practical way, bringing us back to reality.

After a good lunch it was time to start for home. We began our climb up the steep hillside toward Priest's Walk, holding on to clumps of grass. At one point we came upon an animal trail going northeast beneath Priest's Walk. Below it a steep slope slanted down to the same cliff from which Snake Falls cascaded. I said, "Ruth, Fritz and I have been over this trail. If you like we'll go just a little way until we come to that wide ledge and boulder." She was game, so we took the trail leaning in toward Priest's Walk, away from the precipitous slope. After reaching the boulder we retraced our steps and resumed climbing on the original trail. Next came a surprise: where the path crossed a stream it had been partly washed away. So I tied the rope to a tree and around my waist and made my way across the gap clinging to tree roots and jumping the last five feet. I tied my end of the rope to another tree. Then Ruth made it across holding on to the rope and then to me. Another great opportunity! We had to leave the rope there. Finally we came to Priest's Walk.

Only then did we realize that our clothes were streaked with black mud and slime from our wet, sliding, rainforest adventure. Fortunately we did not meet anyone who knew us on the Kodai streets. Ruth's mother took our messy appearance with good grace. Ruth told her about the ramble, omitting the cliff trail detail.

It was time for tea, quite a ceremony in Ruth's home. Christina preheated the pot, used loose tealeaves, poured milk, and put sugar into the cup first, then the tea after it had steeped in the pot covered by a cosy. She served it with biscuits and dates, of course. What a great and refreshing way to end the first and best ramble we ever had in our Kodai High School days. All good rambles should end with tea!

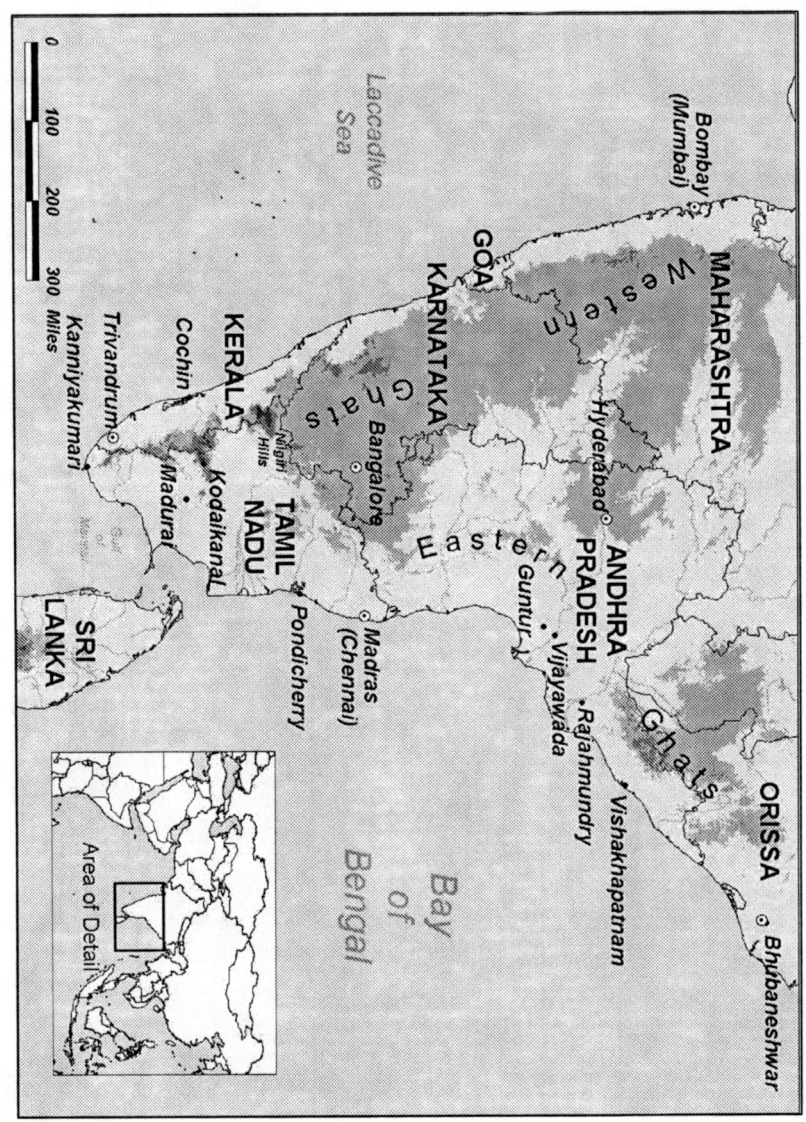

Map of South India

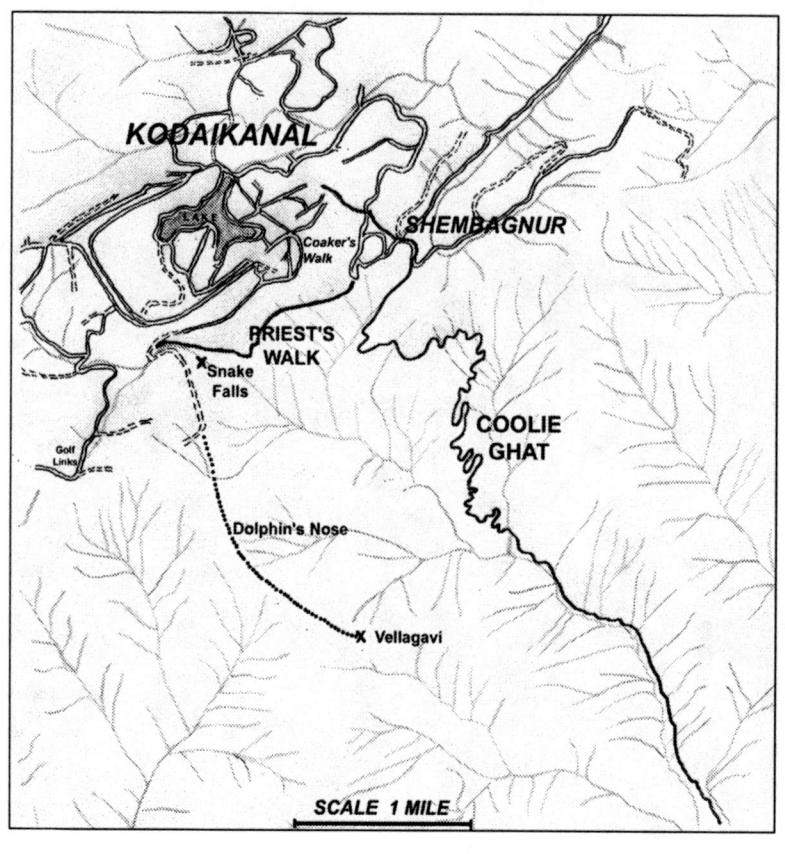

Map of Kodaikanal with trails to Priest's Walk, Snake Falls, Coolie Ghat, and Vellagavi

CHAPTER 2

A PLEASANT RAMBLE AROUND PRIEST'S WALK, DELIGHT IN DANCING, AND MEETING FEAR IN THE FOG

Priest's Walk, an old pony trail, ascends more than 1000 feet from Jesuit Sacred Heart College at Shembaganur to the Jesuit monastery near St. Mary's Church at a high point of Kodaikanal. The upper part of Priest's Walk twists its way through Pambar Shola. In this lush and rugged shola on the edge of the escarpment, huge old boulders and massive slabs of granite-like charnockite, fallen from the cliffs, lie on both sides of the path. Through the years a variety of ferns, vines, and hardwood trees have taken root in crevasses and even on top of leaf-mold covered rocks. The animals best suited to this forest are barking deer, jackal, monkeys, black Nilgiri langur, brown langur, chipmunk, flying squirrel, and the very large and striking, multi-colored, Malabar squirrel. Jungle fowl, black Nilgiri wood pigeon, the whistling schoolboy thrush and the red-cheeked bull bull are among the many species of birds.

We looked forward to going around Priest's Walk! The year before we had followed Pambar Stream to the Jump Off. Now we would view the shola and falls from above. We were in eleventh grade. Ruth was still out of boarding. Her mother, Christina, had stayed over the winter in Kodai because German submarines had made Persian Gulf travel unsafe. Christina gave us permission to go and packed our lunch for this "safe," on-the-trail hike.

I thought it best to walk first to the top of St. Mary's Road, then descend the trail from there. Climbing up past St. Peter's Church we again visited my family's summer cottage, Fern Cliff. I talked with our gardener and looked around enjoying my favorite view.

On the terrace of the Jesuits' property next to ours was a large stone sculpture of Christ on the cross looking out over the valleys and plains below. Next we climbed the steps to St. Mary's Church, which was built at the edge of the cliff. Looking inside we saw several worshipers adoring Christ on the Cross and St. Mary in this place of quiet beauty. Then, walking past La Providence Monastery, we entered Priest's Walk opposite Pambar House, the former residence of the chief regional British officer.

We noted many wild flowering shrubs and vines along the path. The red trumpet flower was the most beautiful. We came upon a miniature waterfall bordered by delicate fern and wild begonias wet with spray, and masses of small delicate yellow lady slippers. Again we talked about God being a great gardener. Next we passed a cliff on the left side that was down the steep slope below St. Mary's Church. Perched like birds on some of the ledges were white banana orchids with roots looking like bunches of hill bananas. I simply had to get some for Ruth and tried climbing up to the ledges. My romantic urge soon gave way to my need to survive, so I carefully aborted the ascent. Ruth's only comment was typical of her frankness, "I thought you should have turned back sooner."

Further along the trail we found a small dainty kind of fern growing out of the shaded most bank. We called it "almond fern" because that's what it smelled like when crushed. To me, it brought back memories of smelling tramped-on hay fern in Pennsylvania.

We came to the point where the trail goes along the edge of the cliff above Pambar Falls. Holding on to a blooming rhododendron tree, we peered over the edge to view Pambar Falls and hear the roar of falling water. The deep undulating "uhg-ha, uhg-ha" call of the Nilgiri langur came to our ears. We saw two of the large black monkeys noisily jumping around the crown of the forest. The rain forest treetops looked like broccoli. We caught our breath and stood looking at each other, very happy to be experiencing this together. We shared memories of our first adventure, the ramble to the top of Pambar Falls. Then we walked hand in hand down several switchbacks and sat for a while on a ledge looking out over the plains. Over to the southwest we could see Eagles' Cliff and Dolphin's Nose, and, below that, the path descending to Vellagavi, the little village older than Kodai, cradled in the lower ridges of the Palnis. We hoped that someday we would hike there together. Eating the lunch Ruth's mother had prepared for us we talked about school, our friends, and the upcoming Valentine's dance. Ruth had promised to be my date! For a time we sat side by side treasuring the closeness, the beauty of the hills and the day, and what we meant to each other. Then it was time to be off.

From further down the path we looked up to "Fern Cliff" and the Christ on the cross statue. I told Ruth how my brother Fritz and I had roved all over this slope working on our "A" level biology project: collecting, identifying and pressing 100 varieties of wild flowers. These we had found along Priest's Walk, in Pambar Shola, along the trail to Vellagavi, in Gundar Valley, and on what we called "bike-hikes" to Berijam Lake, and Vanderavu. We had also collected fourteen varieties of fern in Pambar Valley, along Priest's Walk and below the aptly named "Fern Cliff." These included bracken, tree fern, a small lacy fern we used in making corsages, almond fern, silver fern, an irregular fern, ferns with parallel branches, one with irregular pattern, and another species with alternate branches. Along the trail we found lemon grass and many varieties of ferns and flowers. Two flowering shrubs were ubiquitous, blooming abundantly on the open grassland slopes after we left the shola: the wild indigo flora with yellow stamens, and hypericum, the yellow St. John's wort. For me, finding and pressing flowers had been a passing interest, but for Fritz it would become a lifelong passion. He became a Ph.D. botanist, and with his botanist wife, Alice, has identified and photographed hundreds of varieties of wild flowers in various countries.

Nearing a big rock, half way down the trail where there were several large eucalyptus trees, we looked up the slope again at Fern Cliff. I told Ruth how Fritz and I used to roll rocks down the slope. On weekends we'd invite our friends to stay with us and, after dinner would search the hillside for rocks to roll, sometimes using a crowbar to pry loose larger rocks. Watching Priest's Walk to make sure no one was on it, we would thrill to the spectacle of rocks rolling, smashing through bracken, sometimes bounding way up twenty feet or more into the air and then leaping over Priest's Walk to disappear over the cliffs below. What fun! I had hoped Ruth would catch my thrill for rock rolling, but she did not. In fact, she wanted to get away from the area quickly, wondering if there might not be "other fools up there ready to roll boulders down upon us!"

The final portion of the walk sloped gently through a eucalyptus shola of very large trees, some perhaps 90 years old. Here and there we could see sawpits where selectively cut logs three or more feet in diameter were being hand sawed laboriously into beams and boards. In several places men were burning charcoal. Mounds of eucalyptus wood cut from the branches were covered with clay and fired very slowly, giving off a creosote-like smell. In another spot, *eucy* leaves were being boiled and eucalyptus oil distilled. The strong aroma was enough to clear up a cold. This beautiful and productive forest was owned by the Jesuit Sacred Heart College, as were some pear orchards on the slope east of Shembaganur.

From Shembag we walked up the Ghat Road returning to Kodai, and there shared our adventure with Ruth's mother over cups of tea with dates and cookies.

Valentine's Dance plans were in the air and our class was in charge of the arrangements. We invited chaperones and planned the decorations, snacks, and musical selections. Ruth and I had danced together often, but never on a date.

Dancing had come to Kodai School sometime around 1939, about the same time World War II began in Europe. The first dances were held off campus and sponsored by the parents of students out of boarding because dancing was not yet allowed on the school grounds. Brother Jerry had attended one of the first dances on campus when he was a junior in 1940. French chalk had been liberally applied to the hardwood gym floor, and 78-rpm records carefully selected. He had taken his girlfriend, Connie Dudley, to the dance. Since Jerry was our role model, when he told us about dancing it occurred to Fritz and me that some day we also might enjoy this kind of sport.

In those days Kodaikanal School had only seven years of elementary education. The seventh year was called seventh-eight-grade. When Ruth and I were attending that class, one of our classmates, Nancy Hatch, arranged for us all to learn how to dance. Her mother, Emily, had been a dancer and actress on Broadway and was quite concerned about Nancy's social development. One afternoon Nancy invited everyone in the class to tea at her house. She informed us boys that we would be having dance lessons taught by her mother. At first we resisted. At age twelve we were not yet interested either in dancing or in girls. Nancy, however, persisted. The following Wednesday we found ourselves at Nancy's house.

Emily put on a 78-rpm foxtrot record, demonstrated the step, grabbed me as her partner, and away we went. She held me rather closely. I could hardly breathe and thought I'd die, but soon she traded me for another partner. What a relief! We got used to it, and soon were dancing with other girls, but holding them as far away as we could. Week after week we learned to waltz, foxtrot, polka, do the Lambeth Walk and the Virginia Reel.

Nancy was stylish. One day, back in sixth grade she had been showing off to the other girls a very full skirt she was wearing for the first time. She stood on her desk, twirled around fast, as the girls all "ooed" and "ahed" at the sight of her flying full skirt. We boys watched with studied indifference. As the skirt whirled at its highest and fullest our teacher, Miss Van Deusen, walked into the room. She blushed and was aghast! "Nancy, get down!"

At the end of the period she told the boys she wanted all of us to come over to her apartment for breakfast the next morning. The following day she would have the girls over. At breakfast she told us that boys were different from girls, that we should respect girls, and not stare at their legs or try to see their underwear. The next day during her session with the girls, after a good breakfast, she told them they shouldn't show off their legs and undies to the boys. We compared notes with the girls, finding that neither had learned anything new, and that Miss Van Deusen had been embarrassed about the whole thing. Maybe that was the first attempt in Kodai to impart sex education.

Miss Leila Van Deusen was probably the best teacher we had in grade school. She taught English so well that both Ruth and I claimed that we were fully prepared for college English by what she taught in Sixth grade. She made up grammar-based games and underlining exercises. We had contests between teams that greatly motivated us to learn. Later in our lives, Miss Van Deusen would be our neighbor and become like a member of our family.

* * *

After Ruth and I entered tenth grade, in 1942, we attended on-campus dances. Almost everyone came, with or without a date, and everyone danced with many different partners. Even if you took a special girl to the dance, you danced with her only for the first dance, the dance before intermission, the dance after the intermission, and the final two dances. You could also sit together with your special girl and have a snack during the intermission. The boys made it a policy to dance with every girl in the class at least once.

We held our partners at a respectable distance when we danced. We called this our NBC (no bodily contact) rule. Even when dancing to the song *Dancing Cheek to Cheek*, we did not dance cheek to cheek. But we did have a lot of fun together.

Decorating the gym for the Valentine's dance was a cooperative effort. We boys went into the hills to gather wild rhododendron blossoms. The girls would make hearts of the beautiful red blooms, and pin them to the navy blue gym drapes. For other seasons we gathered flowers from the many beautiful gardens in Kodai, bringing in the flowers on our bikes.

It was fun making our own corsages with the help of some of the parents and staff. We used delicate ferns and rosebuds, gardenias, or orchids. I learned to make good corsages and tried hard to find orchids, which Ruth particularly appreciated.

Once during a religious education class, our teacher, a staunch conservative Baptist, informed us that dancing was sinful. We had lessons about the evils of dancing and then a debate in the library along with the junior class. Our teacher was firm, "Christians should not take part in dancing because it is provocative and promotes lustfulness, and can certainly lead one into temptation. I don't think it is possible for a couple to talk about God or religion while dancing." So, at the next dance, we talked about religion with each of our dance partners, doing this deliberately to prove him wrong. Actually, that added to our fun. We got to know each other better as we shared our faith and beliefs while fox-trotting and waltzing.

The Valentine's dance was great! The hall looked beautiful, and so did Ruth. She wore a lovely evening dress, red with white design, and a corsage I had made of banana orchids. Our swing orchestra played a few numbers for the dance. Brother Fritz played the violin, Ruth the piano, I the flute, John Wilder the clarinet, Elinor Potee the drums and Dirk Muyskens the trombone. Someone played the trumpet. I remember playing *Smoke Gets in Your Eyes* and several other numbers just after the intermission. Then the record player replaced us so we could dance.

As we danced some of our favorite songs together Ruth softly sang the alto parts. She loved close harmony, and the Andrew Sisters were her favorites. Dancing the final waltz, I held Ruth a little closer than usual and thought, "Ruth is my dearest friend, and I hope some day to marry this precious girl." Of course, I didn't tell her of my thoughts. We were just fifteen.

By this time everyone knew I was smitten with Ruth. A notice appeared in the school newspaper, the *Highclerc Herald* after her first perm, "What goose has curled her feathers? And who, oh who, is Schmitt by them?" (The name Gosselink means, little goose). I was so embarrassed!

For several years the junior-senior boys dorm was at Jumisba, a half mile from the main campus. We held the first ever dorm dance there, inviting enough girls so there would be a girl for each Jumisba resident. That was great fun! After the last dance the housemother led us in evening prayers. We sang one of our favorite hymns, *Crossing the Bar*, with Ruth at the piano:

> Sunset and evening star
> And one clear call for me!
> And may there be no moaning of the bar
> When I put out to sea.
>
> For, though from out are borne of time and place
> The flood may bear me far,
> I hope to see my Pilot face to face
> When I have crossed the bar.

What a way to end a dance! Why was this song about death such a favorite of ours? We loved its harmony and peacefulness. We related to the words as we all had come to India by ship, leaving behind grandparents, aunts, and uncles on other shores to return to our friends in India, crossing the bar.

In the fall of that year, we had a most memorable dance during the monsoon season. As usual, we guys had on our Sunday best: suits, good shirts, ties, and Sunday black shoes. Just as the dance ended it began to pour! We took our dates back to Boyer Hall dorm by the covered walkway, said goodnight, and then went to the junior high dorm, Boys Block, by a covered walk. The rain did not let up. We could not get our good clothes wet. It was nearing midnight. What to do? Someone suggested, "Hey you guys, let's leave our clothes in some of the junior high boys' rooms and run home through the rain in our drawers!"

"Yes!" we replied. We stripped down to our briefs, hung up our clothes, and ran the half-mile to Jumisba barefoot through pouring rain, shouting and laughing. What a blast! The next day we wore old clothes to breakfast, then changed into our best in Boys Block and attended church dressed to dance.

Dancing with my favorite girl, Ruth, and other good friends, was a great part of Kodai life. Nancy and her mother were right. It was good that we learned to dance. It gave us a taste of romance and brought us closer to each of the girls.

* * *

Once Ruth's mother left for Basrah and Ruth went back into boarding we could not hike together, so we looked for ways to spend time together without chaperons or others around. The practice rooms in the rear of the gym were an ideal meeting place. Ruth would accompany me as I played the flute. Between practicing Dvorak's *Humoresque* and *Oh Danny Boy* we would take time to kiss. However, soon other music students suspected what was going on. They had various ways of disturbing us. When our music would stop, we'd hear loud steps coming toward our door. So we'd start playing again. Sometimes when we'd stop playing, everyone else would, too. The silence was quite intimidating. Occasionally there would be a face at the window—some nosy 5th or 6th grader.

After one such session I said to Ruth, "Why don't we meet tonight during study hall and go around Coaker's Walk?" At that time late in June, I was still out of boarding so could manage.

"That wouldn't work. I just can't sneak out of study hall," Ruth said. I suggested that she could leave at about 8 p.m. and go to the bathroom saying she wasn't feeling very well. Joyce DeBruin, her best friend, could explain that she'd gone back to the dorm and could take her books back for her. Meanwhile, we'd go around Coaker's Walk, enjoy viewing the jewel-like lights of Periyakulam on the plains, and have time alone. We'd return by 9 p.m. when she could join the girls going back to Boyer. The signal was to be a jackal howling. We thought it would be fun.

Promptly at 8 p.m. I stood beneath the Monkey-up tree and howled like a jackal. Ruth excused herself, and off we went through the little gate by Airlee cottage and past the English Club toward Coaker's. By the time we got to East House a dense fog had settled over the road. We talked and laughed, enjoying our adventure. Suddenly we heard rapid steps and the clicking of a cane coming right toward us—click, step, step—click, step, step. We froze in terror. Both of us knew! Out of the pea soup fog came Papa Phelps, our principal, just fifteen feet away. Being a perfect gentleman, he doffed his hat and said, "Good evening, people," rapidly walked past us, and was swallowed up by the fog. Then we remembered that his wife had been quite sick and was a patient at Van Allen Hospital above Coaker's Walk where he had been visiting her. Now we were doomed!

After his sudden appearance out of the mist there was no more laughter for Ruth or me that evening. We never got as far as Coaker's Walk, but just stood on the road in the fog speculating about how we would be scolded and punished. I knew I would be compounded after returning to boarding. To be compounded for a month was the ultimate punishment. You had to stay on the school grounds. That meant no going to the bazaar, no hikes, no walks around the lake! You couldn't even accept an invitation to go out to a friend's house. It meant being caged like Mr. Musil. Mr. Phelps had compounded me once before when I had gone on an unauthorized hike with in-boarder friends, while out-of-boarding. I had served the sentence after re-entering boarding.

Our evening had been ruined. As students, we were all but terminated! In deep despair we quickly returned to the campus. Ruth neatly joined the girls returning from study hall. The next day we waited for the Principal's summons. A day went by, then another, and another. "He's thinking up something monstrous!"

From then on we were on our best behavior. We studied harder, practiced our music carefully, and our deportment for the rest of the term was flawless. Papa never did call us in, nor mention our meeting to us. The anxiety we went through and the good works resulting from our penance were far greater than what compounding us would have achieved. I shall never forget those terrifying footsteps and the clicking of Papa's cane coming at us in the fog.

Mr. Phelps was a great principal. He was a teaching and coaching principal. If one of the teachers in the grades or high school fell sick, he would be the substitute teacher. He taught Trigonometry, and sometimes subbed for our Latin teacher. He was a Boston Red

Sox fan and coached us in baseball, his favorite sport. He was principal for the whole time my brothers, sister Molly and I studied in Kodai and carried the school through the difficult war years. He was also in charge of finance, the recruitment of staff, and, as counselor for high school students about college selection, he personally gave I.Q. and placement tests. He was also in charge of discipline. All through those years he taught us how to "play the game."

Ruth's first evening dress

Kodai "Andrew Sisters" – Ruth, Elinor, Audrey

Ruth's family: George, Christina, Ruth, Jim, and Chuck

Sam's Family: August Frederick, Marian, Jerry, Fritz, Sam, and Molly at "Fern Cliff," Kodai, 1941

CHAPTER 3

CLAMBERING AROUND PILLAR ROCKS AND HIKING TOWARD VEMBADI PEAK

Pillar Rocks is located three miles southwest of Kodaikanal, where the Ten-Mile Round dips down past the golf course to the edge of the escarpment. It is a scenic, rugged, and very challenging place. Four huge monolithic pillars rise up to 500 hundred feet from the steep sloping hillside presenting a spectacle that cannot be forgotten. The pillars are topped with scrubby trees draped with moss. It brings to mind the Biblical "rock" images of God:

"The Lord is my rock, and my fortress and my deliverer, my God, my rock in whom I take refuge." (Psalm 18) "Lead thou me to the rock that is higher than I." (Psalm 61)

A trail goes from the Ten-Mile Round road to the edge of the first and inner pillar that is accessible. It leads to a cleared area just before the pillars and crevasses begin. From there one path goes down to the Devil's Kitchen, where a steep trail branches off toward the bottom of the pillars. Another trail, going east, leads to the Pit, and a branch of that path enters the cliff area where the first pillar separates from the hillside, creating a very deep dark crevasse.

A bunch of boys in our class had a fascination with Pillar Rocks and often explored there on Saturdays or Sunday afternoons. We had found a new way to get down into the Pit, which involved squeezing between huge rocks that held up a giant slab above us. We explored the large cavern named the Devil's Kitchen. To enter it we had to climb down about sixteen feet using a pole or rope. Some previous expedition had wedged into place an old dried-out tree trunk. Climbing down the old tree we reached the floor of large roomy cavern, with a ceiling perhaps 60 feet above us. We explored the Kitchen. Opposite the entrance from where we had descended, we climbed up through the Chimney, which resembled a steeply sloping mine shaft, exiting near the top of one of the pillars. We discovered a tunnel crossing under the path at the top of the Kitchen. We explored very carefully, as several of the sinkholes and tunnels ended at the ceiling of the cavern.

One Good Friday afternoon five of us procured some thick clothes line rope from our house and went to Pillar Rocks to gather edible birds' nests. We had read in an encyclopedia that swift's nests were considered a delicacy in China, and that these were found in caves. The swifts build their nests by regurgitating a jelly-like substance onto the cliff side within a cave or crevasse. As the layers of jelly-like substance build up, the swifts use sticks, pine needles, and leaves to make an ordinary-looking nest. More jelly is put between each layer to give strength so that the nest stays in place on a sheer cliff. One of our teachers had informed us that swift's nests could be found at Pillar Rocks.

When we arrived at the crevasse between the first pillar and the main cliff, it was decided that one of us could be let down to gather birds' nests. Shining flashlights down into the abyss, we saw hundreds of nests on the cliff side, and noted there were ledges running along the cliff that a person could stand on while harvesting the nests. We had not thought to bring a bag. Dirk Muyskens said, "That's all right, we can stuff them in our shirts." Then, they all looked at me.

"Sam, you are by far the smallest and lightest one here. We can let you down on the rope to the ledges," Hank Moyer said.

"How do you know the rope is strong enough?" I mildly protested. So we tested it by having a tug of war. The rope broke. Then, after one of the guys tied a good knot we had another tug of war and it held. Having eliminated the one bad spot in the rope, they assured me it was safe. I put a loop under my arms, and they carefully lowered me down twenty or more feet until I came to the first ledge. I balanced on the six-inch wide ledge with the rope securely around me and proceeded to pick birds' nests. Many had eggs, which I put in the pocket of my shorts. I stuffed about fifteen nests into my shirt. "O.K., pull me up carefully—don't let the rock edge fray the rope!" I said.

Their pulling was jerky and uneven, and I began to sway out over the abyss and then slammed into the cliff, breaking most of the eggs in my pocket. They pulled me up as best they could, and I arrived angry and sore. My shorts were wet from the broken eggs and goo was running down my leg. Ugh! At least we had plenty of birds' nests.

We took the birds' nests back home. I asked Mom to make birds'- nest soup. Mother was so kind. Looking back at this I realize how the whole idea of cooking up bird vomit must have been disgusting to her, yet she did as I asked with calmness and grace, cooking the mess with lots of pepper and herbs. We strained out the pine needles, twigs, etc, and eagerly tasted it. It tasted of salt, pine needles, herbs, and pepper—nothing special. What a great disappointment!

The disappointment was short lived, as we looked forward to celebrating Easter. My brothers and I were always out of boarding with Mother before Easter. Mother would leave Dad touring his many villages and congregations on the plains, come to Kodai in mid-March with my sister, Molly, and settle into Fern Cliff. Dad would join us the end of April and stay five weeks, which included our three weeks of May vacation.

My first sister, Katherine Marie, had been born in 1933. I remember that she had been ill and had serious health problems and convulsions at Kodaikanal during the summer of 1936. A few days before Christmas of 1936, while we were living in Yeleswaram, she had severe convulsions. Mother and Father took her immediately to Rajahmundry hospital, where she died during the night. The next morning Father came to get us and told us what had happened. We went into Rajahmundry, viewed the body of Katherine Marie, and attended her funeral. That was my first experience of the death of a loved one. At the funeral of Katherine Marie we sang her favorite hymn, 472 in the *Lutheran Common Service Book*. She had sung this every night as her good night prayer.

> Now the light has gone away
> Savior listen while I pray
> Asking Thee to watch and keep
> And to send me quiet sleep

Let my near and dear ones be
Always near and dear to Thee
O bring me and all I love
To Thy happy home above

Every Easter I thought much about Katherine Marie, and how she might be experiencing eternal life. I had planned to help mother color eggs on Saturday and then go to help decorate the gym with lilies. But I woke up with an itchy head, felt little things crawling, and was scratching myself all over. Examining me, Mother found that I was full of bird lice. "Horrors, you are lousy!" she exclaimed. Thus I came to know the origin of the term "lousy." I surely was, and so was my bed! Since the next day was Easter, Mother wisely decided I shouldn't have the kerosene treatment until Monday.

Easter festival was stirring, joyful, and triumphant as usual. The girls all had white dresses, and the boys were in white shirts and pants, "white kit." For the processional into the gym, which doubled as our chapel, we sang, "Low in the Grave He Lay." There were calla lilies everywhere, and a special cross, made of white banana orchids. We joyfully relived the events of that first Resurrection morning. Each class sang a special anthem. The high school chorus sang an Easter Cantata. Between anthems and hymns, which we sang with joy and vigor, there were lessons read by students, and a sermon, followed by the offering and prayers. We recessed singing "Jesus Christ is Risen Today." I thought of sister Katherine Marie as we sang this.

Throughout this joyful celebration I felt lice crawling over me, and tried not to scratch or squirm. After the service Ruth came to greet me. She looked like an angel in white, but I was distracted and snapped at her. "Don't touch me! I can't tell you why here, but I will later." She gave me a strange look as if to say, "What's eating you?" Little did she know that many lice were and that I felt lousy.

The next day I skipped school, took a kerosene bath, tied up my hair in a kerosene soaked cloth, and went for a hike to Upper Bear Shola by myself. I sat on a grassy knoll getting lots of sun. Meanwhile mother cleaned my room. When I returned it smelled of kerosene and detol disinfectant. Later that week I told Ruth what had happened.

That summer, during May vacation, I asked Ruth if she'd like to ramble around Pillar Rocks with me. She happily consented provided we would be very careful and not collect bird's nests. We set a date.

Just walking there with her was a joyful experience for us. She was fun loving and such a good friend. We had little jokes and stories between us that only we could appreciate. Leaving the Ten-Mile Round as it crossed Levinge Stream, we took the old pony trail directly to the top of Pillar Rocks ridge and then descended the forest road to the silent, deeply shaded place in the glen—the base camp from where every expedition and exploration must start. I had promised Ruth we would not explore but stick to known trails and places.

Down we climbed into the Devil's Kitchen using the ladder-like tree trunk, then up through the Chimney, where we paused for kissing and hugging in perfect privacy. Returning to Base Camp, we next descended into the Pit by the rocky way then crawled up the steep slippery opposite side. Taking a trail to the top of the pillar, we surprised a barking deer that came springing past us. Then we took in the view from the edge of the first pillar, looking over to the second pillar that seemed to be so close. Kodai oral tradition tells of a Catholic priest who died there attempting to jump from the first to the second pillar.

I took Ruth to the place where I had been let down to gather birds' nests from the deep crevasse, and we dropped a stone and counted the seconds before it landed. She was horrified to think I'd been lowered into that abyss. She gave me a long hug, then said in her frank way, "How could you be so stupid?" To my disappointment she did not seem to regard my act as brave.

A strange ammonia-like smell pervaded the crevasses and caves at Pillar Rocks. It comes from bat and swift droppings decomposing through the years. "Ruth, hundreds of feet below there must be deep beds of guano, a fortune that has built up for centuries." I said.

"But I ain't *guano* go for it!" Ruth's answering groan gave me deep satisfaction.

By noon we had finished our adventure, and I promised to show Ruth the *other*, better view of Pillar Rocks. We took the trail going up to a point further west on the Ten-Mile Round, then had a picnic in the pines at the top of the hill named Darn Good by Kodai

School bicyclists, who came roaring down the higher hill and coasted up Darn Good hill. After lunch Ruth and I talked about the various adventures we had enjoyed together as the breeze whispered through the scented pines.

After our picnic we took a path along the ridge to the cliff side. From there we had a beautiful view of the pillars framed between rhododendron trees growing on the edge of the precipice. We threw some rocks over the cliff and counted the seconds it took for them to hit bottom. I remembered the formula $16t^2$ for the distance of freely falling objects. A drop time of seven seconds meant 784 feet to the bottom of the cliff. Ruth did get into this rock game, but never could I persuade her to roll rocks down the Fern Cliff slope above Priest's Walk.

We walked back, hand in hand, by the pony trail to Levinge Stream and then by road to our house. What a perfect day! This time, we finished it off with tea with my mom and dad. Dad was meeting Ruth for the first time. He kidded her, saying seriously, "Ruth, haven't we met before at Kodai Road Station?"

"No, I was never there when you were," she replied.

He smiled and said, "Neither was I there when you were there." Mom and Dad could both see how fond I was of Ruth, and what a friendly and enthusiastic girl she was!

* * *

Ruth and I graduated with our class of fifteen members in May 1944. Both of us took part in the graduation program. She presented a paper about Zoroastrianism, the religion of the Parsees; the theme for our senior class reports had been "The Religions of India." Then she and I played *Humoresque* together. As we had practiced together often (the practice rooms were still our trysting place), it was natural that we should play together for graduation.

Following graduation Ruth went with the DeValois family on a trek around the Eighty-Mile Round pony trail. Henrietta DeValois was a cousin to Ruth's mother. Ruth was staying with the DeValois family, since her parents hadn't been able to come to graduation due to the presence of submarines in the Persian Gulf. I wished I could have gone on the Eighty-Mile hike but could understand why the family did not invite me.

Their hiking expedition turned out to be a tragedy. While jumping over a little stream near Vanderavu, Henrietta DeValois developed a hernia that strangulated. She was in agony. They were forty road miles from Kodaikanal, with no vehicle and the road was very bad. A camp porter was sent into Kodaikanal to get medical help. Trotting through the night and using many shortcuts, he made the 30-mile journey by morning. A rescue party with a doctor came in a van to bring Aunt Henrietta and her immediate family back to Kodaikanal. The others, Ruth included, took two days to hike back. Henrietta died, as gangrene had set in. Ruth and the others were shocked and saddened to hear about her death before reaching Kodai.

Several days later Ruth came to our home for dinner. She told us about the trek and the tragedy from her point of view. Mom and Dad listened with sympathy and showed much care; I could tell how much they liked her. On the way back to where she was staying Ruth talked about the tragedy again. She could not get out of her mind the sounds of her aunt in agony that had kept them awake all night. I had never seen Ruth so shaken and grief stricken. She cried as I held her and tried to comfort her.

After I returned home that night I told Dad and Mother how much Ruth meant to me, and that I hoped some day it would be possible to marry her. Dad's response was, "Well Sammy, she's a nice girl, and we like her, but you are going back to the States this year, and she is not. There is a war on. You may not see her for years, and you will find new friends and develop other interests. We'll see how things turn out."

* * *

I wanted to have one more hike with Ruth before leaving Kodai. We decided to go on a long trek—to Vembadi Peak by way of the Ten Mile Round and Berijam road, beyond Green Hut to the trail leading to Vembadi. At 8,207 feet, it was the highest point in the middle of the Palni Range.

We left early in the morning with plenty of lunch, fruit, and raisins for snacks. As we walked, Ruth told me about her plans to stay in Kodai for another term, to take typing, music, and other courses. She had been requested to assist in teaching piano to beginners under the guidance of Mrs. Caspari, who had introduced an innovative method of teaching piano using colors and numbers. Then, war conditions permitting, Ruth would go to be with her parents at Basrah. She and her family hoped to come to America together after the war. We talked about my plans to study at Gettysburg. We wondered if Fritz had made it safely to America. He had left in April, and we had heard nothing about him and did not even know the name of the ship on which he had sailed from Bombay.

It was a beautiful morning. We had crystal-clear views, but didn't dally as we had a long way to go. After Green Hut, going west, we gradually ascended the Vembadi trail, now overgrown from disuse and difficult to follow. After awhile, because of wild raspberries and high bracken, we couldn't follow it. We climbed up to the top of the ridge hoping to find easier walking where the grass wasn't so high. On the way we flushed out a sambur, the largest of the Asiatic deer that had bedded down right in front of us. The huge buck, with magnificent horns, went crashing up over the ridge. What a bonus!

We kept hiking, gradually climbing higher. Then it clouded up and soon we were in thick mist. I said, "Careful, Goofy, here comes Papa Phelps." We had a good laugh. As we waited for the fog to lift, sitting side by side in the bracken, we quite naturally came into each other's arms. Knowing that we would soon be separated, we clung to each other for a long time. Alone in God's garden again, surrounded by mist, all the years of our growing love seemed focused on that precious moment. Even then, Ruth, true to herself, came to our rescue with her often-used line, "Oh Sam. Oh my! Well, I guess it's time for lunch."

Looking back at that moment, I am thankful that Ruth had the strength of character to set and keep boundaries. She was right.

After lunch, since the fog was thick as ever, we thought it would be wise to turn back. The weather was not improving, and there was no way we could see or reach the real peak in this fog. We had already walked over nine miles, and could not wait indefinitely for the clouds to lift. Going back we followed the trail we had made through the bracken. We felt badly that we had not succeeded in reaching Vembadi Peak. However, the hike had brought us still closer together and was well worth it. I was sure at age sixteen that I would love only Ruth forever.

The next week I left for Bombay. I traveled with my classmates Dirk Muyskens, John Wilder, and Harrison Moyer. Mom and Dad,

Molly, Ruth and some of our classmates came to the bus to bid us goodbye.

We went first to Bombay and waited there for the next ship. Some other missionaries had already been waiting there for several weeks. It hurt a lot to leave my family and Ruth. Yet I was excited about going to America to join my big brothers and to start college. Then too, I was confident I'd see my loved ones again.

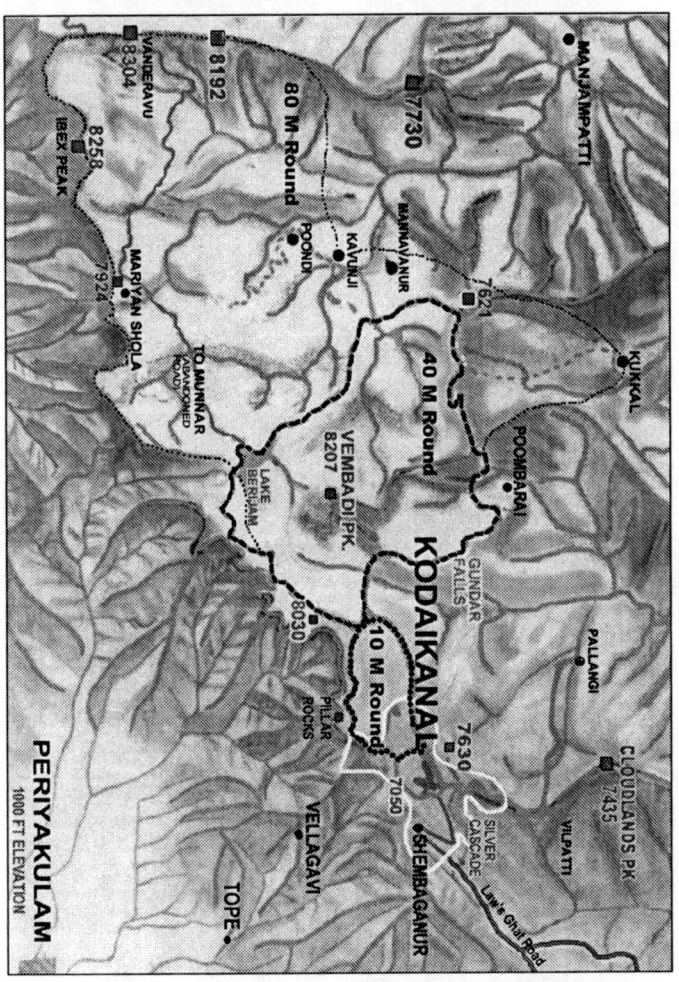

Map of Kodaikanal and the Palni Hills Range with 10 Mile, 40 Mile, and 80 Mile Round

Pillar Rocks

View of Southwestern cliffs on the way to Doctor's Delight

CHAPTER 4

WALKS AROUND PELLA, BELLA SYLVA, AND GETTYSBURG

I needed to see Ruth. She was in Pella, Iowa, going to Central College. I was 900 miles east of there, studying at Gettysburg College in Gettysburg, Pennsylvania. Since our Kodai parting after graduation Ruth and I had seen each other only once, at a small Kodai reunion over Easter of 1946, in Oberlin, Ohio. There Ruth and I had met more as old friends than as "boyfriend and girlfriend." We did not have an opportunity to talk just with each other, as friends were always with us. Since then we had written occasional letters. Both of us were adjusting to the States, to college, and to making new friends.

Mom, Dad, and Molly had come back to the States in August, 1945, after Germany had surrendered. I had received a telegram about their arrival from Aunt Katie while working at a restaurant in Atlantic City with Kodai friends. I made a beeline for Chambersburg. Mom and Dad rented a house on Washington Street, and, finally, our family could be together again except for Fritz, who was overseas. Father spent much of his time away from home doing deputation work in Mohawk Valley, New York, visiting his supporting churches, and one in Greensburg, Pennsylvania. I came to Chambersburg as often as I could. We looked forward to spending the summer of 1946 together at Bella Sylva.

As soon as college was out I went with Father to Bella Sylva to clean and make ready the cabin for our family, painting the bed rooms downstairs, the parlor, and the hallway. We worked so hard! To our frustration we had to spend a lot of time repairing the road with wheelbarrow, pick, and shovel, finding and breaking up rocks with a stone hammer to fill in the deep ruts. After a week of work, Father had to leave to attend a mission meeting he did not wish to go to in Chicago. He was ordered to attend. Before leaving, he gave a list of things he hoped I could finish before his return. He never came back. Three days later my cousin John came walking down the road and with sadness told me that Father has been killed in the Lasalle Hotel fire in Chicago on June 5. What a shock! John took me to Chambersburg to be with Mother and Molly.

At that time, brother Jerry was studying in the University of Pennsylvania Medical School, under an army program. The dean called him into his office and said, "Jerry, you are needed at home. Get a pass from the sergeant major and go right away!" He never told him that Father has been killed. Jerry bought a newspaper before boarding the train in Philadelphia, and as he rode home happened to read about the fire and see Father's name in the list of the victims. He was so deeply shocked! Mother was almost lost without Father, but was helped and comforted by the presence of her children and sisters and many missionary friends who came to visit. Fritz, in Korea with the occupation forces, did not arrive home for several months after Father died. It was a hard time of grieving for all of us.

After Father's death I had called Ruth and talked with her for a long time. She wrote several kind, comforting letters as a sympathetic friend. Yet she seemed to be cool toward me, and was probably glad to be free from the bondage of being my special girlfriend. She could now go with others, as I did occasionally from the time since I had come to the States in June 1944. Ruth probably wondered if I really loved her after so long a time and so many new experiences. Yet I could not get her out of my mind. I really had to see her again!

In January 1947 there was a break between terms. On the 30th I put on my long winter underwear, packed a small suitcase, and persuaded Aunt Katherine to drive me to Carlisle, where the Pennsylvania Turnpike began at that time. I started hitchhiking to Iowa. A helpful trucker took me all the way to Gary, Indiana, where we arrived late at night. From there I took a bus to the Greyhound station in Chicago, where I slept till early morning. Then I took another bus to the west side of Chicago to continue hitchhiking. It was cold! Fortunately, people had mercy on me. I arrived in Pella that evening.

Ruth had arranged for me to stay with the Olcotts, who had served in the Reformed Church of America (RCA) Arcot Mission in South India. The Gosselink family was also RCA. Bill Olcott had been our Kodai classmate in grade school. The Olcotts gave me a warm welcome and a room in the attic where several college students were boarding.

After unpacking I went in search of Ruth, finding her after supper. She was with Joyce DeBruin (her roommate from Kodai days), Dave Wilder (who was attending nearby Grinnell College), and Dirk Muyskens, (on leave from the Navy). Dirk had attended Central before being drafted. We had a great mini-reunion, and stayed together the rest of the evening. The next morning, a Saturday, Ruth and I spent most of the day walking around the college and town and talking. It was bitter cold, but we felt happy and brought each other up-to-date on all the happenings we had experienced since June 1944.

I told Ruth about my horrendous trip home. The first available ship at Bombay had been the USS Randall, for men only. Harrison Moyer couldn't come, as his sister was with him. I boarded with John Wilder and Dirk Muyskens. On the way to the docks we passed a huge area of rubble, part of the Bombay harbor and town that had been leveled when an ammunition ship had blown up in April, just hours after Fritz's boat had cleared the harbor. Thousands of people had been killed. It was the worst disaster of the war for India. As we cleared the harbor the Southwest monsoon struck our transport full force. Almost everyone got sick. We were miserable for several days. In our hold were 350 civilian men packed into three tiers of bunks. As there were 2000 troops on board from the China-Burma-India Theater, they could give us only two meals a day, in shifts. Our shift was 6 a.m. and 6 p.m. We ate standing up at long stainless steel tables, chest high for me. The food was great, but we missed rice and curry. There was not much to do between meals except to read. On good days we could go on deck. We saw boxing matches. In one lounge at the only piano a black GI played on and on every day. Everyone loved him. It was the best Jazz I have ever heard. We first went toward Cape Town, then under changed orders we headed southeast to land in Melbourne in July, mid winter in Australia. All the troops went ashore for two days and had a rip-roaring time. The 350 civilians in our hold were not allowed off, being a "poor security risk." This upset us. Crossing the Pacific to the United States, we were not allowed to bathe or wash clothes for the last ten days because of a water shortage. Forty-six days after leaving Bombay we arrived in San Diego, California, filthy and with no clean clothes. We were met by the American Express Agent who took us straight to the train station in Los Angeles and put us aboard a train to the East Coast by day coach. The train was crowded, something like 3rd class in India! We took turns sleeping on newspapers on the floor. My ticket from Los Angeles to Harrisburg was 66 US Dollars. The charge from Bombay to San Diego on the transport was a dollar a day, or 46 US Dollars for room, board, transportation, and entertainment.

When I arrived in Chambersburg at Aunt Katherine's apartment, she wondered who this filthy young tramp was. When it dawned on her that it was her nephew, she gasped, "Sam, come in! First take a bath, then I'll get you something to eat." She brought me clothes my brothers had left when they had joined the army.

Before closing the bathroom door I asked, "Where is the Dutch cleanser?" Mother had coached me carefully and told me she'd be mortified if I ever left a ring around the bathtub in her sister's home. Aunt Katie howled with laughter about this and so did Ruth when I told her.

Especially interesting was Ruth's account of her family's long visit to Jerusalem after V.E. Day, and their stays in Cairo and Port Said. From there, in the summer of 1945 she and her mother boarded a freighter for the States, saying goodbye to her Dad, to Jim, and to Chuck. The reason for this was because so many Americans were trying to get back to the States at the end of the war with Germany, travel agencies crowded women into one boat, and men into another. Several days later Ruth's Dad and her brothers took passage on a fast freighter which arrived in New York before Ruth and her mother did. Shipping authorities were still security-minded and would not give out any information. By chance, one day they saw Christina and Ruth's freighter coming up the Hudson, and so were on hand to meet them as they disembarked. What a grand surprise!

* * *

That evening alone in the Olcotts' home, Ruth and I talked by the cozy fire, sharing our past and mulling over our future. Finally I told Ruth that I loved her, wanted to be committed to her, and would "try to give up going with other girls." We kissed and hugged for the first time in two and a half years. Then I asked her to accept my fraternity pin, which she did. Ruth was so happy, and I was bursting with delight!

As she had to be back in the dorm by 10:30 p.m., we hurried to the campus and there met Joyce and her boyfriend, Jim Dunham. After dropping off our girls Jim and I hung out together in a coffee shop eating Dutch letters, a Pella specialty. Dutch letters are pastries filled with almond paste, each baked in the shape of an alphabet letter. Pella is a Netherlands Dutch town.

Then I suggested to Jim that we serenade the girls, Kodai style, and I dragged a reluctant Jim to the back of the dorm where Joyce and Ruth roomed together. There, below their second floor window, I howled like a Kodai jackal.

The window opened and Joyce called out, "All right, you guys, don't gloat just because you have no curfew. We know you are happy, Sam. Ruth showed me your pin, and she is so happy! Now quit howling and git before the police come after you."

Sunday after church Ruth and I had dinner at the Olcotts, with the Kodai gang, feasting on chicken curry and pilau rice. What a happy time it was for all of us! Our friends were all delighted about Ruth and me, especially our old friends Joyce, Dirk, and Dave.

I started back early on February 4, after four wonderful days of affection with Ruth and the joyful renewal of our relationship. I was so excited that I don't remember any details of the trip home. When I thanked Mrs. Olcott I told her that if I had left anything behind to just dump or burn it. Ten days later I received a parcel containing a pair of woolen pants I had left in the closet. There was a note attached from Mrs. Olcott that said, "I don't like the smell of burning wool." She also graciously invited me to stay with them any time I came to Pella. She seemed to sense our destiny.

Ruth and I kept letters going between Pella and Gettysburg. It was hard being so far from each other, but we managed fairly well until the middle of spring. That is when I met Geraldine.

I first saw Geraldine studying in the library with her older sister, Lois, and was very attracted to her. I asked Geraldine for a date, and soon we became close friends. I enjoyed going out to her family's farm. It was good having someone I could see often and go with to sporting events and dances and to study with in the library. I never dreamed of the anguish this would cause later.

Ruth and Joyce went to Denver for work and adventure during the summer of 1947. They ended up working in the airport restaurant as waitresses and enjoyed going into the Rockies on days when they could get away.

Mother and nine-year-old Molly were planning to return to India that Fall. One Sunday after dinner Mother told us she had been called by the Board of Foreign Missions to be housemother of Kennedy Hall at Kodaikanal School, and she had gladly accepted. She and Molly would be leaving in late October. Providentially, Fritz and I had decided to spend the whole summer with them at Bella Sylva, our ancestral home.

Fritz and my project was to build a new outhouse. During World War II no one stayed at Bella Sylva for four years. Porcupines had chewed their way into the old pine outhouse, eating out the seat and the floorboards. Dad always said they liked outhouse wood because it was flavored with salt from human sweat and waste. By the summer of 1947 the old outhouse had collapsed into the hole. We obtained permission to use Aunt Adelaide's four-holer outhouse. Adelaide, Father's sister, had an old log cabin up the hill from us. She didn't mind us using her facility, but family pride demanded that we have our own outhouse.

Fritz was the architect and master builder. First a hole had to be dug six feet deep through hardpan which had lots of pine tree roots. Next we built a rock and cement foundation. We left a space eighteen inches wide in back so that we could rake out the old stuff every nine or ten years. As we gathered tools and materials, we found a lot of old hardwood boards in the barn that had been sawed from our own logs by grandpa back in the 1930s. For beams, Fritz decided to use sugar maple poles which were still standing as dead timber, air dried, and hard as rock. Without power tools, working with hard maple and with the wood we found in the barn was very challenging. Hand sawing was most difficult, nails bounced and bent, and drill bits broke. Learning as we went, we finally finished it. It was roofed with red shingles like the house. We put in a transom for reading light, a bookcase, and pictures on the walls.

All was ready. We invited our neighbors to a coffee party to inspect our work, help us celebrate and use our new outhouse respectfully. Our neighbor, Joe Harrison, looked at our outhouse, stared, scraped at a board with his knife, then exploded, "My God, you built this outhouse out of one-inch seasoned cherry planks. I'll give you 1,000 dollars for this outhouse."

Only then did we realize we had used prime cherry lumber that had been seasoning for nearly twenty years. We named our outhouse The Cherry Among the Pines. We are sure it is the most beautiful and valuable outhouse in Pennsylvania. In 1997 we celebrated the golden anniversary of our privy—50 years of Schmitthenner meditation and expression.

Before mother returned to India, I thought Ruth should get to know her better. So I invited her to visit us in Bella Sylva at the end of summer. When she wrote that she would come, I was so excited. Soon the whole family knew that she was coming. We hoped that she would pass the Bella Sylva test. Molly teased me unmercifully. She and mother fixed up a room for Ruth upstairs and really shared in my excitement.

I picked Ruth up at the Harrisburg train station and we drove to Bella Sylva in Fritz's car. Molly, Mother, and Fritz were glad to see her and welcomed her. For a few golden late August days we swam in the lake, picked blueberries, fished, walked through the woods, and enjoyed grilled suppers with all the fixings at our outdoor picnic place. Ruth and mother got along well. Mother showed her how to make blueberry pie and other special dishes, and how to keep the wood stove going evenly. Ruth passed the Bella Sylva test with flying colors, not minding the outhouse or dumping her own slop bucket each morning. She didn't mind the bats, learned to put worms on the hook, took part in chores like washing dishes, used the stove to heat water, and cleaned her own room. But she never learned how to clean fish; I deleted that requirement from the Bella Sylva test. Best of all, she loved Bella Sylva and compared it to Kodai.

The pine-scented air, the beauty of the lake, nights on the lake watching beaver swimming near their house, cat-fishing, hearing and answering the hoot owl, and counting the number of bullfrogs grumping in the lake brought us closer together. We spent a lot of time boating, exploring the swamp side of the lake, and breathing the fragrance of thousands of pure white tuberous water lily blossoms. We also enjoyed yellow American lotus blossoms and, around the dock, abundant blooms of broad arrowhead flowers. I picked water lilies and made garlands for Ruth.

We went on a ramble around the lake. First we took the path toward our dock, then around to the north, crossing the beaver dam at the lake outlet, until we came to the swimming place. From there we followed a path going west past my cousin John's cabin to the Plessinger house. Then we cut up the slope to the old railroad grade that goes to Lopez, passing the stump of the largest cherry tree ever harvested in North America.

A storm uprooted this giant in 1897. It was 53 inches in diameter, had 297-year growth rings, and contained 4000 board feet of lumber. Twenty-one feet from the stump it branched into two sections, each of which was larger than most other cherry trees on the property. My great grandfather sent a five-foot, 600 lbs section to the New York Museum of Natural History in Central Park. This was written up in two local papers—the *New Age*, Tunkhannock, Pennsylvania, on February 25, 1897, and in the *Sullivan Review*, Dushore, Pennsylvania, March 4, 1897. When the tree was cut the stump had flopped back in its place. Cherry lasts a long time even when exposed to extremes of weather. The stump is still visible now, a century after the tree blew over. From the old roots another cherry tree has grown that is now over 15" in diameter and 60 feet high.

Next we turned south going through woods, winding our way through blueberry thickets, coming to the swampy area formed by the largest inlet of the lake. Beaver had made a series of dams from three to six feet high along this watercourse. Some of these had been washed out. Finding a crossing place was difficult because of the mud, hardtack clumps (a spiraea also known as steeple bush) and blueberry thickets. But finally, following a deer trail, we found a way. We came upon a beaver lumbering operation with dozens of fallen trees and dragways headed in toward the nearest pond. Deer following a trail will jump over logs; beavers chew them out of the way, or sometimes tunnel under them. We saw where beavers had chewed through ten-inch diameter cherry trees with their chopper teeth, going around so that the stump was cone-shaped with each tooth bite like a chisel mark. A few of the trees they had chewed through had hung up on other trees. "Ruth, do you know what happens when a beaver hangs up a tree?" I asked.

She just shook her head.

"They say, 'Damn'(!) They like to dam."

Ruth groaned.

After that we angled east through more huckleberry thickets until we emerged at another railroad grade. Though the rails had been taken up more than forty years previously, we could still see the depressions where each of the ties had been. We followed the railway grade toward Aunt Adelaide's house, coming to a grassy area with many Juneberry trees. Juneberry is called "shadbush" in New York, for it blossoms when shad, migrate up-stream from the sea. It is also called "service berry." The beautiful white blossoms of this tree were the first flowers of spring available to beautify church services in old New England. In Bella Sylva, Juneberries actually ripen in July. Mature berries are deep red to purple and luscious. When baked in a pie or made into jam, the big seeds give a nutty taste and add flavor and special-ness to the creation. Unfortunately, the berries had already shriveled and fallen by the time of our ramble.

After some quiet togetherness in the Juneberry grove we headed for the corner of the lake to the Shooting Rock, a large sandstone-pebble composite boulder in the southern corner of the lake. From there we went toward our cabin, going past the sand spring and the deer spring to our dock path. Two minutes later we arrived home in time for a quick cup of tea and a swim.

We swam twice a day and soaked up the sun on the swimming raft. Our love seemed to blossom, and we were closer together than ever before. The picture of us on the swimming raft in Bella Sylva portrays our mutual love and delight we shared in that beautiful place.

Our five days together went by too fast. Ruth had to return to college. We decided to attend the Labor Day Kodai reunion at Holland, Michigan, together. Against Mother's advice we planned to hitchhike. Mother and Ruth gave each other a fond farewell embrace, not knowing they would never see each other again. Ruth said goodbye to Bella Sylva and the family, then Fritz drove us to Towanda. We began hitching along route 6, the most scenic highway in northern Pennsylvania.

Fortune smiled on us. A veteran and his British bride drove us to the west of Erie. Fifteen minutes after dropping us they returned to give me my wallet, which had slipped out of my jacket pocket. From there we quickly had good rides with kind people. I told Ruth that her innocent looks made hitching easy, and hinted that "hitching" with her would be a great lifetime journey. She just smiled. That evening in Indiana, three black youths in a convertible gave us a lift to the Michigan border. They treated us with respect, but scared the life out of us going over 80 miles per hour.

By 9:00 that evening we were in Holland. We quickly found the reunion site and rejoiced to see our old friends and classmates again. For three days we shared experiences, brought each other up-to-date, ate rice with curry and sambar, played soccer, and swam by day and in the moonlight in Lake Michigan. Everyone was happy to see Ruth and me back together.

Sunday noon we left our friends and hitchhiked toward Chicago. At 5 p.m. in Michigan City we had supper at a diner and Ruth, who had worked all summer as a waitress, said, "I'll give the tip." She gave a generous one. Then we took a train to the railway station in Chicago. Going to purchase her ticket to Ottumwa, the station nearest to Pella, Ruth reached into her bag for her purse, and lo, it was gone! She had left it on the counter when she gave that generous tip. I counted my money. Fifteen dollars was all I had, not enough for her ticket. What would we do? After collecting our thoughts we appealed to Traveler's Aid. The lady on duty treated us with suspicion thinking we were runaway kids. Finally I said, "Look, we want accommodation only for Ruth—we will phone our friends to telegraph money. I'm going to start hitchhiking home now. This is a genuine case! What is Traveler's Aid for?"

The lady made a reservation for Ruth at a for-women-only hotel a mile away. To save money we walked there, past stockyards and numerous bars, lugging our suitcases. Then we telephoned friends in Holland who promised to wire money to the hotel first thing in the morning. I gave Ruth six dollars so she would have something for breakfast and to phone if she needed to, kissed her goodbye, and set out for Bella Sylva at 11 p.m.

After taking a train to Gary, Indiana, I walked to the edge of town and began hitching. It took three days to get home. After Labor Day route 6 was almost deserted. After long waits I had short rides from local people. The first night I phoned to Pella and was happy to hear Ruth and to know she had made it back safely. I slept outside that night, and was accommodated by a kind farmer family the second night. They also gave me a huge breakfast. Finally I made it to Lopez. Leaving my bag with the postmaster, I walked the last seven miles home.

Now I was sure about Ruth. She loved me, she wore my fraternity pin, she had passed the Bella Sylva test, and she got along great with Mother and my brothers and sister. The way toward marriage seemed clear, but I was only nineteen, still in college, and immature. Mother's sister, Aunt Katie, who had never married, said to me, "Sam you are too young. You should be older, have a job and 1,000 dollars in the bank before you can think about marriage." It would be a long wait. Little did I realize how complicated things would soon become for Ruth and me.

After our happy Bella Sylva summer, Mother and Molly moved back to the rented house in Chambersburg. During the summer, many friends, including retired and furloughing missionaries, came to visit us and to encourage mother just as they had the previous year. Mother began preparation for her and Molly's return to India. Fritz and I went back to college. We tried to spend Sundays with Mother and Molly in Chambersburg, even on weekends when we had soccer games.

The weekend of their departure we went by train with Mother and Molly to New York. We boarded the Queen Mary, helped them settle in their stateroom, and said our good-byes. Leaving Mother was much harder than ever before, as now she was without Father. But we knew she would be with mission and Kodai School friends, and felt confident that she would be the best housemother the grade school boys had ever had at Kodai School. I phoned Ruth about Mom's going. Ruth said, "One of her boys will be my little brother, Chuck. Isn't that great?"

* * *

Shortly thereafter I started going out with Geraldine again. She was lovely, unsophisticated, very natural and a joy to be with. She became a soccer fan. After each home game on Saturdays I would go out to her family's farm to be with her. Together we attended football and basketball games. She came to see all my home-wrestling matches. Occasionally we'd have a movie date. When we saw *Gone With the Wind* together it was very emotional for her—how she cried! Her folks were kind to me, and I felt comfortable with them and with her. It was good to have a girlfriend I could see almost every day. She was innocent, pleasant, encouraging, and good company. I enjoyed her engaging sense of humor. We became very fond of each other.

But how could I be doing this? Did I not love Ruth? Were we not destined for each other? Slowly my heart was being torn and my thinking muddled. I could neither think of giving up Geraldine nor change my mind about Ruth.

As Thanksgiving approached, I decided to see Ruth again. Would this visit help me find out which one I really loved? After my last class I got a lift from a classmate to Carlisle and began hitchhiking on the Turnpike again. A very tired driver picked me up and asked, "Where are you going?"

"Iowa," I replied.

He asked if I had a driver's license. When I showed it to him he said, "You drive. Wake me up to pay the toll. I know a good way around Pittsburgh. Don't go over 70 mph. It's very windy tonight."

I drove a steady 60 mph to Irvin where the turnpike then ended. What a way to start! After he dropped me off in western Ohio it began to snow. By the time I arrived in Pella on Thanksgiving afternoon, there were six inches of snow on the ground.

Ruth gave me a warm welcome. We hadn't seen each other since that bad night in Chicago. Again I stayed with the Olcotts; they had prepared a grand Thanksgiving dinner for us. How fortunate and thankful we were for our Kodai missionary extended family— the common heritage, faith, interests, shared experiences, and loving fellowship. We had much to be thankful for that night. Ruth and I were thankful to be together again. Yet, in my mind and heart there were dark shadows. I wanted to tell her about Geraldine, but could not. Being heavy-hearted, I did not say much. Ruth must have sensed that something was wrong.

Saturday, though, was pure fun. Ruth had planned a picnic in the snow with Jim and Joyce. We bought rolls, Pella bologna, and Dutch letters. As we pulled the girls out of town on a couple of borrowed sleds they pretended to whip and treat us like horses. At the far edge of the park, near some woods, we gathered firewood and made a bonfire. With pointed sticks we roasted bologna, and toasted buns. How good it was to enjoy hot food and coffee in the snow and frigid weather. For dessert we stuffed ourselves with the Dutch letters representing ourselves S, S, R, G, J, J, and D. We kidded that since Joyce DeBruin and James Dunham had the same initials, Joyce wouldn't have to change her letters if she married

Jim, which later she did! It was below freezing, so after eating we all backed up toward the fire and toasted *our* buns. Then with numb feet, full stomachs, and overflowing hearts, we rambled back to the dorm through the snow.

I left Pella after church and dinner on Sunday, more sure about Ruth than ever. Yet after a few days, when I saw Geraldine again, I wanted to be with her. She had missed me and wondered how things had gone. Gerry knew all about Ruth, yet I think she hoped that she and I would end up together. As I kept going with Geraldine for the rest of the winter and early spring, I lost touch with reality, thinking, "Everything will be all right."

Years later, after 40 years of pastoral experience, I know that many people caught up in multiple relationships really think they can continue in those conflicting relationships. Inevitably, when reality catches up and breaks the fantasy, there comes the time of tearing, hurt, grief, guilt, and loss. Love demands faithfulness. Anything else leads ultimately to disaster and pain.

As the spring of 1948 came slowly to Gettysburg, I felt obligated to see Ruth again. Now I *would* tell her about Geraldine and would have to make the ultimate decision. Once more I was hitching on the Turnpike bound for Pella. I arrived there on March 23, during Holy Week, feeling guilt and foreboding. How could I have been so deceptive with Ruth, who had loved me steadfastly all along?

Ruth had sensed from my letters that something was wrong and immediately discerned how horrible I felt. Saturday I told her about my love for Geraldine, and we talked over the whole matter, both sharing our feelings. Then with anguish I said, "But I love you most of all."

"Do you really, Sam? You love Geraldine and it is plain that you can't give up going with her. Between us there are years of friendship. I was your first love, but we both have changed and grown apart in distance and understanding. It is not working out. You can't have two loves at once."

She looked steadily at me with hurt hazel eyes and said, "Here is your fraternity pin. I'm sorry." Throughout all of this she was calm and never lost her temper. I was devastated, yet relieved, because finally I had told my best friend the truth. But this hurt so much!

The next day, Easter, Day of Resurrection, we went to Sunday School and church together. Joyce and Ruth both wore white suits with red roses. How beautiful she was! After the Easter service the four of us had dinner together. Then I got my bag, kissed my dearest friend goodbye, and left with great sadness. The joy of that Easter could hardly touch me. That day Joyce wrote in her diary, "Sam and Ruth have broken up. Sam was in a kind of fog all the time."

The whole way back to Gettysburg I was in a hurt daze, hardly knowing what I was doing, and overwhelmed with the sense of loss.

Ruth and Sam on the raft, Bella Sylva Lake

Stump of the great cherry tree (taken years later)

CHAPTER 5

WALKING WITH RUTH AGAIN AT
LAKE GENEVA, CHAMBERSBURG, AND
BELLA SYLVA

Until my graduation from college in June 1948 I spent more time in
study. Geraldine and I didn't spend as much time together; losing
Ruth did not bring me closer to Gerry. Saying goodbye to Ruth had
hurt so much that I realized how much I loved her. Geraldine
sensed my hurt and noticed my lack of lightheartedness. She was
soon to transfer to John's Hopkins for nursing school. Our lives
seemed to be heading in different directions.

Besides striving for a strong academic finish, I had been keeping
in shape by playing soccer every day. The U.S. Olympic committee
had invited me and two others on our great team to attend the
Olympic soccer team tryouts in May. Through the winter and early
spring I practiced almost every day with Fritz. He was better than I.
However, while fighting in the Philippines he had contracted malaria, which frequently flared up. He missed games and was in a
weakened condition when he did play. I played left inside and left
wing forward and had a good left foot, and a high-scoring record.
Fritz was an unrecognized debilitated halfback. I practiced trying to
dribble around him to get shots at the goal. Sometimes he would
play in the goal while I took shots from every angle and distance
with either foot. We practiced running full speed and passing back
and forth. Running a mile every day and eating carefully, I kept in
top form.

In May, I attended the tryouts, and played for three fifteen-
minute periods with different groupings. At the end of the day I

was cut from the squad, but did receive a good letter thanking me for participating. I keep and treasure this.

Still grieving over the loss of Ruth, I had my last date with Geraldine at the end of the spring term. We both felt very sad about breaking up, for we had been good friends and meant a lot to each other. I felt terrible about causing her hurt. She had never done anything that was not honest and honorable. I took the blame for our breakup and assured her that I had the deepest respect for her. It was a very difficult parting.

In a letter to Ruth I told her I was planning to go with Fritz to work for the summer in Idaho, St. Joe National Forest, to help save pines in a blister-rust control program. She replied informing me that she would be at the YMCA/YWCA Camp at Lake Geneva, Wisconsin, for work and training. She had been elected to serve as president of the Student Y for her senior year at Central— quite an honor.

That made me think. Should I try again? Did I deserve another chance after hurting two such wonderful women. I thought, "No I certainly do not!" Yet I wanted to see Ruth again.

Sometime that winter I had read about worker-priests in France who worked in factories on assembly lines along with factory hands in order to experience the dignity of labor and identify with laboring people with the view to minister to them more meaningfully.

I got to thinking, "I've been studying for the past 16 years; I should have factory-work experience, maybe for a whole year, before going to seminary." I had been a pre-ministerial student for my last three years in college, but did not feel ready to continue. I needed to straighten out my life and become more mature.

I wrote to Allis Chalmers in Milwaukee, inquiring about a job. Their return letter assured me that they would give me a job in their foundry for the summer, and perhaps for a longer period.

I told my brother Fritz that I had a job lined up with Allis Chalmers in West Allis, a suburb of Milwaukee, and that I planned to visit Ruth in Lake Geneva, hoping she might take me back. Fritz looked at me and just shook his head, asking, "You mean you'd give up our great western adventure?"

"Yes, Fritz, I have to see Ruth again and ask her to forgive me."

We decided to hitchhike together as far as Chicago. At the last minute our brother Jerry, who had just mustered out of the army medical school program, decided to join us. His aim was to travel to the West Coast and back. We soon found it was difficult for three of us to get a ride together, so we split up. I offered to go solo since I was used to hitchhiking. They were picked up first. Later, somewhere in Ohio I spotted my brothers thumbing on a corner. I got very excited and told the trucker who had picked me up that they were my brothers. Could he please take them also? He could, with the provision that one of us would ride in the back on a smooth bed of cartons. We took turns doing this through the night all the way to Chicago. There we ate brunch together and then split since I was going north to Milwaukee.

After renting a room in West Allis I reported to Allis Chalmers, where I attended a safety course and was told to purchase a pair of steel-toed safety shoes. This was the beginning of my work in the world's largest foundry, the hottest workplace I've ever been in— including India. My crew mixed special kinds of sand and oil that were vibrated into core shapes, baked, then placed in molds. Steel was poured into them to make engine blocks for tractors. I worked hard for two weeks before getting up the courage to visit Ruth.

On my second Saturday I took a bus to Lake Geneva, wondering how Ruth would react to seeing me. After finding the Y Camp, I located Ruth as she was ready to go on duty as a waitress at lunchtime. When she saw me, she was amazed, and then she said angrily, "Why did you come here? Don't you know it's over? You are supposed to be in Idaho. You lied to me!" She raised her voice and was really upset.

"Okay, I'll go soon, but can we talk first?"

Still angry she said, "All right, after lunch. Sit over there and eat, after you pay for lunch at the desk."

She served me with a frown and was really busy for about an hour and a half. After eating I went outside and waited, feeling miserable. Then she came looking calmer and was kinder in her manner. We talked for most of the afternoon. I told her that Geraldine and I were finished and that I was sorry for the hurt I had caused both of them because both had been fair, honest, and kind to me. I was the one who had done them wrong. Then I asked Ruth to forgive me. With real pain she expressed how badly she had been hurt, and how hard it had been to lose her trust in me after so many years of faithful commitment. Then she said, "Well, we have been friends for so long, and I hope maybe we can still be friends." She looked me in the eye with half a smile and a more tender look in her hazel eyes and continued, "I guess you don't have to leave right away if we are going to work at being friends."

Ruth found me a place to stay that night in the boys' cabin with some of her friends. On Sunday we went to the camp church where worship was free spirited with enthusiastic singing. We talked some more before I left for Milwaukee. When I asked, "Can I come again after two weeks?" she looked at me thoughtfully and said, "Yes, I think that might be all right." Returning on the bus, I felt a great burden had been lifted from my heart.

The second visit was very interesting. On Saturday evening Ruth suggested we visit the observatory on a hill above Lake Geneva. The Y Camp had a good relationship with the observatory staff, so we went there and enjoyed looking at planets and stars through a powerful telescope. An astronomer from India named Mr. Rao explained some of the special projects and work of the observatory. During our conversation he happened to mention that he had worked at The Kodaikanal Observatory for a number of years. He was very happy to hear that Ruth and I were graduates of Kodaikanal School. He had known Carl W. Phelps and many other staff members.

Sunday we had a long swim after church. I left with the invitation from Ruth to, "Come again next weekend, and come early in the day so we can do something special."

Ruth had learned that there was a trail around the lake, over fifteen miles long, with much of it passing through private land. We took a picnic lunch and hiked the whole way. That was fun and much like our old Kodai rambles, which we remembered and talked about. This ramble ended with a swim back at the Y Camp that was most refreshing, but we missed our Kodai teas. The next day following church, lunch, and a swim, Ruth kissed me goodbye. This was our first kiss since our breakup at Easter. I whistled all the way home.

On weekends when I couldn't make it to Geneva, I worshiped in a large Lutheran Church in downtown Milwaukee. To my delight I met Myrtle Onsrud, a furloughing Lutheran missionary from Andhra. We talked about our missionary friends and had Sunday dinner together. Little could I know that one day we would be working together in the same synod in the Andhra Church, and that she would be like a member of our family.

One weekend we spent more time than usual on the swimming raft at the Y Camp. It reminded us of the raft at our Bella Sylva lake. That afternoon, while sunbathing there with her friends, I was dozing off when I heard Ruth's excited voice, "Sam, look at this. A double dragonfly! Have you ever seen a double dragonfly?" I opened my eyes to see two mating dragonflies on her leg. I was so embarrassed. The others on the raft were amused. I said, "Ruth, the trouble with you is you know all about the birds and bees, but you don't have a clue about other insects." Then I dived into the water to hide my embarrassment. I heard a splash; Ruth had jumped in and was swimming toward me. Though the water was cold, she was blushing.

"Gosh, I never realized that," she said.

Toward the end of summer the Wisconsin State Fair was to be held in Milwaukee, so I invited Ruth to spend the weekend with me for a change. A woman in our rooming house was going to be away that weekend, so I arranged with her and the landlady to have Ruth stay there Friday and Saturday nights. I met Ruth at the bus station, showed her the room, then took her out for a special dinner. We spent the entire next day at the fairgrounds watching surrey races, horse weight pulling contests, taking in the rides and exhibits, while enjoying varieties of fair junk food. That was a happy day for us "best friends."

The next morning I took her to the Lutheran church in downtown Milwaukee. We worshiped with Myrtle Onsrud and then had dinner with her. She was delighted with Ruth and told us about her days with the mountaineer nurse corps of Berea, Kentucky. Myrtle's friendship with Ruth would continue for the rest of their days.

As that special summer drew to a close, Ruth and I were together again—this time with a love that had been tested and strengthened by hurt, grieving, forgiveness and God's gracious reconciling hand. Ruth was total in the forgiveness and love she gave to me. She never brought up how I had deceived her. I shall be eternally grateful for her forgiveness.

Ruth had one more year at Central College in Pella. I decided to start seminary at Gettysburg in the fall. We would be far from each other again, but this time I would be careful and remember the lessons I had learned. We said our goodbyes pledging our love with hugs and kisses. Ruth promised to come to Chambersburg for Christmas. We'd be at my aunt Katie's place with her sisters, Aunt

Dot and Aunt Elizabeth, and my brothers. I felt Ruth needed to know my family better as we came closer to our destiny!

Early in September I moved into the Old Dorm at Lutheran Theological Seminary, Gettysburg. This same building had been the lookout tower for both the Northern Army, then from the second day of the battle, the Southern Army, during the battle of Gettysburg, July 1-3 in 1863. We lived in the midst of history.

On the afternoon of September 30 I was called into the principal's office and wondered, "I haven't been here long enough to get into trouble; I wonder what he wants." Sitting beside Dr. Wentz was an old missionary friend of my fathers, Dr. J. Roy Strock. He and Dr. Wentz looked at me sadly, then Dr. Strock informed me that Mother had fallen down some stone steps near Kennedy Hall in Kodai and had been badly injured. As there was no doctor in Kodai at the time she had been taken to the nearest good hospital, Madurai, 70 miles from Kodaianal and had died the next day, Sept 28, in Madurai. The following day she was buried in Kodaikanal. So by the time the message reached us, she had already been buried.

I was crushed. First Dad had died in a fire accident. Now Mother was gone. The professors tried to comfort me. I asked about my sister Molly. They told me that Molly was being cared for by Dorothy and Ted Wood, and that we would hear from them soon. I told them brother Fritz was at the college and I had to see him right away. I found Fritz, and we spent the afternoon walking and talking together, then went to Chambersburg to see Mom's sister Katie, who was the only one there at the time. How we grieved! I phoned Ruth and told her; she was shocked and sad. Then we phoned the others. Sometime that same day Jerry received a cablegram from one of our missionaries, Ted Benze, informing us how and when mother had passed away. At the time Jerry was completing his residency at Lankenau Hospital in Philadelphia. He phoned Chambersburg and came over that weekend to join us.

Later we received letters from the Woods, from Carl Phelps and from the Doctor Wilder, who had attended mother in Madurai, giving the details of her injuries and death. Ted and Dot Wood wrote that Molly would be staying with them and would be part of their family. They always had been very close to Mother and Father. Their three daughters, Betty Lou, Shirley, and Patsy—who was Molly's age and in her class—had been like sisters to Molly. While the Woods had vacationed at Kodaikanal during the month of June, Mother had asked Dot and Ted if they would take care of Molly Anne in case anything ever happened to her. Mother had given them a letter asking them to do this. Did she have a premonition? Dot and Ted had happily and graciously promised to take care of Molly. As none of us brothers was married or settled, we could not have taken care of her, so we were most grateful to the Wood family.

Shirley Wood was then in Kodaikanal High School. She spent much time with Molly, comforting her after they heard Mother had died. Upon hearing of mother's accident, Dot Wood set out immediately from their home in Guntur and arrived in Kodai in time for the funeral. Until her arrival, some staff members stayed with Molly. She remembers that Mother Pearl Peery was most comforting, understanding, and helpful. She said, "Molly, when you pray to Jesus, your mother will be there too, and she will hear your prayers."

The school gave a holiday to the children, so they could all go out and gather flowers for the funeral and grave side services. All of Mother's Kennedy Hall boys, including Ruth's brother Chuck, were at the graveside as Mother's mortal remains were laid to rest.

Molly became part of the Wood family, and they made a home for her until she finished Kodaikanal High School and went on to Thiel College in Pennsylvania. From then on, her home was with our Eyster Aunts in Chambersburg.

Three months after Mother's death, Ruth came to be with us in Chambersburg for Christmas. I met her train in Harrisburg and brought her home. Jerry, Fritz, and I were there with aunts Katie, Dot and Elizabeth—quite a full house for a three bedroom apartment. The three of us boys slept in the living room on rugs and couches. What a wonderful time we had! Mother's sisters were all professional women who had never married. They were marvelous cooks and kept a beautiful home. On Christmas Eve we feasted on the best of their Eyster cooking, attended the Lutheran service at 7:30 p.m., and at midnight we participated in the Presbyterian candlelight worship. After breakfast on Christmas morning we exchanged gifts.

The week before Ruth came I had boldly decided to give her a nightie. So I went to the Little Shop on Main Street. How embarrassed I was! The sales lady regarded me with amusement as I told her how tall Ruth was and what she looked like. Then she gave me a black, lacy, see-through nightie, which astounded me. I paid for it and fled. Back at Katie's home I looked at it again and was mortified! It was not right for Ruth.

Katie came home for a lunch break, saw my face, and asked why I was so disturbed. I showed her the nightie and explained what I wanted. "Horrors, this will never do! Give me the sales slip," she said as she snatched the nightie from my hands and hurried off. Within twenty minutes she had returned with a conservative, lovely nightgown that was just right. Then she explained to me the difference between a nightie and a nightgown.

Ruth loved her present. That night we pledged our love for each other and became engaged and immediately shared the news with all, as she appeared wearing the modest nightgown.

After Christmas she returned to Iowa. I promised to be in Pella for her graduation. Then we would go to Bella Sylva.

Early in June I traveled to Pella to see Ruth graduate from Central College, then went with her to Sioux County to visit her aunts and her mother's cousins of the Scholten family. Ruth agreed to spend the summer at Bella Sylva provided there would be someone else around. Even though engaged, Ruth was still her very principled self.

I had finished one year of seminary training and needed a break from school. Since I wanted to be at Bella Sylva, yet needed to earn money to put away for our marriage I decided to do some lumbering on our Bella Sylva property. On our 110-acres of forest there were many large old black cherry trees in their prime. After getting permission from my oldest brother, Jerry, and buying a used jeep on credit, I asked my seminary friend and class mate, Carl Ehrhart, if he could help. He happily agreed. After Carl and I began the lumbering operation, Ruth came to join us as camp cook, a proper designation she very ably fulfilled.

"Ruth, tomorrow I'm going to take you to a wonderful place named Mehoopany Falls. We'll take our swimsuits, a picnic lunch, and spend the day. Just the two of us," I insisted. We had been working terribly hard all week so decided to take all the weekend off to rest our sore muscles. Neither Carl nor I had ever lumbered before. Sawing by hand with a two-handled lumberman saw was most strenuous and made our arms and backs very sore. Carl was too tired to hike with us.

Ruth packed a lunch and we set out for Mehoopany Falls, about two miles from our cabin. This had been a favorite hike of our family for generations. During World War II no one had gone there, and the path had become totally obliterated. I told Ruth how Fritz and I had remade the path the year before. First, we explored the whole area selecting landmarks along the way. One of us would go to a designated landmark and stand there beating on a large empty can with a club while the other painted blazes on trees toward the sound. Then we had cleared brush and fallen logs to make the trail. The first landmark, Kaercher's Lake, a third of the way, was actually a beaver pond. From there we crossed its inlet and skirted the pond, past another swamp on our left going to the high ridge above the stream. At that point we could hear the rushing water of Mehoopany and blazed the path down to meet the stream at an old hemlock tree between the upper and lower falls.

Ruth went ahead on the trail. She would often stoop to remove fallen branches saying, "A path should be neat, and better than we found it." We reached Mehoopany creek and followed it upstream, jumping from rock to rock until we could see the falls. Finding separate boulder "dressing rooms" we changed into swimsuits. At the base of the twenty-five feet high falls were many small potholes and a shallow rocky pool good for wading. We climbed up the side of the falls and went in under the overhanging layer of rock over which water was falling. In the cave behind the falls spongy moss, dripping water and slimly rocks to sit on made for a cool time. We sat on the cold flat stones and stuck our feet out under the falls. Then we shared some quality time together. Though we were alone, with a curtain of falling water making it a very private place, the cold, hard, slimy rocks did not provide a comfortable setting.

After our time at the big falls, we went downstream the short distance to the little falls. There, where the water gushes down about seven feet into a deep dark pool we jumped in to swim. The extremely cold water gave us a shock, but we got used to it, yelling and swimming energetically. We sat on the ledge overlooking the pool as we ate lunch, sharing feelings and thoughts about how a year from now we would be married. Again, we were alone in the midst of God's beautiful creation. The sound of water bringing life, abundance, and beauty to our world gave us joy as we shared in the wonder of the place.

Before going back we had another swim with a bit of wrestling and tickling. I showed Ruth the pool below the big one and related to her an old family legend: men and boys used to skinny-dip in the upper pool, as did women and girls in the lower pool. Ruth would not believe the legend as we could see the lower pool from the rock-filled end of the upper pool.

Behind us, above the ledge, were scores of painted trillium plants whose blossoms had now turned to red seed. All along the stream and the path going home there were bushes full of green blueberries. We did find some ripe Juneberries and ate all we could. We hiked back in the hot sun, going uphill most of the way. When we arrived we yelled for Carl, and the three of us went swimming in the lake. Then we enjoyed tea.

Carl and I worked hard cutting down mostly prime cherry trees with a Simmons lumberman saw. On a good day we could take down and saw into sections three or four old trees. Then we would attach chains and drag logs with the jeep to the loading ramp. Clyde Kester, our friend, sharpened our saw and set the teeth every two or three days. He taught us many skills and gave us safety instructions. O'Leary, another neighbor, a brash, great Irish storyteller, came over now and then to help haul logs with his jeep. We kept beer in the springhouse just for him. For two beers he'd usually be helpful for about two hours, and would entertain us with his outlandish stories. Three beers would produce more stories but no more work. If we had no beer, he'd inquire how things were going and then leave rather quickly.

Leo Dieffenbach, a huge lumberman with arms thicker than my thighs, was the one who bought the cherry logs. Our largest cherry log lay in a depression; although I put chains on all four wheels of the jeep and a load of rock in back I couldn't skid it out. Leo brought over his horse, but Mabel couldn't move it either. Leo then sat on a log for twenty minutes, kind of like the Thinker, and then came up with an idea. "Sam, you chain your jeep to the log and I'll chain my horse to your jeep. That'll move it."

First I went to get Ruth since I had a feeling this would be fun to watch. After she came, I revved up the motor in low range gear, Leo bellowed at the horse and Mabel dug in pulling for all her worth. The log slid up the hill all the way to the ramp.

Ruth often watched us lumbering in her spare time. Each morning after she heard the first tree crash, she would come out with a cup of coffee and sit on the butt log while we sawed away. Usually within fifteen minutes, two or three deer would come and begin eating the tender cherry leaves from the top of the tree we were working on. They were very tame and quite used to us. This gave Ruth much pleasure.

Some evenings Ruth and I would hang out and play games with Carl, and, if it was cool, we'd build a fire in the smokey corner fire place of the dining room, sit on the old family rocking chairs and talk. Other evenings we would go cat-fishing or beaver watching, or both. Ruth and I took off some nights for romantic moonlight walks or for rowing around the lake listening to the bullfrogs and owls.

Ruth's cooking improved. She had learned how to master our wood burning range and how to slide pans over to cook quickly, slowly, or to simmer, and to close the damper to get the oven hot enough to make blueberry pies. She made great pot roasts that cooked while we swam in the afternoon. She cooked a good curry. On hot days she'd use pinewood that burns fast but doesn't give off so much heat. We washed and rinsed our clothes by hand and hung them on the clothesline. We cleaned and filled the kerosene lamps each evening and enjoyed the soft light. Work was hard, and life was primitive, but happy and fulfilling,

Various family members came to visit us that summer—my aunts, brothers, Carl's parents, and friends. Were they coming to check up on us? All of our visitors enjoyed watching the lumbering and the stories of Clyde Kester and O'Leary about dramatic events of the past on Dutch Mountain—stories about logging and hunting camps, about bears and rattlers, and about pulling a mess of brook trout out of Mehoopany, with snips of red flannel on a hook.

All summer we enjoyed swimming in the lake. Since we had no bathroom, only an outhouse, and since we were covered with saw-dust and grime we bathed and swam daily, rain or shine, except when there was lightning. On those days we took pour baths off the back porch with one or two buckets.

One day, while we were still lumbering, we lost our cook. Ruth had been looking for a job in the Philadelphia area for the fall. Dr. and Mrs. Hughes, both doctors in Bryn Mawr, needed an all-around person to cook, drive their two children to different schools, keep house, care for the children, and run the ranch. Ruth had answered their add in the paper. They came with their children to Bella Sylva without giving any warning, because we had no phone. They interviewed Ruth and she accepted the position. So Ruth, the college graduate, took this job to be near me, but not too near. Within two hours she had gone off with the Hughes family, leaving me bereft. We did not even have time for a quiet talk. Worst of all, Carl and I were back to our own cooking!

In a couple of weeks our lumbering was over. I paid Carl his share of the profits, and in the end all I had left was the jeep, but it was debt free. I used it and the trailer for hauling work around Gettysburg. With the jeep I could go supply preaching even in the mountains of West Virginia during the winter.

Leo the lumberman made a good profit. He had paid me the going rate of fifteen dollars per thousand board feet of prime cherry at the loading dock. He sold my beautiful cherry lumber to a casket company, making all of our lumbering a cover-up undertaking.

CHAPTER 6

MARRIED RAMBLINGS AT BELLA SYLVA, KARTHAUS, AND GETTYSBURG

On July 12, 1950, Ruth and I were married in Little Falls, New Jersey, by her uncle Pastor David Bogard. We had a Kodai clan wedding. The bridal party and the ushers were all Kodai kids, including my brother Fritz, Best Man, and Joyce DeBruin Dunham, Ruth's Matron of Honor. The persons we missed were Jerry and Shurlee, who had been married the summer before. They could not attend as they were in the midst of having their first child. Ruth's father, George, and her brother, Chuck, were in Kodai and could not come. They celebrated our wedding in Kodaikanal where Chuck and Molly were attending Kodaikanal School. They had a wedding cake in our honor and invited friends to the party.

But Ruth's mother, Christina, had come all the way from Basrah by plane to take part. Christina's sisters, brother, cousins and son, Jim Gosselink, were there, too. Ruth's grandfather, Gerrit Gosselink, gave Ruth away with a very loud, "I do!" Everyone enjoyed that. Our wedding was followed by a reception tea with sandwiches and wedding cake. Then we were off on our honeymoon in the jeep I had used for lumbering.

Guess where we went? Bella Sylva of course! We arrived as it was getting dark, and quickly went down to the lake for the last of the sunset. Carrying Ruth over the kitchen threshold proved to be a strenuous task, but I managed it.

We lit the kerosene lamps, but had candlelight in the dining room for our wedding supper of hickory smoked ham, baked potatoes and peas. Then we sat on the porch facing the lake to enjoy the beauty and quiet of the Bella Sylva woods before going to bed for the wonder of finally being totally together. Putting it biblically, we became one flesh, and knew each other as we joyfully began life together as husband and wife.

The mountain was deserted. Every cabin was vacant. We had a private honeymoon lake and we rejoiced in being the only two in that glorious focal point of God's beautiful creation. We spent much time on the lake and on the swimming raft. After several days we hiked to Mehoopany Creek, spent some time in the cave behind the waterfall and swam in the pool beneath the lower falls. We felt privileged to have the entire stream and mountain area to ourselves, like Adam and Eve in the garden.

Soon our honeymoon week was over, and off we went to Karthaus, Pennsylvania, where I had been serving a three-point parish for the summer. There we spent the next six weeks in the sparsely furnished parsonage, our first temporary home. Our neighbors and the parish were most welcoming and good to us, keeping us supplied with vegetables and baked goods. Every Sunday we had dinner in one of their homes.

After we had been there over a week and met all three congregations, our neighbor, Leona Flood whispered to Ruth one evening that we should go to bed at 11 p.m. with our clothes on, "Just wait and listen and don't be too surprised." I am glad she gave a warning. At about 11:30 p.m. we were surrounded by loud and raucous sounds: trumpets blowing, people beating on pots and pans with wooden spoons, and various instruments chiming in. Our new friends called it serenading. It reminded me of Gideon's men terrifying the Midianites—no wonder the Midianites had fled in panic. After giving our friends seven or eight minutes for effect, we got up fully clothed, turned on our lights and went downstairs to open the house to our shouting and singing visitors. The whole parish was there and in high spirits. They came with folding chairs, card tables, and lots of desserts. They stayed for an hour of joyful, hilarious fun.

Our Karthaus parish experience, though only for the summer, was a most formative time of my ministerial training. I discovered that I loved and enjoyed ministering to people in many different ways. Ruth took quite naturally to sharing in the ministry and I could see that ours would be a life-long team ministry that would bring fulfillment and joy to each of us. It was at Karthaus that our first child, Bill, was conceived. What a blessing!

We returned to Gettysburg in the fall to an upstairs Gettysburg apartment, 20 Reynolds Street, our own *Gettysburg address*. A few days after we moved in, Ruth's mom returned to Gettysburg from a visit with family in Iowa, and stayed with us for several weeks. I did not mind having my mother-in-law around. She was first up every morning and had coffee ready by the time I awakened. I missed that when she returned to Basrah.

I worked very hard during my final year in seminary. Now I had much higher motivation and a greater sense of responsibility. In October I found myself on a bus sitting next to Dr. Abdel Ross Wentz, President of the seminary. We talked about my call to be a missionary. He was then the chairman of the Board of Foreign Missions of the United Lutheran Church in America. I will never forget what he said, "Sam, if you want to be a missionary you have to be a good one, you can't fool around. Tremendous dedication and hard work are what it takes!" I heard him.

The next spring and summer were very busy. Ruth suffered from pre-eclampsia from the middle of March and had to stay in bed on a special diet. I had to do all the cooking and house cleaning, as well as finish my thesis, prepare my term papers, and study for finals.

One evening there was a knock on our door. Mrs. Wentz, wife of our principal, was there with a casserole and flowers. She said, "Sam, one of the student or faculty wives will be bringing your evening meal each night until Ruth is well." They did! This loving expression of the seminary community helped and encouraged us. We were so thankful to be part of this caring fellowship.

Bill was born on May 3, 1951. He came quickly. We barely got to the hospital in time, and I paced for less than an hour. Ruth was in the hospital for six days. I brought her huge bunches of redbud and dogwood that I shamelessly picked on the battlefield early in the morning. We rejoiced together in having William August, named after his great-great-grandfather, founder of Bella Sylva and builder of our log cabin. Having a baby in 1951 was not a great financial burden for a seminary student. Our doctor charged $100 for the delivery, student rate. The hospital bill for 6 days was $100. There was no thought of health insurance in those days.

In the same month I submitted my Bachelor of Divinity thesis on the topic, "Use of Audio-Visual Aids in Proclaiming the Gospel in Foreign Mission Fields." What I researched would prove to be of great help in my work as a missionary. I took my final exams, and graduated from seminary, then was ordained at the Central Pennsylvania Synod Convention in Philadelphia. After that, I took special courses at the Biblical Seminary, NYC, and attended missionary conferences in preparation for work in India. While I was away, Ruth and little Bill stayed in Gettysburg.

When Ruth and I applied for mission service to the Board of Foreign Missions we knew we could not hope for a call to India. The previous year there had been a policy not to send missionary kids, *MKs*, to countries where their parents had served. However, on the application form we were asked to list countries where we would like to serve in order of preference. At that time the United Lutheran Church had missions only in Japan, India, British Guiana, Argentina, Liberia and Tanganikya, now called Tanzania. I listed my preferences, "India, British Guiana, Liberia, and Tanganikya." I excluded Japan, thinking I would never be able to master the language, especially the writing. In 1951 the Board's policy was changed. Gerry Currens was called to Liberia where his father was serving, and we were called and sent to India.

At the end of summer we spent a few happy and blessed days at Bella Sylva, before leaving for India. Bill demanded constant attention. We called him "Little Boss." We washed his cloth diapers by hand at the cabin, rinsed them in the lake, and hung them on the clothesline. We managed to pick and enjoy blueberries but had no time or way to make it to Mehoopany with baby Bill. Friends and family came to visit and were happy to see us as a family.

In September we were commissioned at St. Mark's Lutheran Church in Trenton, New Jersey, the first church to take on our support. In those days it was the policy to commission only the ordained husband, but I insisted that Ruth should kneel beside me and share in the commissioning. Dr. Luther Gotwald, who was serving as the Board Secretary and had previously served with my Dad in India, agreed and laid his hands on both of us as he conducted the commissioning. We would be co-workers.

Ruth's graduation from Central College

Our Wedding, July 12, 1950

The wedding party

CHAPTER 7

RAMBLINGS IN INDIA AROUND PEDDAPURAM AND KODAIKANAL

"Sam, let's go for a long walk," Ruth requested. "Rajamani can look after Bill. I need to get out into the countryside, away from this red dust and talk about how our life is shaping up here." So we set out on our first ramble since we had come to Peddapuram in South India, where my family had lived from 1930 to 1935.

We had arrived in India with baby Bill on January 8, 1952, after leaving New York in November on a Dutch freighter. The ship took us safely through a terrible Atlantic storm. Every time the freighter pitched and the prow smashed down with a terrible bang, we remembered seeing the crew load 500 tons of TNT in the ship's forward hold in the Delaware River near Philadelphia, the day after we set sail from New York Harbor. However, soon the weather calmed and we had a pleasant sunny voyage the rest of the way, entering the Mediterranean at Gibraltar and sailing past Malta to Port Said in Egypt.

At Port Said we left the ship with most of our things in our cabin and took a bus to Cairo, stopping at road blocks put up by the British, then the Egyptians. This was shortly after the British-French task force had invaded the Suez Canal Zone. Tension was still very high. In Cairo we sensed trouble in the air, but with the assurance of our hotel manager found a good guide and visited the national museum, the pyramids, and rode on camels, taking Bill everywhere with us. We saw few other tourists.

On December 12 we flew across the Suez Canal and the desert of Sinai to Basrah on a DC-4 at about 7,000 feet. As we flew over the Sinai Peninsula our pilot gave a good travelogue. Pointing out Mt.

Sinai, endless wadis and ridges, and the vast emptiness of the desert
he said, "It would have been a good place to wander around for
forty years." In one area we saw where rain had fallen recently,
making the desert green, attracting Bedouins with tents, herds of
sheep and camels. What a sight! As the sun set over the Shatt-al-
Arab River (the combined Tigris and Euphrates Rivers) we landed
in Basrah, Iraq, the beautiful city of date palms. Ruth's mom,
Christina, her dad, George, and her brother, Chuck—a junior at
Kodaikanal School, home for vacation—welcomed us with much
joy. They met Bill for the first time.

We stayed with them until our ship came up the river in January.
It was a grand time, sharing Christmas, Ruth's birthday on December 26, her parents' 25th wedding anniversary, and Bill's baptism by
his grandfather, all within a three-week period. We met and had
fellowship with all their friends—Brits, Armenian Christians, Scots,
Arabs, and fellow American missionaries. We played lots of tennis.
Meal times were special. We enjoyed Arab bread and dates with
every meal.

One day George took me and several British friends to Ur of the
Chaldees, Abraham's hometown, and guided us through the dig-
findings of the archaeologist, Sir Arthur Woolly. George had taught
in Basrah Boys School for three years before his marriage to Chris
in 1926. He had visited Ur many times, while excavations were going on, and had seen the archaeologist's work and findings. We
shared in his enthusiasm and love of Ur. We will never forget the
memory of Iraq as a peaceful, progressive and gentle place: the land
of Abraham and Ezra, date gardens, desert wells, groves of Australian Pine trees—*ethel*, the land of the great Tigris and Euphrates
rivers; the land of Muslims and Christians living in harmony. I am
glad Ruth and her family could show me the real, human, and
hauntingly beautiful side of Iraq. This land has played such a sig-
nificant part in the faith and life of Jews, Christians, and Muslims
through the past 4000 years.

We left Basrah on January 4. Sailing directly to Bombay, we arrived in India January 8, 1952. From there we went by train to
Guntur where we were met by the Wood family with my sister
Molly, Christie Zimmerman, and others. We stayed with the
Woods. Molly and Pat enjoyed playing with Bill. After several days
we traveled 130 miles north to Rajahmundry, my birthplace. The
missionaries who met us there, the Geslers, Dolbeers, Ziglers,

Moyers, Colemans, Sue Glatz, Meta Blair, Hilda Kaercher, Mabel Meyer, Ethel Dentzer, and Hildagarde Swanson, had known me as a boy. They welcomed Ruth and me now as fellow workers and part of the missionary family.

After visiting in Rajahmundry for several days, we went to Peddapuram, where we would spend one year in language study. There we met George and Mary Phillips, with whom we would share a spacious duplex during our first year in India. The first day we decided to share housekeeping, though there were full separate quarters for each family. We shared a cook named Thomas, Samuel the waterman, whose job was to fill the water tanks in the kitchen and each bathroom, and Rajamani, an *ayah*, or *amma* (nanny), who would look after little Paul Philips and our Bill, while we studied language together. George of Georgia and Mary from South Carolina spoke with rich southern accents and used many wonderful expressions.

At the end of our first week of language study, Ruth suggested that we take this long walk. We started walking behind our house, past the high school boys' hostel and beyond. Finding a path that ascended a gentle slope we climbed for more than an hour through fields of sesame seed, horse gram and Bengal gram—red lentils. There were lots of interesting birds—blue rollers, the green jet plane-like bee-eater, hoopoo, Indian oriole, crow pheasant, larks, minas, and hawks. As we climbed up the long slope the fields turned to grazing land. Boys who couldn't have been more than ten years old watched herds of cattle, sheep, and goats. We stopped to talk with them. They laughed at our attempts to speak Telugu. We could hardly understand them.

Near the top of the ridge we came upon a beautiful mango garden. It was like an oasis. How could they have found enough water to raise these trees? Exploring the garden, we found an old abandoned well that must have been seventy feet deep. Some wealthy landowner with vision and a love for fruit trees had spent much and made this great effort to dig the well, set out trees, protect them every day from free grazing goats, and water them for the first two or three dry seasons (from mid-November into June). Now this orchard of 100 or more trees was a fruitful and valuable asset for the patient owner, and a source of delight, shade, and rest in the hot season for anyone passing by. The garden was also a sanctuary for birds of all kinds, but especially for parakeets, doves, and cuckoos. We decided then that after language study, at our new home, we would plant fruit trees as part of our mission to make the world a better place.

After climbing a few hundred yards beyond the mango grove we reached the top of the ridge. From there we had a panoramic view of the Madras-Calcutta rail line, two miles to the southwest. A steam train puffed its way north to Vishakapatnam. Beyond the rail line were irrigated rice fields of the Godavari Delta fed by the Cotton Canal, named after the master engineer and builder of the Godavari Annicut, a low-level irrigation dam. Sir Arthur Cotton designed the entire delta irrigation system covering one million acres, in the 1850's. What a contrast to this dry ridge of rough grassland on which we stood!

Since the sun was getting low in the west, we started back sharing our thoughts about being in India together, problems we had with language study, and the differences between our living style and the living style of the Phillips. We agreed on the need to make a go of living in community with them, learning from them, and being flexible to new ways. We returned home feeling much better about our situation. From then on, at George's suggestion, we had frequent conferences with George and Mary and would bring everything into the open. Thank God, we were able to live together with cooperation and understanding, and form a lifetime bond of friendship.

One night after we had both read awhile and turned off the light, Ruth said, "Sam, listen!" So we listened to the sounds of the road beside our house. A line of more than thirty bullock carts went creaking past our house on the red dirt road. One cart driver was telling a story in a loud voice. At the end of a long sentence or paragraph he would pause, and from carts behind and in front of him, we would hear each driver grunt *Ummm* or *Aayya,* meaning *yes.* This showed that they were awake and listening. —A Telugu proverb teaches, "A storyteller is only as good as the *Ummms* of his audience." Toward the end of the convoy, a cart man was singing a beautiful Telugu lyric—all this to the rhythm of the hooves of the plodding bullocks. We came to treasure these sounds of the road and would fall asleep each night listening to them.

As dawn would break, *kovela* (cuckoo), called *kokila* in Sanskrit, would begin singing to welcome the new day. In Telugu literature *Kokila Ghanamu,* the cuckoo song, is thought to be most romantic.

We found it was so. We would awaken to it, lie there and breathe deeply of the cool air, listen, look at each other in love, hazel eyes to brown, and see the beauty of the dawn. Next we would hear the Muslim call to prayer—hauntingly beautiful. Then the radio of a neighbor would bring to us the sweet strains of Hindu morning praise hymns, sung in Telugu or Sanskrit poetry by two singers, man and woman, singing an octave apart, doing every trill, slide, and grace note in perfect unison. These were classical South Indian *ragas*, melodies composed by Tyaga Raju, a Telugu devotional poet and musician who lived in the early 19th century in Tamilnadu in South India. Many Telugu Christian hymns are arranged to his Carnatic ragas. The early morning in India, especially in warm and hot weather, is the best time of day for prayer and work, and we would take full advantage of it.

Language study with our Brahmin *munshi* (language teacher) was much fun and very helpful. P. Venkata Rao taught us by the direct method by pointing to things, bringing objects, commenting on the snacks we brought. Using great ingenuity he helped us to begin thinking in Telugu. He forbade us from writing anything down for two months, until our pronunciation was correct, after which we could write only in Telugu, which is phonetic. As we advanced he used John 4, the account of the Samaritan woman meeting with Jesus at Jacob's well as the Telugu text, teaching us new words and expressions. We came to respect him when we realized that he, a Hindu, knew the story so well and could explain it much better than we could. The Woman at the Well is a most familiar scene in India.

When the hot season began we took Sri Venkata Rao with us to Kodaikanal and studied with him for three months. Ruth was pregnant again, but very healthy. We played tennis and went on a hikes between study days. We enjoyed the fellowship with other missionary families. Ruth's brother Chuck, finished his junior year at Kodaikanal High School, then lived with us during his May vacation. I went camping with him and his friend Donald Oberdoerffer at Berijam Lake. Molly, also in Kodai School and living with the Wood family, spent much time at our house. So we had wondeful times with our youngest siblings.

By the end of May 1952 we needed a break from our Telugu studies. So eight years after our last romantic ramble together as students in Kodai, Ruth and I again attempted to climb Vembadi

Peak, this time with friends Ruth Sigmon and Dolores Dohlen. Leaving our one-year-old Bill with our *ayya*, we set forth with lunch and flasks of coffee, and the determination to reach the summit. We took a car for six miles to the top of Green Hut, then hiked on the road till we came to the turn-off. After several hours we experienced the same trouble as previously. The overgrown path became more and more difficult to follow. At noon we found a lovely spot with ancient pine trees where we had lunch; we then kept going. I was starting to be concerned about Ruth, now nearly five months pregnant. But she was in good shape and health. Then it began to drizzle. She slipped on wet pine needles and fell. That did it! I insisted we turn back. By the time we returned to the Forty Mile Round the rain had stopped. Crossing the road, we took a forest firebreak trail to the cliff edge and there enjoyed beautiful views of the plains and the ridges descending from the escarpment. To the West we viewed series of majestic cliffs and ridges beyond the high point, Doctor's Delight.

We returned home for tea and toast. Ruth was none the worse for her fall, but we were disappointed that we had again failed to reach Vambadi Peak. Would we ever stand on top?

After returning from Kodai to Peddapuram we settled down to more intense Telugu study and life on the 'plains.' I kept in good shape playing soccer with the Peddapuram High School boys after school hours. Even though I had played three years of varsity soccer for Gettysburg College, two of the Telugu high school boys played better than I could. I picked up a lot of Telugu from these teens, including some expressions that I soon learned were not fit to repeat.

We played on the same field where hundreds of thousands had gathered to see and hear Mahatma Gandhi when he had visited Peddapuram on December 24, 1932. Dad had recorded some of Gandhi's visit on 16 mm movie film, including his arrival by Model A Ford and his reception and speech at the high school soccer field. I was then almost five and remember how we three brothers had sat on the compound wall waiting for Gandhi. When he came in his car with bodyguards standing on the running boards we waved at him. Little did we realize what an historic event we were witnessing. My historian son Dr. Peter Schmitthenner is the present custodian of this valuable film.

Ruth needed exercise too, so we began walking two or three times a week. Following the dusty red-dirt road was hopeless, so we began walking in the fields on the northwest side of the road. This was in the opposite direction that we had taken on our first ramble at Peddapuram. The monsoon was just starting with occasional showers, and farmers were busy plowing and planting dry crops. One afternoon after walking more than a mile, we came upon a number of workers planting chili seedlings. One crew dug holes eighteen inches apart, a second crew filled the holes with water from a large number of pots they had carried nearly a mile, and then women planted six-inch seedlings filling in the holes. We watched this process for half an hour wondering if it was worth it. We also surmised that all over India most chilies are planted this way, with just as much labor involved. We voiced this question to the landlord who explained that it was a very viable operation and that he would make a good profit in December. He invited us to come to his home for breakfast the next morning. At 7 a.m. a young man came to guide us. We were served *idlies* (rice and lentil flour cakes) with coconut and various kinds of *chutney*. Mmm, so good! We had a great discussion with our host and answered his questions about Christ and our mission.

In August Ruth came down with German measles and a high fever. A nearby Brahmin doctor, Rama Rao, came to visit and lovingly cared for her each day. He would not let us take her on the bumpy twenty-five mile ride to the mission hospital, saying that we might lose our child. We were so relieved when she recovered. Dr. Rama Rao had a large picture of Jesus in the entranceway of his hospital, and began each day's work with prayer to God the Father in Jesus' name. He attended English services and thought of himself as a Christian. We had long discussions about baptism, which he thought was not necessary. I presented the view that this is a sacrament which our Lord Jesus taught and commanded and that this is the way we become part of God's worldwide family for all ages. We enjoyed our sessions together where we also discussed the English sermons. Years later I was very happy to hear that he had received baptism by immersion, joining one of the Baptist churches.

In September, Ruth's parents came on leave from Basrah, and visited us after staying in Kodai for a few weeks. They were pleased that we were expecting another child. Mr. George, as the Arabs called him, spoke at a special program in the high school and preached at the English service. They met our friends and enjoyed special occasions with our missionary community in Rajahmundry.

One day we went with the Gosselinks and the Phillips family to Uppadu, a beach on the Bay of Bengal near the port of Kakinada. What a disappointment! As children we had stayed at a lovely brick beach house and enjoyed a pristine beach safe for swimming and wading. Now, fifteen years later, the remains of the house were in the surf, much of the beach had been eroded, the bay was full of jellyfish, and a fishing village had been established, polluting the sandy beach where we used to swim. Sea erosion had been caused by the dams and canals of the Godavari restricting the flow of mud and sand which previously built up the delta. India's growing population demands rice, irrigation dams, more fish, fishermen, and fishing villages. In spite of the changes we enjoyed a good time together watching Paul and Bill react to their first experience with unlimited sand and the ocean.

On October 22, 1952, in Rajahmundry Hospital, Hans was born in the same place where I had been delivered. I scrubbed up and was watching when Dr. Zigler and his nurse wife Jean, assisted by several Indian nurses, delivered him. He came head first, hollering lustfully as soon as his head appeared. This one would be noisy and talkative! He surely was, and is.

Returning to Peddapur with baby Hans, we set to work preparing for our early December language exams. Even with her pregnancy, illness, nursing Hans, and running the household smoothly, Ruth scored one point higher than I did on the written exam and equal to me on the oral exam. I was proud of her. And I was told that she was proud of me.

Our first Christmas in India we celebrated in Peddapuram with a new baby and the Phillips family, and with our new friends and congregation at Peddapuram. What a wonderful, warm, loving fellowship we had! The people of Peddapuram had gone out of their way to make us feel welcomed and loved. It was a great and blessed first year of service.

Our Commissioning as Missionaries at St. Mark's, Trenton, NJ

Dinner with Ruth's family in Basrah, Iraq, in the court yard of a friend

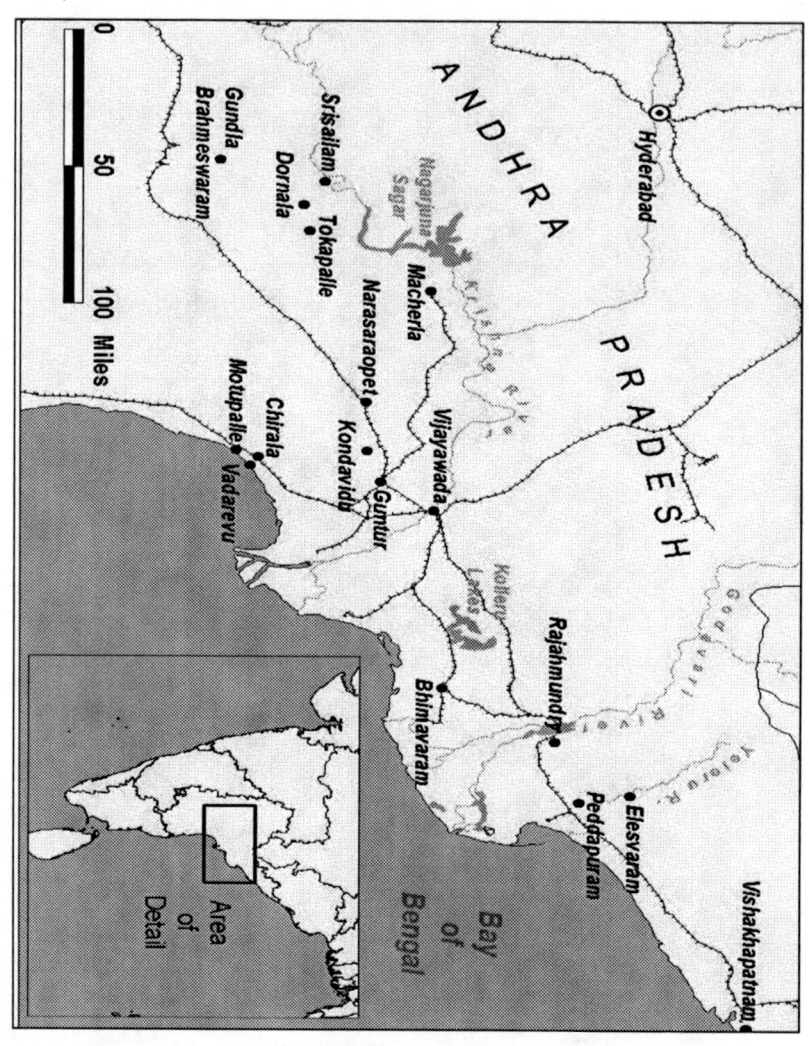

Map of Coastal Andhra Pradesh in areas we worked from 1952-1981

CHAPTER 8

FAMILY WALKS DURING OUR YELESWARAM YEARS

After celebrating Christmas at Peddapuram we packed up and moved to Yeleswaram on New Year's Day, 1953. This was the place where my family had lived from 1935 to 1945. What a home-coming we received! Gospel workers and teachers of the four par-ishes my father had served, plus the local congregation, and Pastor K. John Whitteker Kameswara Rao were all there to greet us. Marku was there. He had worked as waterman for Mother and Fa-ther, and for Uncle Ted Benze before him. His wife Krupamma, now 38 years old, was holding twin baby boys the same age as Hans. She was my old friend. As a teenager I used to go back to her house to eat hot curry and rice with *charu* (pepper water) on days when mother didn't have curry for lunch.

The oilseed *gonagu* trees and *casurina* trees my Dad had planted lined the driveway. At the back of the house were the cork or *konda malli* hill-jasmine trees that I remembered. Two sour orange trees, which I used to climb and pick from, were still in the front yard. I asked Marku, "Where's the temple tree (*frangi pangi*) my Father planted?"

He said, "Mr. Wicklund didn't like that kind of tree and had me cut it down." I told him to find another seedling and plant it right away. He shrugged his shoulders, saying *"chittam"* which means, *your will*, or *yes, I will*. He probably thought, "These missionaries! Why don't they think alike? One plants, another cuts down." What he said was sometimes true about other matters as well.

We settled easily into the wonderful house built by Hank Moyer's father, Henry. He had been in seminary with my Father and was still working as evangelist in the Rajahmundry area. Our home had three large bedrooms and two bathrooms upstairs. A small bedroom with a bathroom, a large office, spacious living room and dining room, a breakfast porch, and some storerooms were downstairs. The kitchen was detached from the house to spare the house from the smoke and heat of the charcoal and wood stoves. The same furniture my family had used during my boyhood was still there. How satisfying and joyful it was to be back home!

Life was pretty primitive in Yeleswaram. Without electricity or a fridge, keeping milk and other food from spoiling was a problem. We reactivated the old ice-ball box. When that stopped working we kept milk in wet sand in a crock in the coolest, darkest storeroom. Carrots, beets, and other vegetables stored the same way stayed cool and lasted longer. But milk often went sour, so we adopted the Indian practice of making yogurt with leftover milk each evening. After six months we were glad to receive a very efficient kerosene-powered Electrolux refrigerator and felt that we were living in luxury.

We settled in, knowing we would be here for five years. This meant we could enjoy the fruits of our labors, fix the house, plant a garden and trees, and make the place our home. About six weeks after our move, after I had toured and surveyed my whole parish, I took a day off. I worked making house and yard improvements. At afternoon tea with Ruth and Bill, I said, "Ruth, let's take the children and go to Timmaraju Tank for a walk. You'll love this place. I'm anxious to show you around."

Since Bill was not yet two, and Hans just three months old, we drove the car through town and one mile beyond to the huge artificial lake made by two dams. In India an artificial lake is called a *tank*. The Timmaraju Tank was supposedly the second largest *tank* in the whole of Andhra Pradesh. The dam on our side of town was fifty feet high and nearly a third of a mile long.

We walked along the *tank bund* (embankment), noting the many varieties of ducks, black storks, Asian open-bill storks, cormorants, white egrets, stilts, and red and yellow-wattled lapwings and sandpipers. All of the birds were feeding along the shore of this two-mile-wide body of water. Two major streams flowed into this *tank*, filling it to overflowing during every monsoon season. Hills framed three sides of the *tank*. One of them, Nagulakonda (Snake Mountain) snakes along for miles to the north and east into Vishakhapatnam District. Seven of the congregations in my Jaddangi parish lay in the early morning shadow of Nagulakonda. I told Ruth about my first visits to these congregations as we strolled the length of the bund. I carried Bill on my shoulders while Ruth carried baby Hans in her arms.

We went past very large *neem* (margosa) trees to the seventy-five foot wide masonry overflow, now dry since the monsoon season had ended in November. I showed Ruth the hillside where Fritz and I used to hunt for birds, and we visited the spot where Fritz had shot a king cobra and the python it was killing. Several large Malabar hornbills flew over us squawking shrilly. The foothills meet the fertile plains at this spot. Water from the hills which receive more rainfall is stored here for the irrigation of rice and sugar cane fields over thousands of acres nearby Yeleswaram and the coastal plain beyond.

We walked back, amazed at the beauty of the sunset. It was good to be together with our children in this beautiful area. It bordered on very wild jungle. In small scattered villages people lived close to nature, gathering forest fruits, soap nuts, wood, leaves, fiber for rope and bamboo for building and many uses. I found the villagers to be caring, hospitable, honest, and hungry to hear God's Word. Serving joyfully in this place Psalm 16: 5,6 came to mind:

> The Lord is my portion and my cup Thou holdest my lot.
> The lines have fallen for me in pleasant places
> Yea, I have a goodly heritage."

What does heritage mean? Surely more than inheriting one's parents' genes and characteristics, more than childhood experiences and memories of the good things our parents have done with and for us, and more than family legends, written and oral. It is even deeper than the land, deeper than places like Kodaikanal or Bella Sylva, our patrimony. I view heritage most clearly as a matter of faith received and affirmed. I rejoice in my heritage of faith, thinking of my parents and forebear's faith. The words of Isaiah 51:1 come to mind, "Look to the rock from which you were hewn." For Ruth and me, heritage was what God had reserved, promised, and given to us as an undeserved gift, by his grace. We received it in faith with joy and thanksgiving. This is the blessing that Ruth and I shared. We realized that we were called to be "joint heirs of the grace of life" (I Peter 3:7). We also lived in hope that our heritage would be further fulfilled.

My work took me all over, and sometimes deep into the hills. Some tours would be for ten days or more. Ruth could not go on any of these journeys, hikes, or long rambles during these years, as she was nursing or carrying a child for four of our five years in Yeleswaram. Naturally Ruth would be lonely when I went away for longer periods. She kept busy with the children, continued language study, became involved in the women's work of the church and soon had many good friends—the pastor's wife, and teachers of the school among others. She spoke Telugu all the time, especially words involved in housekeeping, cooking, and purchasing.

My Telugu was more theological and biblical, and more seasoned with colloquial village expressions. Mortha Sudarsanam, the catechist with whom I worked, encouraged me to take on more of the Telugu service each week, and soon had me preaching in Telugu, first for ten minutes, then twenty, and then for half an hour. This was considered the minimum for a "real sermon." Prayer language, more formal in Telugu, was harder to learn than preaching.

Sometime in the middle of our term, Miss Ella Hansen, the missionary in Samalkot (twenty-five miles away) who worked with Bible women, left for furlough and Ruth was asked to be in charge of the five Bible women in our conference. Bible women had at least an eighth grade education and two years of Bible training either in the seminary or in the Bible Women's training School in Rajahmundry. Many of them were widows, others were wives of Bible trained teachers or catechists. Their ministry was devoted mostly to bringing the gospel to higher caste Hindu women. They were to visit twelve to fifteen Hindu homes a week, making the rounds in several villages, year after year. Usually they became close friends with many of the Hindu women. They gave thorough Bible instruction and teaching about the life and meaning of Christ in each interested home. For scores of Hindu families in our area, whenever sickness occurred the mother of the household would send for a Bible woman as her prayers and comforting visits would bring them hope.

Ruth could not devote much time for this work, but when I could be home with the children doing office work she'd take the car with our faithful driver, Yohan, and go visiting with the Bible women or attend women's rallies. She refused to take on leadership roles and encouraged the women teachers, pastor's wives, and Bible women to be officers and leaders in the women's work of the church.

My times at home were busy, as I was in charge of eighteen village schools in the agency area. Part of my job included supervising about forty village schoolteachers, most of whom were remarkable persons dedicated to their work. They led Sunday worship, services of burial, and healing prayers for their congregations. They were letter writers for the people in their village, served as role models, and settled disputes among their people. These men and women teachers had received two years of teacher's training after they completed eighth grade. More than half of them had a year of Bible training as well. Working with them was for the most part a joy, but there were problems also. During the time I was there the government changed requirements so that new teachers needed a high school education, and secondary teacher's training of two years. Many of our teaching staff went back to school to upgrade. They could go for further education receiving from the education department, "leave with lean on post," for up to four years. This guaranteed their old teaching position when they returned.

Within two miles of our home there were great places for short rambles. When I was home we would go for an evening walk two or three times a week, often to Timmaraju Tank. We also enjoyed walking half a mile to a small rocky hillock overlooking the Yeleru River. The range of hills rising from the other side of the Yeluru River resembled ridges of the Alleghenies, stretching southwest for miles. This range and Nagulakonda (Snake Hill) going northeast from Timmaraju Tank are part of what are called the Eastern Ghats, the foothills of the Deccan Plateau. The first range is 800-1000 feet above sea level. The height gradually increases to over 4000 feet in the higher foothills further to the west. This wild hilly area named The Agency has been assigned to a special government agency since World War I to protect the hill tribes and reserved forest from exploitation by merchants and land grabbers of the plains.

The lower slopes of the hill on the opposite side of the river were adorned with beautiful clumps of bamboo, a most useful and sought-after forest product. Bamboo is the roofing material for most villagers. Sugar-cane clumps are propped up with it. It provides material for fencing, baskets, wattle framework for mud walls, mats, tatties (room dividers), and yokes for carrying water. Other uses of bamboo include farm implements, bows and arrows, fishing rods and fish traps, scaffolding and the manufacture of high-grade paper. We could hear wild chickens calling from bamboo thickets, and were delighted by the fern-like appearance and sunset reflection of the lacy bamboo fronds on the river. In the dry season we waded in the river with the children, staying till sunset. In the flood season we would watch whole trees being swept along the rampaging river. At that time fishermen were busy hooking a certain kind of large fish migrating up the flood-swollen and muddy Yeleru from the sea just thirty-five river miles away.

One day during the floods we took a path upstream from the hillock along a rocky ridge. From above we could see the river sweeping over fields in a low-lying area. The flood came to the edge of a mango garden where Fritz and I used to swim and hunt doves. Not far from that garden was a lone huge old mango tree in the midst of flooded rice paddies. I told Ruth the story of three men who had been stranded in that tree by a flash flood in 1936. Dad had set out to rescue them. First he went around the village collecting stout rope. Then, making a raft of bamboo, he tied the rope to the raft and to a tree on the riverbank, then swam with the raft toward the tree as two men paddled. After great effort, as they neared the tree, they came to the end of the rope tied to the shore. Dad called to the men in the tree to jump one by one. He managed to catch the first two but missed the third who was swept away. However, that man survived. He somehow kept afloat, and half a mile down stream was swept into a flooded mango orchard. Again he caught a branch and climbed to safety. Our whole family had witnessed the awesome flood and heroic rescue from the spot where Bill, Hans, Ruth, and I were now standing.

Many of the poor came to us for medical help. At first we referred them to the local doctor of the government dispensary. But they would return saying that he was unkind and demanded money which they did not have. We were reluctant to begin this kind of ministry, for which we had no training, yet were compelled by the urgency and need. Taking advice and supplies from Dr. Virgil Zigler and his wife Jean, a nurse at our mission hospital in Rajahmundry, we opened a small dispensary on our office porch five mornings a week. Ordering medicines from the Methodist Mission Tablet Industry at Bangarapet, we began dispensing pills for diarrhea, malaria, and headache. We treated the boarding school boys and girls for headache, scabies, malaria, eye infection, cuts and bruises, and worms. Serious or persistent cases we would refer to the Rajahmundry Mission Hospital, helping them with bus charges. Each month we sold 8000 malaria chloroquin pills at cost, giving written and oral dosage instructions for using. Forest areas showed a very high incidence of malaria. Some of our teachers bought chloroquin pills in bulk to dispense in their villages.

Ruth and I took turns at dispensary duty when I was home. After a long tour I would take a week of dispensary duty myself. We treated infections with sulfa powder and even treated several boys who had been bitten by monkeys. Achamma, a poor widow, came on her hands and buttocks with the most horrible leg infection I had ever seen. She refused to go to the hospital. We cleansed her putrid infected sores, applied sulfanilamide powder, and bandaged her legs. We treated her every day, often together, and prayed for her. She stayed on a side porch of a nearby coffee hotel because of the compassion of the owner. She was perfectly cured after two months, and walked around joyfully. The kind proprietor gave her work cleaning the coffee hotel. She visited us often just to thank us. Because of her we had more patients. After two years a kind doctor was transferred to our village, so our ministry tapered off. But we continued to sell malaria pills and treat boarding school children.

One winter afternoon, as we sunned ourselves on the rocks at our river overlook, I told Ruth and the children the story of my exploration of the river. At age fifteen, on my last vacation at Yeleswaram, my parents agreed that I could go exploring by following the river up to the favorite picnic spot where our family would go for afternoon swims and campfire picnics. Dad said that they would come by car to meet me at the picnic place in the evening.

I began the adventure at 6:30 in the morning on a pleasant, cool January day, following the river with my 22 rifle and lunch. The river fascinated me, and the changing pleasant scenery lifted my spirits. It took hours to reach the great arc of the river that we could see easily from a hill near Yeleswaram. Though the car journey to the picnic place was only six miles, I am sure I walked more than twelve river miles by lunch time, yet seemed to be only half way there. I saw dense jungle, great trees, endless bamboo thickets, tribes of monkeys coming to the river to drink, water birds of all kinds, shrieking Malabar hornbills, deer tracks, and tiger tracks. I walked faster up river, following the tracks until they went up over the riverbank. I wondered, "Is it looking at me? Is it hungry?" I walked faster, constantly on the alert. Finally just before sunset, I heard the roar of the waterfall and rapids of the *Kollaturu,* the onomatopoetic Telugu name for the rocks and rapids of our picnic place. Then I met Dad carrying a flashlight. He had come downriver looking for me, knowing it would soon be dark.

All this I shared with Ruth and my children, knowing that some day we would let them explore new and wild places and experience thrills, danger, challenge, and discovery.

One pleasant December we went to Donnagadda Stream, two miles further up the road. Donnagadda flowed into the Yeleru about three miles west of our Yeleswaram home. I had played and hunted there as a lad. Dad used to put us to work, promising an *anna* for every live minnow we caught. We would take these home and put them into the water tanks of each bathroom and the kitchen. The minnows ate the mosquito larvae that were constantly hatching in the house. Four or five minnows would keep the water tank clear. Jerry, Fritz, and I had made sand dams and fish traps to catch dozens of small fish for this mosquito control program. I taught this game to Ruth and the children, and we had great fun. Ruth questioned the effect that minnow turd might have on the purity of the water. I assured her, "Ruth, we boil and filter our drinking water. The minnows live in our bath water. Let them do as they please. The little bit they do sinks to the bottom, and has no smell. It's better than having mosquitoes." She agreed. So Bill, later Hans, and then Chris all became adept at catching minnows in the gentle Donnagadda Stream.

The *anna* coin is no longer in use in India. Under the British Raj, India had 16 *annas* to the *rupee,* and twelve *paisa* to the *anna.* School children had to learn their multiplication tables up to sixteen. During our Yeleswaram stay the Government of India decided to adopt the decimal and metric systems. They did this wisely over a three-year period with lots of newspaper, radio, and special education efforts. The first year the new *rupee* with value of 100 *naya paisa* was introduced. The next year merchants had to replace their measures and weights with liters and grams. That was wise and helpful! Previously each region of India had *sear* measures of different capacities. The government traded new measures for the merchant's old measures, like the thief in *Aladdin*. The use of liter measures and gram weights made interstate and foreign trade far more efficient. The third year Linear measurements also became metric. Cloth merchants now sold by the meter, miles became kilometers and the Fahrenheit scale was converted to the Celsius scale.

While I was enjoying interesting experiences serving my fifteen village congregations, Ruth and the children had exciting times during my absence. One night a mad jackal, foaming at the mouth, came into our compound. It chased and roughed up our dog, then went into the outside latrines of the girls' hostel. A brave girl closed and bolted the door on it and called our driver, Yohan, who came with his shotgun and shot it from the top of the wall. When I got home and heard the story, I took our dog to the vet in Rajahmundry, thirty-five miles away. He quarantined our dog for two weeks until sure it was safe.

Another time a village elder named Chakravathi came to our well. He drew a bucket of water to wash his face and feet after his dusty journey. As he reached for the bucket his wallet slipped from his vest. He grabbed for it, only to fall into the well along with the rope and bucket. Ruth and the children saw this happen! Everyone yelled and men came to the rescue with another rope and bucket and hauled him to safety. *Chakravathi* means turner of the wheel, or great king. I teased him later about turning the wheel pulley of the well and getting anointed.

Another night while Marku and I were away on tour a panther came into our compound, broke into Marku's chicken coop, and killed and carried away his chickens. After our return I sat up three nights in a row watching for the panther, using a goat for bait. But it never came back.

Occasionally, missionary families like the Colemans, Moyers, Hilda Kaercher, or the Geslers would come for a visit. Hans' baptism was a big and happy event and the Colemans came for that. Our local pastor, Rev. K. John Whitteker Kameswara Rao, baptized Hans and the twin sons of Marku and Krupamma. Then we had a feast in honor of the event. Pastor Kameswara Rao, a Brahmin, had been the Telugu teacher in Samalkot Girl's High School and the Telugu *munshi* for Miss Pauline E. Whitteker. Miss Whitteker had lived just two miles away from our Peddapur home when I was a child. We called her "Aunt Pauline." She died very suddenly of typhoid fever, at age 47, in 1933. She had led Kameswara Rao to faith in Christ. So when Kameswara Rao was baptized by my father he took the name of Pauline's father, John Whitteker, who had served as pastor of Trinity Lutheran, Lancaster, Pennsylvania. After Pauline's death the high school was named Whitteker Girls' High School. How fitting that the person my father had baptized could now baptize my son! Grace comes around.

Another welcome event was the day George and Margaret Gesler arrived with a truck bringing a diesel generator along with a building crew. They constructed a small engine shed and the cement slab on which the generator would rest. Our home was wired, and ten days later we had electricity for the first time. We turned on the generator every evening at 6 p.m., and turned it off at 11 p.m. We kept all our kerosene lamps for late night use and as back-ups. In hot weather it was good having fans to keep the children cool until they fell asleep.

Christine was born in Rajahmundry Hospital at 7:30 the evening of October 6, 1954. Doctor Zigler and his wife Jean, a nurse, did the honors. I missed Chris' birth by just an hour. We had moved Ruth and the children to Rajahmundry where she could stay in the hospital compound. I had returned to Yeleswaram that morning to pay salaries, collect our mail, and bring some records up-to-date, as Ruth had showed no signs of delivering. On the way back I had a blowout. After changing the tire I had another blowout just twelve miles from Rajahmundry. Having no second spare or tire irons, I persuaded two road workers to help me remove the tire using crowbars. I had an old patched spare tube, which I placed in the best of the two blown-out tires, then pumped it with a hand pump. Just as the tire became fully inflated, the whole valve assembly blew off and out into a field. I locked the car and after a long wait managed to flag down a lorry that took me to the outskirts of Rajahmundry. From there I took a cycle rickshaw for five miles to the hospital to find Ruth with our new daughter. "What took you so long?" asked Ruth, feeling sorry that I had missed the birth, her easiest so far. But she thought my story was highly amusing.

We weren't in Yeleswaram very long before I planted many trees to make the compound more fruitful and beautiful: one row of grafted mango seedlings, a parallel row of Batavia oranges and several jack fruit trees. Jackfruit, similar to breadfruit, is a huge ball-like fruit sack with a layer of prickly skin encasing dozens of sections of succulent fruit, each with its own seed. The unripe fruit and seeds can be cooked in a curry, and the ripe jackfruit is delightful, but smells so strongly it turns some people off. Around the border of a low corner of the compound I planted thirty teak taproots, which looked like long skinny carrots. All these trees grew well. Between the rows of trees our cook, Prakasam, planted sesame seeds that blossomed white and produced a bumper crop. The seeds were taken to an oil press and we had a good supply of sesame seed oil, known in Telugu as *manchi nooni*, the good oil.

Once when Bill was asked what his father did he said, "Oh he works for awhile in the office. Then he goes outside and watches the trees grow."

Between the Yeleru River and Donnagadda Stream, the road to Addatigalla climbed several hundred feet into rugged rocky hills. Scrambling up from the road, we could reach a ledge of rock from which we had the best view of the Yeleru River and the whole area that I had explored while in high school. In flood season we could see the river flowing out of the hills from the northwest in the distance, then turning in a great arc coming east toward where we were. We enjoyed spectacular panoramas of hills, bamboo forests, and colorful sunsets reflected on the river. At this beautiful spot Ruth and I would share our experiences, thoughts, plans and hopes while keeping an eye on the children. Their favorite activity on this hill was throwing and rolling rocks down the hillside.

One evening when I had just returned from an exciting journey deep into the hill tribal territory, Ruth had a better story to tell than I. Our community had several large tribes of rhesus monkeys which would frequently invade our compound and steal sour oranges. They would also pluck and eat all the leaves of our papaya plants, gorge on tamarind fruit, and do a job on our garden. Boys would chase them with old-fashioned slings, (David's type), shooting baked clay balls at them. The monkeys often came around our well to drink water from the pools in the cement apron of the well and then play along the walls and timber of the well. One day one of the monkeys was bumped in this rough play and fell into the well. Some of our neighbors witnessed this, and again everyone came shouting and running. They persuaded Bushanam, a skinny man who did occasional work for us, to be let down by rope and bucket to rescue the drowning monkey. One of them expressed their common urgent concern to him. "We can't let it die there, too many people use this well. Bushanam, you weigh the least! You must do your duty!" So Bushanam stood with feet in the bucket holding onto the rope while they winched him 50 feet down into the well. Meanwhile the monkey had managed to climb up about six feet, gripping indentations in the broken brick. When Bushanam was let down to water level the monkey jumped on his head, scampered up the rope, and took off. Bushanam went into shock and was so frightened that he wouldn't let the men pull him up as he could hardly hold on. He kept shouting that he would die. Finally the men rescued him.

Our short evening walks meant so much to us. It was at such times away from the office and the demands for our time and help that we could catch up on each other's lives. We would share, listen to each other, and rejoice together that God had led us to this land, made us a family, and enriched our lives by His grace and the people to whom we ministered.

Our family continued to grow, and 1956 was a very special year for us. Molly was to graduate from Kodai in the first week of May. Our fourth baby was due toward the end of May. Ruth's Mom and Dad wanted to come for a visit in June. The question was how could I juggle all of this with my work and vacation schedule?

Ruth went to Kodai in the middle of March to spare the children from the intense heat of summer and to open our cottage. I followed her in May, a week before Molly's graduation. Molly spent time with us, even though she was part of the Ted and Dorothea Wood family and was soon to graduate with her sister, Pat Wood. We took part in Molly's graduation. Leaving the family in Kodai, I went to Madras with Molly, said goodbye, and saw her off to America. She would make her home with Aunt Katie and attend Thiel College in the fall.

I returned to Yeleswaram, and during the hot dry time of May I, together with a group of evangelists, toured all my parish villages that were hard to reach during the monsoon season. I visited homes, and led services of baptism and communion. Every night we'd find a mango tree under which to pitch our tent. The mangos of the large shady wild hill mango trees are very small, but sweet and good. Ripe mangos would fall on the tent throughout the night. One of our evangelists, Bonku Joseph, kept getting up and gathering them, before the goats or pigs could. For breakfast we would have four or five small mangos each, coffee, and cracked wheat *oopma,* a spicy dish with nuts, onions, and hardboiled eggs. The mangos kept us regular!

Meanwhile, back in Kodai, Ruth's mother, Christina, came early from Basrah to help Ruth with our children. When Ruth went to Van Allen Hospital and quickly gave birth to our fourth child, Christina sent me a telegram, "Peter Lee born May 21, all well." My clerk sent it to our camp by a boy on a bicycle. As soon as I received the good news I cycled back the thirty miles to Yeleswaram, leaving the tent, equipment, and bullock cart for the others to complete the tour. They could come back at their leisure when they'd had their fill of *konda* (hill) mangos.

I arrived in Rajahmundry in the midst of a huge gathering of pilgrims coming from all over India to celebrate *Pushkaram* by bathing and worshiping in the Godavari, one of the twelve holy rivers of India. 1956 marked the special pilgrimage year for the Godavari. As I stepped off the bus, a health officer immediately gave me and all other passengers cholera immunization. He used the same needle for the whole busload, just wiping it off with methylated spirits after each jab. Another officer gave me a certificate stating I'd been injected, which I kept diligently. Perhaps a million extra people were in town. I went to our mission residence, Riverdale, to view from the riverside wall thousands of pilgrims taking their holy baths in the Godavari. Everywhere pilgrims crowded toward the river or returned, wet clothes clinging to their bodies, to their hotels and *satrams*—rows of small unfurnished single 8' by 10' rooms, attached to temples, bathing ghats or hospitals, where whole families can camp, usually at no cost, while traveling on a pilgrimage. Never before or after have I been in the midst of such great multitudes.

Getting on the train was a work of careful planning and great physical strength as no reservations were available in any class. I gave my suitcase to a coolie, who took charge giving me clear instructions, "You get on as best you can in this third class coach. Forget that you are a polite and kind missionary or you will not travel. I will follow and then pass your suitcase over the heads of others to you. Pay me now, for there will be no chance later." I forced myself on with the stream of humanity trying to make it into the compartment. My coolie followed and handed my suitcase over others' heads yelling, "Give it to the white guy!" I stood about twelve feet into the compartment holding my suitcase on my head for over two hours until, at Eluru station, the mob thinned out enough for me to put my luggage down. Two hours later, at Vijay-awada I got half of my seat on the edge of a bench and slowly shoved. The row of women sitting there shoved toward me until we all gave up and I settled for half a seat. A pretty girl in her twenties, squashed next to me, was very uncomfortable at first. What could we do? After 10 p.m. she finally fell asleep. I contemplated about the role the railway has played in India to abolish untouch-ablility. This was a perfect example of how travelers jammed in together have to give up their prejudices, revulsion, and normal social restraints. The next morning before reaching Madras the girl and I talked in Telugu and I told about the birth of Peter. She was happy for me and seemed quite relaxed.

A day later, after another overnight train ride from Madras to Kodai Road—this time with a sleeping berth—and a fifty-mile bus trip, including the twenty-nine-mile long Ghat Road, I arrived in Kodai. Mother Gosselink was so glad to see me! She was totally exhausted from taking care of our three children and walking a mile each way to visit Ruth a couple of times a day. I went to see Ruth residing in the "blue room" at Van Allen Hospital. Ruth was nursing Peter when I arrived and looked very happy. From her bright flower-filled room she had a glorious view of the plains below, as the hospital was built on a high point above Coaker's Walk. We shared many happenings and feelings that afternoon.

After another a few days Ruth's dad, George, arrived from Basrah. We spent three wonderful weeks with Ruth's parents in Edmonstone, one of our Lutheran cottages in Kodai. The children loved their new little brother and having their grandparents there. George and I took the three older children on rambles to Lower and Upper Bear Shola, the lake, and Coaker's walk. We took lots of pictures. Now our family was complete, and we celebrated this with Ruth's parents in peaceful, beautiful Kodai, Ruth's favorite place. Grandfather George baptized Peter in the Kodaikanal School Chapel after the Sunday service. What a blessed family time! At the end of June we returned to Yeleswaram.

One November evening in 1957 we climbed our river-view hill to find many rocks had been blasted and swathes of trees clear-cut all the way to the river. The ledge had been leveled and there was white paint all over the rocks on both sides of the road and river. The government of Andhra Pradesh was studying the possibility of putting a large dam at this location to provide more irrigation and sufficient water for Vishakhapatnam, the ever-growing seaport eighty miles to the north, India's primary naval base. We learned there were also plans to establish a steel mill in Vizag. We were stunned and felt our beautiful viewing spot had been violated.

The Yeluru as we knew it was a pristine living river bordered by bamboo and framed by hills. Along its banks in the Agency area were more than fifteen quaint villages, each with picturesque houses, traditional workplaces, and a rich culture and history. Would all this, along with beautiful groves of mango and tamarind trees and places of worship, just be obliterated? India's growing population was creating pressure for many changes, and at that time there were no ecology-minded organizations to study and oppose harmful changes.

After lunch was usually siesta time for our family, for Prakasam, our cook, and Marku, who filled the bathroom and kitchen water tanks and served as our gardener. My office clerk, our *ayah*, and everyone else rested for an hour. One day when I was home taking my siesta Ruth got up first, then called to me, "Sam, come here! Something mighty funny is going on." Quickly I went to join her on the porch. There, 100 feet from our house we saw an amazing sight. More than fifty hawks were circling, swooping, and calling in their shrill way. Dozens of crows joined them. I noticed that chickens from the residences behind our home were congregating underneath the diving hawks which they normally feared. What strange behavior! Slipping into my sandals I went to have a closer look.

Marku had come and was also watching the show. He said, "*Ussulu!*" Then he caught something and brought it to me. It was a large winged white ant, a termite. He showed me where thousands of these large potential queens were emerging from a termite nest in the ground. Most would lose their wings right away and be picked off by chickens, birds, and chipmunks. Crows caught them with their beaks and hawks swooped to catch them in their talons. A tribe of monkeys came to join in the feast, sitting around the termite-mound vents grabbing handfuls of these succulent creatures. What endless abundance! *Ussulu* began pouring out of many more termite hills. In the evening people came with lanterns and metal shields, brushes, baskets, and grain measures. Swarming termites would fly toward the light, bang into the shields, and fall down to be brushed into the baskets, then put into the measures after the food gatherers picked off the legs and heads. The *ussulu* were roasted and eaten. I ate them, too. They tasted like cashew nuts.

After Peter was a year old we went several times with other missionary friends for evening picnics to Kollaturu, our favorite river place. It was still beautiful, but not as clean as previously as herds of goats had been there earlier in the day. In my youth it had been so wild that goat herders had avoided the place. I missed some of the best old trees which had been cut down. We waded, played in the sand, and caught minnows in a small branch of the river. Then as evening fell we sat listening to the sounds of the jungle and of the river flowing over rock. Among the bamboo on the opposite shore jungle fowl called, then roosted. The day ended as the mountains and clouds joined to give us an indescribably colorful sunset that ended with the deepest darkest red imaginable. As darkness fell we built up our bonfire, enjoyed our evening picnic, toasted marshmallows, and told stories. How fortunate to be able to share so much of my own rich heritage with Ruth and the children, and friends! A verse from *O Worship the King* came to mind that night:

> Thy bountiful care, what tongue can recite
> It breathes in the air, it shines in the light
> It streams from the hills, it descends to the plain
> And sweetly distills in the dew and the rain.

God's care, his wonderful beautiful creation, the gift of the ever-flowing life-giving river, and our experience of his love all came to us during those Yeleswaram days.

Travelling by train from Rajahmundry to Kodaikanal

Ruth, Hans, and Bill

Lumbering with elephants in Kodaikanal

Picnic at the Yeleru River at Kollaturu

CHAPTER 9

VISITING BASRAH, CHILDREN'S FIRST BELLA SYLVA RAMBLINGS, AND HARTFORD

After completing six years of ministry and learning, we were given a furlough from May 1958 to September 1959. We first flew from Bombay to Basrah to be with Ruth's parents. They had made good plans. After several days they took us for a picnic in the desert to see the wells of Zubbair. We picked up Arab bread, *qubbis*, after watching the baker make it. He slapped the flattened dough on the inside of a hot clay oven and then peeled off the freshly baked pita or *tandur* bread.

From another shop we bought juicy lamb kabobs; Christina had made salad and cake. We crossed the desert on a fairly clear track, passing grove after grove of ethel (Australian pine) trees. Our destination was a place of six wells dug by hand to a depth of thirty feet. Arab farmers were busy lifting up water with a pulley, using yokes of oxen to pull the large leather buckets and pouring the water into ditches that irrigated a few acres of vegetables, water cress, turnips, eggplant, okra, and tomatoes. Between the vegetable plots the farmers had planted tree seedlings. George explained to us that after four or five years these trees are big enough to find the water table, after which time the farmers move on to a new spot, dig more wells and repeat the procedure, gradually turning the desert into useful woodland. There was a good water supply near the surface of this low level area. We had a cheerful picnic and enjoyed seeing the children play in the nearby woods. We continued to watch the nearby Arabs working to irrigate their gardens. They were happy as they worked to turn the desert into a garden. It was like prophecy being fulfilled before our eyes.

Early morning the day before we were to leave Peter managed to reach over from his crib and get hold of a medicine bottle containing daraprin, a malaria prevention drug, which all of us had been taking for the past few years. Only a few pills remained in the bottle. I found him with a mouthful of white stuff, and rinsed out his mouth. Then we tried to make him vomit giving him salt water, then raw egg. He kept it all down. I told George's doctor friend about it that evening during a dinner party. He took it very casually, saying, " Probably he'll never have malaria."

That night Peter began to have spasms, then very strong convulsions. It was frightening! We rushed him to the hospital, where doctors worked on him for several hours until he calmed down. The neurologist told us it had been a close call. He had known of children dying from too much daraprin. He asked us to return at 9:30 in the morning. At that time he checked out all of Peter's reflexes and found him to be without brain or nerve damage. We were so thankful! Writing a prescription he asked, "Does he take pills?" For the first time in eighteen hours we broke into laughter.

That afternoon we flew to Baghdad, and on to Rome. There we tried sightseeing with the children. The Colosseum and St. Peter's were boring and meaningless to them. We soon realized our attempts were a lost cause, but there we were, booked at a good hotel for five days. For the next four days Ruth and I took turns going on bus tours while the other looked after the children in one of the nice parks.

From Rome we went by train to Naples and then sailed for the U.S. aboard the *Constitution*. We had a great journey. While passing Gibraltar we noticed a huge cloud that seemed to come from the peak of the rock and spread over the Mediterranean. On the Atlantic side there was no cloud. Evidently the difference in temperature of the rock and the warmer Mediterranean condensed the cold moisture-laden air from the Atlantic into a cloud. Later, while passing the Azores, we had a grandstand view of a volcano erupting repeatedly—what a sight! The children were impressed. We were met in New York by Jerry, Shurlee, and their three children, and Aunt Adelaide, Dad's sister, with whom we stayed in Manhasset, Long Island, New York. In the summer of 1958 we went to Chambersburg for a few weeks with Aunt Katie, and then we headed for Bella Sylva for three months.

At mid-summer we went to Mehoopany Falls with a bunch of siblings, cousins, and friends. Bill and Hans made it without much help. Chris needed occasional assistance, especially at the stream and on the way home, and Peter had to be carried much of the time. Ruth was very patient and encouraging, getting me or someone else to help and carry when needed. It was a time of adventure and discovery for the children. How much fun it was to take them to the cave behind the falls. They waded and splashed around, having a great time. Watching them, Ruth and I remembered the times we had come to the falls before our marriage and on our honeymoon. We felt joyful that we could share this ramble with our children and pass it on to them.

We generally stuck close to home, boated around the lake, explored the swamp in back of the beaver house, swam and fished a lot, and took short walks to visit neighbors, to Kaercher's Lake, or in the woods near the house and the lake. Exploring down our lake outlet, we found several new beaver dams where the boys caught record numbers of sunfish and perch. Bill and Hans leaned to swim pretty well and could swim to the raft and back with confidence. It was a good summer. We had followed our aunt's advice, "Don't travel with the children, let others come visit you."

Early in September we moved to Hartford, Connecticut. I enrolled in the Hartford Seminary Foundation's Kennedy School of Missions, registering for courses I needed for my work: Christian Education in the Asian setting, Anthropology, Linguistics and Hinduism. My first term experience in India helped me relate well to the courses I took which were most beneficial. Ruth took courses in New Testament that helped her a lot. Bill and Hans attended first grade together; Chris and Peter went to the seminary nursery school.

At Hartford we had a wonderful year of study and warm fellowship with missionary families from all over the world. Life-long friendships developed, and later we rejoiced to see some of the missionaries become renowned teachers, dedicated leaders, and most effective missionaries in many parts of the world.

CHAPTER 10

ADVENTURES AROUND NARASARAOPET AND KOTAPAKONDA, ENJOYING PRIEST'S WALK AGAIN, KONDAVEEDU, AND KODAI HIKING CLUB

Returning to India at the end of July 1959, we flew all the way for the first time. In the Bombay airport we were delayed three hours by customs procedures to clear my rifle and ammunition. Missing the bus, we took a taxi to the Methodist Guest House. Our Sikh taxi driver and I had a spirited, friendly discussion about the meaning of the Sikh's beliefs and the basic faith of Christians. Several hours later there was a knock on our door. There was our taxi driver holding a shopping bag containing the Swiss cuckoo clock we had purchased in Zurich. After delivering three other passengers he had noticed it on the back window ledge where I had placed it. Refusing a tip he said, "We must live our faith." It was a clear sign for us: welcome home to India.

Meals are an enjoyable aspect of traveling. We noticed how prices and tastes vary greatly from place to place. Our last meal in New York had cost 15 dollars for the family. The mutton curry and rice meal in Bombay was priced at 15 rupees or 2 dollars. The next day, while traveling by train through the scenic Western Ghats toward Madras, we ordered four vegetarian curry and rice trays at 1 rupee each, and for 53 cents had more than enough for the six of us. Traveling through the night and most of the next day, we arrived late at Central Station, Madras, and rushed to Egmore Station to make our connection on the Trivandrum Express. As we were stowing our luggage, the train engine whistled signaling departure.

Quickly, I bought six *sambar* rice packets wrapped in banana leaves for 25 *paisa* each. That meal—totaling 1.50 rupees—was judged by Ruth and our children as the best of all that we had eaten on our travels. Our family had been well fed and delighted with 20 cents worth of good Indian food!

We went directly to Kodai to enroll Bill and Hans in second grade. Ruth planned to stay for a month to help the children grow accustomed to school, then ease them into boarding. We settled into Woodhaven, the only wooden house in Kodai. It would be our Kodai cottage for the next thirteen years, until Chris graduated from high school.

Before I left for the plains and Narasaraopet, Ruth and I went for a ramble around the Ten Mile Round, taking the pony trail shortcut past Pillar Rocks. At Darn Good hill we walked toward the cliffs to view the mist enshrouded Pillar Rocks from the west, sharing memories of our teenage visit. We reviewed the happy year we had spent in Hartford, where Bill and Hans both received a good foundation in first grade. We talked of God's goodness in making us a family with wonderful children. We were thankful that our lives had been enriched by loving friends and co-workers. By then we were walking in a cloud heavy with moisture. The pre-monsoon mist and spray kept us cool without making us too wet. In the dense fog it seemed as though only we existed; we were together in harmony as we shared many good memories. We arrived home happy, in time for tea with the children.

The next day we visited the school, met the second-grade teacher, Bertha Lange, and saw Phelps Hall, the dormitory where our boys would stay. The following Sunday, we said our goodbyes. This was always hard, but was an inevitable part of missionary life. I took the bus to Kodai Road Station, the train to Madras, and, the following night, one to Guntur and then one to Narasaraopet, where our home would be for the next six years.

A month later I drove into Guntur to meet Ruth, Chris, and Peter, and took them to our new home. Ruth was delighted with my story about moving our things from the Rajahmundry storage. First we moved the furniture and stored things by lorry from the *godown* mission storehouse to Riverdale, then by river boat across the mighty flooding Godavari, next by canal to Nidadavole, then from there by lorry to Narasaraopet. Other missionary families in Narasaraopet were our friends the Lomperises of our mission; the Edbergs, Swedish Baptists, and the Dexters, American Baptists.

Chris and Peter liked their new home and had their own rooms downstairs. They soon made friends with the compound kids and were delighted to be living by the railroad line going from Guntur to Hubli, located on the West Coast of India. They watched for each train and waved at the engineers. Often the steam train engineer would whistle back.

We settled in comfortably. The many surrounding old *neem* (margosa) trees had a cooling effect upon the residence. We loved the upstairs sleeping porch with its attached bathroom. As we rested together that first night, Ruth poured out the story of leaving Bill and Hans in boarding. She had said goodbye to them in their dorm and then left for the bus station in tears. Ruth began to sob as she continued her story, "As the bus came down past the school gate, Hans and Bill were standing on the school gate just looking at me and the bus. They didn't wave. I burst into tears and cried almost all the way down the *ghat*. You know Sam, being separated from the children is the hardest part of missionary life." She wept in my arms for a long time. I could picture the scene and shared in her anguish.

One afternoon we four went with Marge, Lompie, and Susie Lomperis—Susie was Chris' age—to see Kotappa Konda, a hill seven miles away that we could see from our house. What a lovely, peaceful spot, with its sacred *tank* for bathing and hundreds of stone steps leading up to a Saivite temple. Though not large or famous, this temple had a fascinating story. It was the focus of a huge pilgrimage every *Maha Siva Ratri*, Siva's Great Night. A trail ascended beyond the temple to a small shrine on the summit of Kotappa Konda.

We climbed up the steps to the temple, the children with their light bodies jumping and running ahead. Outside the entrance, on one side of the holy place, was a row of stone cobra images representing *Subbarayudu*. These were darkened by many layers of oil, tumeric, coconut, and *ghee* (clarified butter) anointings. Subbarayudu wears a garland of live cobras and is considered to be Lord Siva's son. He is linked to the god of fertility of ancient Hinduism that predates Buddhism. Incense smoke wreathed around these idols. A bare-chested priest greeted us at the temple entrance. He had Saivite horizontal ash markings on his forehead and a sacred thread going from his left shoulder across his chest to his waist. From him we heard this story of the local goddess, Golamma of Kotappa Konda:

> *More than 400 years ago a young maiden* gopi *used to bring her cows to this hill to graze. One day, when going after a cow that had wandered near the top of the hill, she came upon a* sanyasi, *or holy man, in prayerful meditation. She made discreet obeisance to him, took her cow, and left. The following day she took a pot of milk and some food with her. As the cows grazed, she climbed to the top of the hill and offered milk and food to the holy man. He spoke not a word, but gestured a blessing and she left happy. Thereafter, each day she climbed the hill to offer milk and food to the holy man, showing utmost devotion and faithful concern for his welfare. After many months this girl in some miraculous way came to be with child. The holy man had never even touched her or spoken to her. She simply became pregnant because of her constant devotion to the deity. She faithfully continued to bring him milk and food each day.*
>
> *Being very heavy with child during her ninth month she became totally exhausted making the daily climb. So she bowed to the guru and requested, "Reverend Guru, I cannot make this difficult climb, but must serve you each day. Kindly come down part way so I can continue to serve you."*
>
> *For the first time the sage gazed directly into her face and nodding his head in agreement he spoke, "All right, you lead the way down to the place where you wish to serve me and I will follow. But do not for any reason look back!"*
>
> *To this she agreed, and then began to descend. She heard his footsteps following her, soft padding, then firm striding steps, then heavy footfalls, thumping, ringing, pounding, ever louder, blasting, earthshaking, thundering huge roaring steps that made the mountain shake. In her innocence and terror she finally could take it no longer and looked back over her shoulder. She saw the huge towering Lord Siva with glory and terrible power on his face pounding the rocks to dust with each step! In that moment she gave birth to a son. Instantly she and the son both turned into stone, and above them on the path, Lord Siva also turned himself into stone. This is the story and glory of Kotappa Konda.*

As we came down from the temple with the children I walked with Ruth, not behind her, but I pounded out each step as loud as I could while she giggled.

On the day before Maha Siva Ratri, Siva's Great Night—a lunar festival that happens during our Lenten time—we drove out to the mountain in the midst of thousands of pilgrims. It took an hour to drive the seven miles. The road was full of elaborately decorated bullock carts drawn by one or two yokes of beautifully groomed prize oxen with brightly painted horns and vermilion powder on their foreheads and shoulders. These were bearing *prabhas*, twelve to sixteen foot high panel-like shields made of bamboo frames covered with tapestry or cloth painted with pictures of gods or adorned with cinema posters of gods. When electric lines obstructed the way men with bamboo poles with a board across the top would lift the lines so the *prabhas* could pass. There was singing and drum beating. Some *prabha* carts carried diesel generators which powered strings of lights and gramophones, or radios blaring out cinema hits and Hindu devotional songs. Each individual *prabha* was held up by guy ropes with six to eight men holding up the *prabha* along the seven-mile journey. Excited children and youngsters ran everywhere, heedless of the traffic and danger. What a colorful and grand festival!

As we came to the foot of the mountain near the *tank*, we saw a newly constructed community of thatched and tented shops and temporary shelters. Timber merchants were selling house beams and rafters. Cloth merchants, restaurants, snack shops, and fancy goods—nearly everything available in our town bazaar was there. It is considered most auspicious to purchase household goods and articles, timber for a new home, and clothing during Maha Siva Ratri. By the next evening 200,000 people would be there. A police contingent with a temporary headquarters shelter, the fire department, a medical contingent with doctors and nurses on duty, and the sanitary department were all there working hard to keep the place clean and safeguarding the pilgrims. Christian evangelists were there also. Our church had erected a tent and outside had set up a Bible and bookstall. Inside the tent preachers took turns teaching about the life and teachings of Christ. Many Hindus came into the tent to listen and ask questions. We sold many Gospels and Bibles over the three days of the festival. For years no Hindus objected to this gentle quiet presence of Christian witness at their festivals. By the end of the 1970s, however, Hindu Maha Sabba fundamentalists raised serious objections, and our tent ministry was discontinued as we did not want to have a law-and-order problem with so many thousands present. The Indian constitution gives freedom to practice and propagate one's religion. Yet, in all hon-

esty, wouldn't Christians be indignant if Hindus were to sell literature and preach outside churches during Christmas and Easter festivals?

Ruth and I again slowly climbed the hundreds of steps to the
temple as part of the pilgrim throng. We turned to take in the view
of the pilgrim city, the multitudes, and all the activities. There were
couples seeking to have children bathing in the holy *tank*. They
would buy and break a coconut and hand it to a priest seeking his
blessing. He would tie the woman's sari to her husband's *pancha*, a
man's sarong-like garment worn for special occasions. Then the
man would find a rock of six to ten pounds, put it on his head, and
walk tied to his spouse all around the mountain—eleven kilometers. Carrying the stone symbolized that he carried Kotappa's sacred mountain around his shrine, while linked to his wife. Next,
still tied together, the couple would climb to the shrine.

I whispered to Ruth, "maybe we could try for one more child."
She said, "Don't you think we have our hands full now? Besides,
you probably could not lug that rock around the hill."

Lining each side of the eight-foot-wide steps were bands of beggars with every kind of deformity known to humankind. Each had
a patch of old cloth onto which people were dropping alms. Giving
to the destitute is an obligatory ritual and indicative of a pilgrim's
devotion and purpose. Many people carried with them three or
four-liter containers of puffed rice and threw handfuls on the
cloths. Others dropped coins. When thousands do this the rice
piles up, and the coins add up.

Halfway up to the temple was a wider platform. There we saw a
sadhu, or holy man, wearing a saffron-colored robe talking to several disciples. Ruth and I joined and greeted them. He asked us,
with a perfect BBC English accent and warm smile, "Well, what do
you think of our *pilgrim's progress*?" We had a great discussion with
him. Then he stated, "I love the New Testament and stories and
teachings of Jesus. I especially appreciate the Gospel of John.
When Jesus taught, 'I am the way, the truth, and the life,' what did
he mean?"

I witnessed to my faith, and said that I believe Jesus meant that
there are many religions, philosophies and great teachers, but only
Jesus is divine, God who came in person to dwell among us. He
offers us forgiveness of sin, salvation, and eternal life as his gift of
undeserved grace. We cannot earn salvation. Therefore, He alone

fully embodies the way, the truth, and the life. To this, our *sadhu* friend said, "That is your belief and opinion, but I understand it to mean something else. When Jesus said, 'I am,' he was expressing that he is *Atman* or the essence of reality—the world soul. Realization of the innermost self, *Atman*, is the way and truth and life. Inner self or soul is the only reality. All else is illusion." To this I answered, "That is your faith and your belief, but that is not how Jesus' disciples understood or taught what that means." After further sharing our thoughts and faith we wished each other peace.

I hoped to meet him again, but never did. I was curious about him. Who was he, and what did he do before he became a *sadhu*, probably at age sixty? He could have been a college professor or top administrator. His English was beautiful and more correct than mine, his manner warm and sweet. But I had an inner feeling that I should not ask him or his disciples about himself, for a true *sanyasi* dies to his former self. At or after age 60 he renounces the world publicly, and with his family members present he conducts his own funeral obsequy, leaving home and family without any money or kit to begin his new life.

We continued our pilgrim's progress up to the temple. There, off to the side by the images of Subbarayudu, the snake god, were more than a dozen women lying prostrate in the dust with their hair spread out in front of them. People had thrown dust and ashes over them. They appeared to be asleep or in a trance. Clay lamps filled with *ghee* were burning in front of the idols. We were told that they would sleep there for hours until they dreamed that Lord Siva had appeared to them and promised them children. Meanwhile, their husbands waited nearby, munching snack foods, smoking, laughing, talking, and playing cards with each other. See the 'fun of it?' as Indian's like to put it. The men needed no divine help; being childless was, of course, the women's fault.

The entrance to the temple was jammed with people. Police and boy scouts tried to have people stand in queues; some people had been waiting four hours to gain entrance. Once inside devotees would give coconuts, *laddu* sweets or bananas to a priest. They would then receive prayers and have Siva's crown placed on their heads with a blessing chanted in Sanskrit. The priest would give back to them half the coconut and half the sweets and fruit they had offered and send them to the exit. The returned blessed food, called *prasadam*, was later shared with family members back home.

Climbing down, we met a young couple ascending the mountain. The rather thin, weak young wife was complaining, "I'm so tired, I can't go any further." Her robust, energetic mother-in-law grabbed her by the arm and shouted, "We've journeyed all this distance! Spent all this money! Now, *ekku!* (*Up you go!*)" and she and the girl's husband kept her going up to the temple. The mother-in-law had to have a grandchild!

At the festival bazaar we saw families buying brown sugar-puffed rice brittle. The beggars were recycling their puffed rice, selling it to the "sweet" shops where it was processed into various snack foods. Ruth decided we'd not buy puffed rice for cereal from the local market until three months after the festival.

One year we stayed at the festival until 11.00 p.m. on Maha Siva Ratri. *Prubhas*, powered by diesel engines, were colorfully illuminated, and dancing girls performed on some of the larger flatbed bullock carts. Shops did a roaring trade throughout the night and seemingly endless queues of devotees waited for temple entry. There was every kind of entertainment: minstrels, ballad singers, acrobats, bands, a small circus, and cinemas drawing many thousands of customers. On Siva's holy night the worshiper should pray, keep vigil by staying awake throughout the night, visit the temple, and give an offering. Many hundreds of Muslims and Christians also attended, because for them Maha Siva Ratri at Kotappa Konda was not just a religious festival. It's like a state fair with all-night mall shopping, music, entertainment, and excitement for all. We left and drove home in good time, meeting not one person along the road; all were at the holy mountain, Kotappa Konda.

For the six years we were in Narasaraopet, nearby Kotappa Konda became our favorite rambling place. We went there for picnics with friends, and with our children when they were home for winter vacation. The older boys and friends often biked there for the day. We saw it every time we drove south, east, or north; it dominated the whole area. For us it was a symbol of good family times, Hindu faith and celebration, ancient mystery, and for much of the year, a quiet, beautiful place.

* * *

Ruth went to Kodaikanal before Easter in 1960, took Bill and Hans out of boarding, and settled in our Woodhaven Cottage. I came in

May for several weeks and again in August when Ruth's mom and dad came. We went on short rambles with the children to Upper Bear Shola, around the lake and Middle Lake Road, and went crabbing with them in Bear Shola Stream—which bordered the mission property. After Ruth's parents joined us we all went around Priest's Walk together. It was good to see grandparents and children enjoying our special ramble. As we were descending a hairpin turn, a group of nuns dressed in white habit were coming up the trail toward us. Peter, then four years old, became very excited. "Mommy, Mommy, look at the angels," he said in a high clear voice. The nuns' laughter filled the valley and hillside.

From the Jesuit Sacred Heart College we slowly walked up the Ghat to the cemetery. We found the grave of my mother, the children's grandmother. The white marble cross-shaped stone is inscribed:

Marion Eyster Schmitthenner
November 5, 1895 - September 28, 1948.
"Blessed are the pure in heart for they shall see God."

This verse was also engraved on my Father's cross-shaped gravestone in Chambersburg, Pennsylvania. Mother had asked for this. The flowers that Ruth and I had planted earlier were now in full bloom. On a hillside overlooking lower Bear Shola Stream, with high pine, cedar, and acacia trees, the cemetery is a beautiful, peaceful place with views of the hills. Nearby were the graves of Kodai School teachers: Auntie Powell, our beloved first grade teacher, and Mario DiGiorgio, who had been the violin teacher and orchestra conductor during our high school days. Christina was glad to visit the grave of Mrs. Henrietta DeValois, her first cousin. They had been brought up together in Boyden, Iowa. Ruth and I recalled how devastated she had been by the experience of her aunt's agony at Vanderavu and her tragic death.

We walked uphill all the way to Woodhaven for tea. Mother Gosselink poured tea in her proper British manner—preheating the pot, pouring boiling water over loose tea leaves, putting milk and sugar in the cup first and serving it with snacks both sweet and savory. Oh how refreshing!

* * *

In late October Bill, Hans, and Chris returned to Narasaraopet with the other mission children for their winter vacation. The house was filled again with joyful noise. Our life became less routine and more interesting as family outings were planned. One day Ruth came into my office and said with a smile, "Let's go to the Kondaveeds tomorrow with Lomperises. Marge wrote me a note saying they were going there with their kids for a picnic, and would love to have us come along. They say it's a fantastic old Reddi fort in the hills near Phiringipuram. I'm sure the kids will love it! So take a day off."

For nearly three centuries powerful Hindu Kings of the Reddi caste ruled the whole Guntur region from Kondaveedu. Reddis are not from the princely warrior Raju or Kshatriyya castes, but were fierce fighters from one of the farming castes of the Sudhra Varuna. They had ruled this area as part of the Hindu Vijayanagar Empire that dominated most of South India until the Muslims took over the area in 1579.

Konda means *hill*, and *veedu* is the word for *street*. Usually the plural is used, so I call *Kondaveedu* the *Streets in the Hill Fort*. In Guntur District there are many rocky granite-like hills rising abruptly from the coastal plain. Kondaveedu is on one of these steep hills, only 700 feet high, but rugged, with many cliffs and much bare rock.

We approached the hill by way of the town of Kota which means *fort*. The village itself was surrounded by a moat, now partly filled in. A great stone fort wall, about twenty-five feet high with twenty-four turrets, protected the old settlement. The fort walls extend right up to the hill, merging with sheer cliffs. Inside Kota was a Hindu temple, which had been converted into a mosque. Over the original temple *sikhara*, or center peak, a Muslim dome had been constructed, and minarets now graced the four corners of the old temple courtyard wall. Idols had all been smashed. This temple-mosque is no longer used for worship.

We began climbing the steep rock-paved eight-foot wide road which occasionally ascended in series of steps. Bird life was abundant and many Indian robins (a small black bird with white on the wings), bee-eaters, shrikes, drongos, blue rollers, minas, red-vented bull bulls, swifts, purple sun birds, and two varieties of dove flew around and hopped in the bushes along the trail. When we had climbed halfway we turned to enjoy a bird's-eye view of the village.

To the northeast was the Hindu section of the village where Brahmins, Reddis, merchants, tradesmen, and farmer castes lived, each in a different section. In the middle dwelt the Muslims with their two-minaret prayer wall. And to the southwest, a little distance from the others, were the huts of the Christians and Harijans, now called Dalits—the *oppressed*—who came from the lowest grouping of Hindu society. Technically, Dalits do not have a place in the caste system. They have been oppressed for many centuries.

Closer to the hill was the five-room village school, built in a neutral place and convenient to persons from all communities— *Community* in India means *caste* or *religious group*. We could also see a number of fertile fields located on the far side of the village under the protection of the walls of the fort.

Further up the trail we passed through a gateway with a very cleverly engineered second line of defense that took advantage of steep cliffs. For the rest of the day we were within the second perimeter of defense. Ascending through a rocky pass, we came to an old travelers' bungalow. The watchman in charge, who lived in *Kota*, which means fort, told us that before the railway system made it possible to escape to a hill station British collectors and sometimes missionaries used to stay at this travelers' bungalow. There was always a good breeze coming up the valleys through the two gateways and passes leading to the bungalow.

We saw a small graveyard with the grave of a baby of the Stokes family. Hudleston Stokes had been collector of Guntur District in 1842 when our first missionary, Father John Christian Frederick Heyer, had come to begin work in Guntur. Collector Stokes, a devout Anglican, encouraged Father Heyer to stay in Guntur to establish the mission and schools, and gave him many acres of land, funds, and every possible help.

After a snack and coffee on the guesthouse porch, we entered the level area in front of the rest house which had been built on the foundation of the old palace. Two polished stone slabs with lions in bas-relief graced the base of the stone stairs. We followed the path past a temple and the thick-walled *treasury* to the first *tank*. The high masonry dam made of huge stone blocks was still intact. Irrigation channels going from the dam toward the guesthouse enabled us to picture how vegetable and flower gardens once had flourished here on the terraces which now were filled with thorns and scrub. The palace had royal baths and fountains.

We spent the day exploring. We could see two more *tanks*, with solid cut stone dams further up in the large basin. All three lakes still had plenty of water late in December, though there had been no rain for six weeks. We climbed a path with steps cut from the solid rock until we looked down on the highest *tank*. From there we had a panoramic view of the inner fortress. The highest lake had a fortress of its own, a third and ultimate line of defense. Going down the 30-degree rocky trail was slow work; a stumble would result in rolling down a long steep slope.

Clarence Lomperis, who knew Urdu well, talked to some Muslim goat-herders and the watchman. (Urdu is the Arabic language of most Muslims in India) They told legends and interesting facts about the place. We learned that the fort had never been taken by force of arms. It had been besieged by a Muslim army for months in 1579. The Muslim commander had several Mahratta Brahmins in his employ to write histories and to keep accounts and records. In those days most of the Muslim warriors were illiterate. For a huge sum of money one of the Brahmins, who was also a priest, offered to betray the Reddi princes. Acting as intermediary, he invited the Reddi leaders to a feast and peace talks. There was some kind of sedative in the food which was shared by the Muslims and Reddis. Then the priest took the half-drugged princes into the temple one by one, and led them to the *garbhalayam*, the dark innermost holy of holies. There he pushed them down into a forty-five foot deep pit, the well of death, dug for that purpose. With all their leaders slain, the confused Reddi defenders surrendered. There is still a deep hole in the ancient temple *garbhalayam*.

Our children, gently cautioned about snakes, ran ahead to explore the fort. They climbed up to one of the fort walls at the edge of a cliff and threw down rocks and insults at the "dirty invaders." We found places where many people had lived. There were stone foundations, grindstones, rice-pounding stones, and other stone implements. Something in a crevasse beneath a four-foot high boulder caught Ruth's eye. She found pieces of beautiful blue patterned china—once a dish of a Reddi king?

Near to the travelers' bungalow was a temple built up against a monolithic rock peak. The temple structure was held up by neatly shaped monolith stone pillars with a simple cornice design. The inner room of the temple was a holy of holies cave hollowed out of solid rock. I had been reading an article about temple architecture entitled, "The Mountain and the Cave." The idea is that the Hindu temple *sikhara* (peak) represents the Great World Soul, *Paramatma*. Directly under the *sikhara* is the small dark room where the idol of the god of the temple dwells, called the womb of the temple; the *garbhalayam* represents the inner most reality of each individual soul, *atman*. So the figure of the womb-cave *garbhalayam* and the *sikhara* mountain was the actual design of this unique deserted temple, overgrown by wildflowers, vines, and thorn bushes in the hill fort of the Reddis.

* * *

The next summer, when we vacationed in Kodai, we noticed that the Kodai School students were not hiking as we used to. One day Alice Martin, our neighbor, talked about this while we were enjoying a tennis, coffee, and doughnut social. "My kids just sit around on Saturdays," she lamented. "They hang out sitting on the swings at school where they will just develop bigger bottoms. I wish we could get them interested in hiking." We all agreed that a hiking club was needed. Sam was asked to be the leader.

It was late April 1961, just before Kodai School's May summer vacation. Ruth had come up with Peter from Narasaraopet in March to take Bill, Hans, and Chris out of boarding, and to celebrate Palm Sunday and Easter with them. Our children had always loved to hike. So we encouraged them to invite their friends and scheduled the Hiking Club's first expedition, a climb up Perumal, for Saturday morning.

Perumal is a massive peak, rising to 7328 feet in the lower northeast Palni Range about seven miles from Kodaikanal. This symmetrical cone dominates the Kodai skyline and can be seen from many hillsides. It has always influenced the thought and culture of those who dwell in the Palnis. Ancient dolmen dwellers built nearly all of their dolmens and settlements on ridges and in valleys where they had a view of Perumal, indicating great reverence and orientation towards the holy mountain. Many boys and men in Kodai are named Perumal. It is also the name of a deity. Mount Perumal graces the seal and stationery of Kodaikanal School. Thousands of wonderful photos have been taken of various views of Perumal.

Peru means *big*, *mal* means *mountain*. "You are a fool if you have not climbed Perumal, and a fool if you have climbed it more than once," says a local Kodai proverb. So Ruth and I, who had climbed it often, were fools, and now we hoped to begin the process of converting more fools.

Long before dawn, Saturday morning, we drove in a convoy to Neutral Saddle at the base of Perumal, elevation about 5000 feet. Missionaries of the Madurai Mission seeking a cool and healthy refuge first settled in Neutral Saddle, then went higher to Kodaikanal to avoid malaria. Our hiking club would begin with the blessing of all the parents joining in the hike. We had at least six families and over fifteen children, now excited about the adventure.

"No warm ups," I told them. "You start right in climbing and soon run out of breath. Hopefully you soon get your second wind. Yes, it comes, and you keep climbing." I repeated for everyone the mantra that my dad used to say when hiking up a long hill, "Slow and steady wins the race." Within half an hour our hikers were divided into three groups. The older boys and girls who had some hiking experience were walking up the hill at full speed. Second came the smaller children, light of body, and not fazed by the steepness or breathing problems. Puffing parents made up the third group. Actually, we considered ourselves to be in pretty good shape since we played lots of tennis and walked everywhere in the town, several miles each day. But we had more weight to pull up the mountain and were encumbered with brunch, coffee, and water. Also, we thought too much about the formidable nature of the continuous climb of over 2300 feet, while the children climbed with no concerns.

As the head of the hiking club I felt obligated to be with the smaller children. Leaving my peers, I hurried to catch up to the five to ten-year-olds. Ruth came more leisurely with her friends. I marveled at how effortlessly the children hiked. Dawn was painting the sky when our middle group attained the summit. In those days there were eucalyptus and wattle plantations on the lower slopes, but no trees near or on the summit. Thus we had a 360-degree, clear, vast view of the clouds which had settled in the valleys all around the holy mountain during the cold night. The colors and beauty of dawn from that majestic viewpoint made the climb most worthwhile.

After enjoying the sunrise, we sang a grace:

God has created a new day, silver and green and gold
Live that the sunset may find us worthy His gifts to behold.

Then we fell upon the potluck brunch, filled up on coffee, juice, and water, and told stories. I related to them how years ago we would hang out on Perumal for a few hours, explore down the ridges on the northern side, and, when the sun was high enough, flash mirror messages back to Kodai friends on Coaker's Walk. Sometimes at Kodai we would look through a telescope at those hiking up Perumal.

After brunch the new hiking club planned their next hikes. We would go to Wiffy stream and swim and, the following week, hike the long way to Gundar Falls. "Yes, let's do it!" the children exclaimed.

I sat next to Ruth and told her I'd missed climbing with her. We looked over the north and east slopes of Perumal and planned a future all-day hike. First we'd climb Perumal, then descend the northern slope until we hit the long ridge going east, and then descend the arc shaped ridge around to the south until we met the Ghat Road. It seemed like an ideal kind of ramble—but not one we'd do with children. There was no sign of a path on the ridge As often happens in Kodai while on a good hike, plans are made for later explorations.

Wiffy Stream is actually the upper part of Gundar Stream, draining from the massive ridge running from the Green Hut Hill to Vembadi Peak. Every tributary of the Gundar Stream originates in a *shola*, or high altitude rain forest. These *sholas* in the well-watered valleys cannot spread to the ridges because of frequent grass fires. The fires are spawned by the long dry season and herdsmen's periodic setting of fires to burn off the mat of dried bracken and grass before the monsoon season in order to have new meadows of fresh green grass. Rhododenderon trees, being fire resistant, flourish on the upper slopes and ridges, attaining a height of 10-15 feet.

The next Saturday Ruth and I found ourselves with the same children climbing the two-mile long Observatory Hill Road. India's foremost solar observatory is located at the top of the 7630 feet peak overlooking Kodai. From there the Ten Mile Round skirts Gundar Eucalyptus Shola, which for years was the largest stand of *eucy* trees in Kodai. Going around a series of sweeping curves, we had a continuous overlook of the deeper part of Gundar Valley, with the Poombari Road (Forty Mile Round) going across on the other side at the base of the massive Vembadi Ridge. We pointed out these features and places to the eager children. I also showed them banana orchid rocks above the road.

The children wanted walking sticks, so I cut some wattle poles. They helped debark them, then happily marched on with their "third" legs. A mile before the zigzagging Poombari Road descends we took a short cut path going directly down to Upper Wiffy Pool. We were there in two and a half hours hiking time. Changing into swimsuits, we spent the rest of the morning wading, swimming in the deeper holes and climbing down the side of Wiffy Falls–carefully–to Lower Wiffy Pool, examining and plunging into pot holes, and having a great, wet, and sunny time. The kids called us Uncle Sam and Aunt Ruth. Ruth and I have always felt as close to our India mission family children kids as we do to our own nephews and nieces. Hiking, swimming, exploring, and picnicking with them made it a very special day.

Wiffy Pool was named by very early hikers who came across a dead, foul smelling donkey beside the pool. Now, however, flowering trees waft a delightful orchid-like fragrance. A low dam, just five feet high is located at the pool above the falls. An irrigation channel has been dug from there into the hillside to convey water three or four miles to fields outside the Poombari settlement. What a feat!

Going up to the Ten Mile Round on the way home, we were tickled to see how easily the children climbed the steep short cut. They kept calling down to encourage us, "Come on, slowpokes. You're supposed to be teaching us how to hike!"

"'Puff puff,' went the little engine. 'I think I can, I think I can,'" we said. Then they yelled, "They made it!"

Vacation had begun. As we walked home taking in the views of Gundar Valley we asked them, "Do we take the big Gundar hike to that valley this week?"

"Sure, let's do it," they said. So we decided on Wednesday and asked them to invite their parents. We would need more adult hikers for that major hike with up to 15 children.

Wednesday dawned a beautiful day. The hiking club gathered at the lake bund. Again the observatory hill gave us the warm up and second wind we would need for the rest of the day. Passing the observatory we walked on the level Ten Mile Round for less than a mile, then turned at a small stone hut onto a lumber road going into the Gundar Eucy Shola. We followed the road until, after several zigzags, it came to the edge of the forest. Finding a path through the 30-foot wide wattle belt bordering the Eucy Shola, we came out on a grassy hillside to enjoy a magnificent view of Gundar valley. It had rained the night before, clearing the air. We could see clearly the great valley below Poombari, the massive plateau to the northwest beyond lower Gundar Valley with its two villages, Puttur and Perriya Puttur, and a freshly recharged waterfall between. Beyond that were the higher Kukkal Leech Shola and Kukkal Rock and the distant hills west of Manjampatti, in the State of Kerala. In the distance, perhaps eighty miles to the west, were the cloud covered Nilgiris.

We followed the trail down and down. Descending a few hundred yards, we crossed an underground stream. One of the children stepped in a hole and had to be helped. When the underground stream seriously floods it comes up through such holes. We could see where floods had left driftwood and brush on bushes and trees three feet above the level of the present path. We continued down until we crossed the stream coming from the observatory peak area. Here fragrant single-petal white wild roses, with blooms four inches in diameter grew in profusion. Rhododendron trees were everywhere. We also saw lots of asparagus fern. "We can collect some on the way home," Ruth suggested.

Following the northern side of the stream, we continued toward the junction where it met the main Gundar stream. There, by the path, was a herd of cattle cared for by two boys, ten or eleven years old. They told us they lived near the observatory and every day would take the cattle down into this valley to graze. One of our boys pondered about their presence and their work, "We think this hike is a big deal, and we bring knapsacks of food and drink for this adventure hike. But these kids do this every day without all this stuff, and in bare feet, too. Wow!"

Crossing at the junction was difficult because of the rains. We were glad we had enough grownups along to help the small ones ford the stream. Above the crossing was a lovely and full waterfall. We followed the main stream down. Because of cliffs and falls we had to cross and re-cross the stream. At each crossing and it took time to help the "little people" over. Wildflowers and flowering trees made this a pleasant venture. Numerous and interesting pot-holes had been formed by the water in the solid rock streambed. At times the way was a bit hazardous. We were very careful! Finally we came out above the long sloping slide-falls rushing into the main pool. We descended at the edge of the slope on wet leaves and slippery grass with little to hold on to. Going very slowly, helping the younger ones, we finally made it.

The pool was a gem of a place, completely hidden from any viewpoint other than the top of the falls. Above the pool there are several large potholes more than eight feet wide and over seven feet deep. I showed the kids to swim first in these warmer pot-holes, then slide down the smoothest falls into the big, deeply shaded, cool pool. Whoosh! I suggested, "Swim fast until you warm up!" How refreshing it was!

After lunch I guided a few of the older children, Ruth, and one of the parents downstream for half a mile of rugged boulder jumping. We came out above the great falls. What a sight! As mist swirls up from the valley and the chasm yawns, it feels like being at the edge of the world. No plains or fields are visible below, only rugged un-inhabited jungle. Ruth and I sat and listened to primitive sounds, rushing water, the hum of insects, and the silence of creation's dawn. We threw a few logs and rocks down over the falls. The wa-ter drops about 900 feet here in a series of falls. Approaching the falls from below is almost impossible.

On the way back we found some bison dung in the woods beside the stream. Ruth asked in amazement, "How did that get down here?" Bison (*gaur*) are huge and weigh over a ton, but are agile and able to climb very steep hills. We saw a four-foot-long thin green tree-snake crossing the stream on a boulder just in front of one of the boys. What a beauty! Nilgiri black imperial pigeon called from the *shola* across the stream. Then we rejoined our group.

After another round of tea to hydrate us for the long climb back, we set off carefully climbing the slippery trail beside the long falls. We made a game of counting potholes. By the time we reached the junction we had counted more than seventy, each distinct. Some were double, several halfway down the falls had sides that had given way, and most still had numbers of rounded smooth stones in the bottom which would continue to grind away when high monsoon waters churn them into motion.

From the junction the hike straight up to the edge of the *eucy shola* looked formidable. It was nearly as long and steep a climb as Perumal, only now we were tired. It began to cloud over and soon it was raining.

"Don't worry, it always rains when you're going home from Gundar. It makes the climb cool," I yelled so all could hear. And it did make the climb easier. We passed rock orchids that were starting to bloom above the path. But the rocks were steep and made slippery by the rain, so we left the orchids for God and the young cow-herders to enjoy.

Soon we were soaked, and our water-filled shoes sloshed with each step, but the climb kept us warm. We sloshed our way down the Observe Road, and went to our homes, happy.

Our family trooped into the warm kitchen. Gnanamma had two five-gallon tins of water heating on the wood-burner range for baths. Ruth and Chris bathed first, after which the boys and I had pour baths. Then we had tea, cinnamon toast, and cookies. What a day!

Pencil sketch of Mount Perumal from Coaker's Walk of my father's collection, made in 1930

Bill and Hans with our milk buffalo at Narasaraopet

House built by Peter

Ruth and Chris

Ruth, Joan Nabert and bill above Kondaveedu Fort lakes

Ruth viewing Kondaveedu Temple

A Prabha *on the way to Kotappa Konda Temple*

Attending village church dedication with Grandma *and* Grandpa. *Our children were always safe, but often surrounded by friendly, curious, and kind people*

CHAPTER 11

HUNTING, WALKING AND WORKING WITH RUTH IN THE NALLAMALAIS, NARASARAOPET, PALNAD, AND KRISHNA VALLEY

The Nallamalai, or Black Hills Range, located in Kurnool District is one of the most desolate forest regions of Andhra Pradesh. The Nallamalais extend from south of the Guntur-Hubli rail line to beyond the Krishna River in the north. The Guntur to Kurnool road crosses the northern section of these hills. From the village of Dornala a road built in the 1950's branches off to the Srisailem temple and the nearby Srisailem Hydroelectric Dam, where the Krishna River has dug a great 1500 feet gorge through the Nallamalais. Except for rough forest tracks there are no roads other than these two crossing this vast area.

Bamboo and teak are the chief products of this great forest. One of the other valuable hardwood trees, the manduru tree, has hard, ebony-like wood which is used for pillars in temples and the homes of the wealthy. Wooden clarinets made of this beautiful dark wood give the best tone to play *nagaswaram*, the cobra's song.

Along the two main roads and the railway are a number of villages. But in the forest there are only small settlements of Chenchu tribal people, who keep mostly to themselves. It is surprising to find a part of Andhra Pradesh so sparsely populated.

Mr. Abraham, Superintendent of Police, once invited Ed Nabert and me for an overnight hunting trip to a secluded forest bungalow at Gundlabrameshwaram, midway between Dornal and Chellamma on the rail line. The bungalow had been built by the British Forest

Department as a hunting and forest inspection lodge. We drove there one winter night from Chellama Station in two jeeps Mr. Abraham provided. We had no success in hunting and froze with temperatures of 40-45 Fahrenheit.

Since then I had wanted to show Gundlabrameshwaram to Ruth, so we scheduled four free days with Ed and Joan Nabert for the adventure. Our Peter, six years old, and Joey Nabert, then five, came with us. Their siblings were in Kodai boarding. We set out in our four-wheel-drive station wagon with our trusty driver Solomon. After driving more than 100 miles on the plains we entered the foothills of the Nallamalais, passing through beautiful but sparse forestland. This was a dry area where trees grew slowly, spaced at a non-competitive distance from each other. In every valley or moist depression there was bamboo in abundance. Kepok, the wild cotton tree, was the largest of the forest trees. Tamarind trees, which provide one of the spices needed in every India kitchen, were everywhere. Chenchu tribals traded dried pressed tamarind for other needed commodities and used the ripe fruit, mixed with the ash of tamarind wood, as part of their staple diet.

One small and slender variety of tree, the *Cochlosperum Religiosum*, was laden with large yellow blossoms that gave off a luscious fruity smell. As the name indicates, the flower is often used for temple offerings. Seeing one such tree near the road, Ed and I shook it, bringing down a shower of blossoms which we gave to our sweethearts and children. Driving slowly on the forest trace, up and down mountain ridges of this pristine forest, we were delighted by scenic views, the quiet unfolding of nature, and the serenity of the wooded hills.

We arrived at the hunting lodge we had reserved with the Forest Department feeling confident that we would have a great hunt. As we sipped tea with the local forest ranger, he informed us that hunting was now restricted in this special area. Then, noticing our disappointment he gave us permission to shoot jungle fowl, the ancestors of all the chickens in the world. We drove around in the early evening and shot four of the many wild chickens we saw. Solomon plucked them and made jungle chicken curry and rice for us.

After "meals" (meaning rice and curry to Indians), our ranger came around again. Accepting a cup of coffee, he said, "You can go tonight with flashlights to spotlight game. No problem. I will come also."

We told Joey and Pete a bedtime story, tucked them in, left them in the care of Solomon, and got in the jeep. Our ranger friend said to Ed, "You should bring a rifle just in case." So Ed brought along his 30-30. I drove and Ed sat in front with a flashlight clamped to his rifle. Ruth, Joan, and the ranger were in the back seat. We went about five miles, slowly, now and then shining our lights, seeing several antelope and a spotted deer. Then a leopard crossed the road to Ed's side about 100 feet in front of us. Driving slowly to where it had crossed, I stopped. Ed shone his light. Just 50 feet away the leopard sat on its haunches watching the road, transfixed by the light. "Shoot it!" whispered the ranger. So Ed did just that. The leopard dropped and lay still. We waited five minutes. It didn't move or twitch; clearly it was dead. We carried it to the car—it weighed less than 100 lbs. There we admired its beautiful coat of black rosettes on orange, with some white in the belly. Ed was ecstatic. His first leopard! He lit up a cigarette and accepted the cup of coffee I poured from the thermos. Joan came around the corner of the jeep looking perturbed. "How could you shoot such a beautiful animal?" she asked. Ed was crushed. He spilled his coffee over his hunting jacket and dropped his cigarette. Ruth agreed with Joan, though in a more gentle way.

Early the next morning I skinned the leopard. Having done two of my own, I knew just how to do the head, face and claws. We saved the skull with the teeth and salted down the skin. Then we paid some bamboo cutters to haul the carcass half a mile into the forest and cover it with branches and rocks. The forest ranger came by in a terrible mood. "A messenger has just come by cycle with a note that the Conservator of Forests is coming tomorrow," he said. "We must do away with all evidence. I have set two men to clean up all the chicken feathers, and to dig up the bloody ground. There will be terrible trouble if he finds out about this." He was having all kinds of regrets about giving us permission to shoot chickens and the leopard. Wrapping the skin and skull in burlap, we stowed them under the jeep seats. All would be well.

That afternoon we drove without guns seven miles to a place where I had previously seen a stand of magnificent teak trees. An old sign described it as a "Natural Grove." On the way back we stopped at the stream half a mile from the lodge. Walking along its banks, we came to a sandy place. Joey and Peter took off shoes, socks, and shirts, and had a great time playing in the sand, wading, sitting in the water, and splashing each other.

Suddenly Ruth pointed to the other bank and said, "Look at that long white 'feather thing' flitting through the trees!" We crossed the stream for a closer look. It was a rare bird, the paradise fly-catcher. With a white tail nearly three times the length of its body, the male twists and turns as it flies, creating an exotic spectacle.

That evening after supper and more stories for Joey and Peter, we decided to go game spotting again. Our ranger friend came over to see us on our way, making sure we had no guns. He couldn't come with us, as he was preparing reports on the bamboo harvest for the Conservator of Forests.

We had driven only half a mile to where the lumber road crossed the stream where the children had waded when a magnificent tiger stood facing us. We stopped within forty feet of it. It yawned, stretched, and then walked off to the side of the road. We went forward slowly, then spotted it with our flashlights. It walked slowly to where the road branched, took the right fork, and then strode along majestically. We followed at a respectful distance, enjoying its swinging gait and rippling muscles, and noting its obvious masculinity. A large mature tiger can weigh up to 400 lbs; this one may have weighed 350 lbs. Now and then he would turn, look at our jeep with annoyance, raise his eyebrows, open his mouth showing all his teeth, and then proceed on his way. We followed him for two miles. Finally, sensing that game was close by, he sprang over a low stonewall, and was gone. We just sat there awed by the experience. "Wasn't that so much better than what happened last night? We saw a tiger in action in fullness of life and beauty. I'm glad you guys couldn't shoot it." Ruth said quietly. We had to agree.

The following morning we packed up to leave, paid the rent, thanked the ranger, tipped the watchman, and departed. We stopped near the stream where the children had played to look at the tiger tracks, then visited a stone shrine only five feet high, which sheltered an ancient deity carved in the Buddhist style and a Siva Lingam. The shrine was probably a Buddhist holy place long before it was Hinduised by the installation of the Lingam. A Lingam is a stylized cylindrical shaped phallic symbol representing the god Siva. Lingams are placed wherever Siva is worshiped. Where important and holy streams originate and flow there are usually

Hindu shrines. The Gundlabrameswaram stream is the source of the Gundlakamma River which flows into the Bay of Bengal near Ongole. This small river, sacred to Buddhists and Hindus, is also a symbol like the Jordan River for Telugu Baptist Christians.

On our way home to Narasaraopet we followed the Gundlakamma River for twenty miles. I told Ed, Joan, and Ruth about the mass baptisms that had taken place years ago in this historic river near Ongole, a site renowned in Baptist Churches. There, 3536 men and women were baptized by immersion in the Gundlakamma from the evening of July 2nd until the afternoon of July 4th, 1878, by six ordained Baptist preachers, as missionary Rev. John E. Clough, stood on the riverbank coordinating an event reminiscent of Pentecost Day. Their names were recorded according to their villages. For a few days, prior to that, the candidates had each been examined by clergy and evangelists. The baptism ingathering continued at the Gundlakamma River for six more weeks until a total of 8691 had come to Christ through baptism. The detailed narrative of this ingathering is described in John E. Clough's book, *Social Christianity in the Orient*.

* * *

In early spring of 1964 our fifth year in Narasaraopet was drawing to a close and the time for furlough grew near. Ruth and I went to climb Kotappa Konda to talk over plans, our life, and ministry. My work as evangelistic missionary and synod treasurer had been most fulfilling and joyful. Now that our children were all in boarding at Kodai School, Ruth often toured with me. Together we worked with pastors and Bible women in the villages, and stayed overnight in the homes of friends and fellow workers and in quaint old travelers' bungalows. The Lord had blessed our ministry together in many ways. Our relationship and love for each other had grown deeper. We and our children had adjusted very happily to our life and work and the community at Narasaraopet. We now believed it would be good to stay for another year, making it a second six-year term. We held hands going down the mountain and agreed to pray, write and plan for that and then see if the Andhra Evangelical Lutheran Church and the Board of World Missions of the Lutheran Church in America would approve.

Both the AELC and the board agreed, and our children were happy about our decision. We had another blessed year in Narasaraopet. By this time we had moved across town into the house the Lomperis family had vacated when they went on furlough. Following my pattern, I planted neem and tamarind trees which grew well in that compound.

During this time Ruth Sigmon had been assigned to Narasaraopet. Our children were delighted to have Auntie Ruthie with us for festival days and rambles at Kotapa Konda. She brought much joy to all of us with her enthusiasm. We delighted in her way of walking full speed. Her Telugu was excellent, and Bible women rejoiced in working with her.

We had been involved in the founding of three congregations at new government projects. The first was at Nagarjunasagar, where a mighty dam was being built across the Krishna River halfway between Guntur and Hyderabad. This church, initially started as an interchurch ministry, had evolved into separate Lutheran, Baptist, and Church of South India congregations. The Lutheran work kept growing until three strong Lutheran congregations in different areas of the project had been established. They built permanent church buildings and were flourishing.

The second was at Bandlamotu, in the southwest part of Guntur District, where India's Department of Mines had recently established the nation's largest lead mine. At the request of the officers at the mine we had opened an English Medium School for their children. At the same time we had gathered a congregation of the many Christians who had been attracted to this site by the promise of steady, well-paid work. They came from surrounding villages where there was not enough work opportunity for *dalit* (oppressed caste) Christians. Many Christians of other denominations working at Bandlamotu also gladly worshiped with us, thankful there was a church in such a remote area.

When Ruth and I visited the second time we were taken through the mine by a Christian engineer. He showed us old, narrow mine shafts dug two centuries previously by engineers of Hyder Ali and his son, Tipu Sultan, rulers of Mysore during the late eighteenth century, who had fought long and bravely against the British. This place, more than a hundred miles northeast of the old Mysore border, had been their main source of lead for bullets. The old mine shafts, so skillfully engineered, had been cut straight through to the richest beds of ore. The engineer expressed his amazement, "How did they do it back then?"

We then walked to the historic fire pit near the village named Agnigundala (fire pit). Oral tradition relates that several hundred years previously a mineshaft here had collapsed, killing a number of workers. As the recovered bodies were cremated in this large fire pit, the wives of the victims had committed *sati* by jumping into the fire to join their husbands in eternity.

Later that afternoon we worshiped joyfully, celebrating communion with the new congregation and dedicating their newly constructed thatched prayer chapel. We then continued on our way to Srisailem, the third government project where we had new work.

That evening we stopped at Tokapalle Public Works Department T.B. (*Travelers' Bungalow*). The lodge, about half a mile from the village, was near an irrigation *tank*, that was full of ducks. Walking on the *tank bund* we watched the sunset and then moved into the bungalow. The walled-in compound had its own good well and a grove of neem trees. A refreshing breeze was blowing down from the pass in the hills through which both the road and the Teegaleru, a branch of the Gundlakamma River, descended. Hunting for insects through the leaves under the neem trees were Indian Pita birds. *Navarang,* nine colors, is the Telugu name for this small but very beautiful bird.

The old watchman and his son cared for the bungalow as they had been trained to do by a British officer. Everything was clean and neat. In the bathroom he poured two five-gallon cans of hot water into an enormous zinc bathtub so that *madame* could have a hot bath. Our driver, Solomon, cooked a good supper. That night as we were falling asleep under mosquito nets we could hear the call of the stone curlew which gives alarms in dry scrub-jungles from dusk to dawn. We also heard the "chuck-chuck rrring" of the nightjar, a bird related to the whippoorwill of North America.

At dawn Solomon was up brewing coffee. After a cup of coffee with a banana we went for a leisurely hunt through cotton and chili fields at the foot of a rocky ridge which had been deforested by the dwellers of Tokapalle in search of timber for homes and firewood. Ruth took binoculars. I carried my rifle with a scope. We spotted a herd of ten *jinka,* the black buck antelope, about 400 yards away. But they were skittish, and stalking over the chili fields was difficult. Then we saw animals in front of us moving from the fields to the hillside.

"Wow, Ruth, look there with your glasses! Three wolves!" I exclaimed. We watched them for quite a while. They went about halfway up the rocky hill and then disappeared, probably into their den. They were the reason why the *jinka* were so wary. Further on we came to a little pond that was full of birds. Often you can see more birdlife in a small pond than in a big body of water. We saw stilts, red-wattled lapwings, grey wagtails, and spotted sandpipers. Hanging from the acacia thorn trees, weaver birds nests swayed in the breeze. I noted birds seen in my copy of Salim Ali's *Book of Indian Birds* which I often carried with me. Ruth was so happy to be sharing this dry hunt with me. On a dry hunt one takes along a gun but is not primarily interested in shooting. We were content to see the beauty of nature, study birds, enjoy the early morning, and walk along empty-handed but full-hearted.

After breakfast we set out for Srisailem. From Dornala we ascended the new *ghat* road to Srisailem, crossing ridges of the Nallamalai Range. The first several ridges had been denuded by village woodcutters. But later we entered a protected reserved forest which became wilder and thicker with each passing ridge. Beneath a banyan fig tree a small herd of spotted deer feasted on small ripe red figs. Further on we went through stands of bamboo, alive with jungle fowl. Several miles before we reached the *sikara*, or peak, overlook of the Srisailem temple area, known as the *Devastanam* (God's place), we stopped to shake down the fruity yellow flowers of a cochlosperium tree near the road, to enjoy their fragrance and beauty. There Solomon spotted curry leaf bushes. Together we picked bunches of wild curry leaf sprigs to take home for our neighbors. Wild curry leaves are tastier than the cultivated variety and quite a treat!

We arrived in Srisailem Friday morning at 10.00 a.m. First we visited and inspected our large English Medium School. The children in grades one through five gave a grand performance of recitations, songs, and drama, and showed us their drawings of plant, insect, and animal life, and other exhibits. They were mostly children of engineers and merchants at the project. We had rice and chicken curry with the pastor, and then we spent more time in the school. In the afternoon we drove five miles to the thousand-year-old famous Saivite temple site and settled into a nearby well-equipped "pilgrim" guesthouse which we had reserved. Ruth and I strolled through the *Devasthanam*, exploring the temple and talking to priests and pilgrims until dark. We met an old widow wearing saffron, who had been living for years on the temple grounds. Her life consisted in worshiping and helping pilgrims. She reminded us of Anna, the prophetess who saw and adored the Christ child. (Luke 2:36-38) who "did not depart from the temple, worshiping day and night."

The Srisailem Temple, one of the three great Saivite temples in Andhra (Telugu country), was built in the ninth century with great blocks of stone. Two years previously I had made a special study of Saivism in Andhra Pradesh to present to our mission historical society. I had studied the Srisailem temple history and the hundreds of bas-relief scenes carved in the five-foot by three-foot stone panels of the outer wall. I had taken pictures for a slide program depicting the life and meaning of the Srisailem temple. The Devastanam government officer had shown me the Srisailem Temple Ready Register, the official government records of the temple. Carefully recorded and periodically reviewed and updated, this large register records the history of the temple and research done by archeologists and historians. It lists the inventory and location of all temple properties—gold bars, jewels, land, and other treasures. And it records the annual income of the temple. The temple priests whom I had come to know had been most helpful. They showed me the *Sthala Puranam*, the scripture of this holy place, which records all the myths, legends, and colorful happenings of the deities and devotees associated with this sacred place. Every major temple in India has such a *Sthala Purana*.

Each of South India's great temples, which attract many thousands of pilgrims every year, is administrated by the Government Department of Temple Endowments. The British established this practice to bring peace among rival factions of Brahmin priests and regional leaders who exploited pilgrims and fought over the fabulous riches that came from pilgrim offerings. All temple entry fees and fees paid for sacraments to be performed are collected by the government. The rates for each sacrament and ritual are listed on a bulletin board by the office near the temple entrance. The worshiper pays for entrance and for the needed sacrament, some of which are the naming of a child, the sacred thread ceremony, marriage, the ritual of anointing the idol with pots of water or *ghee*, or worshiping with 1000 sacred bilva leaves. The worshiper and his party show the receipt of payment to the priest who then performs the needed sacrament, chanting in Sanskrit sacred verses from the *Vedas* and other Hindu scriptures. I have never seen a priest use written scripture or a songbook. They know a wide variety of detailed liturgies and scripture verses by heart. The Government Devasthanam office pays the salaries of all priests and temple complex workers, but the priests are allowed to keep a portion of the extra thank offerings given to them personally.

On Saturday, an engineer named Solomon Raju, a member of our congregation there, took us on an extensive tour of the dam site. He showed us caves upstream from the dam-site which were being filled with concrete. In one of the caves, not yet filled, we met a *sadhu*, or holy man, who took us back into the cave with a flashlight until we came to a small stream of water. He related the wonder of this sacred stream, "This is flowing from the Krishna to the Ganges River by an underground way. Prayer shawls, marked with the worshiper's names, dropped here by bathers have been found months later in the Ganges at Varanasi. This flows into the sacred Sarasvathi River." Stories similar to this are told in many places in India where devotees bathe in holy underground streams flowing through caves. The Sarasvati, one of the 12 sacred rivers of India, is now just a stream that flows and disappears in the desert sands of Rajasthan in North India. But the Sarasvati is believed to be a divine and holy underground river. Many other subterranean streams are said to join it until it merges with the converging Jumna and Ganges Rivers at Allahabad.

On Sunday morning we worshiped with the congregation at Srisailem. Pastor Are Samuel John, one of the best preachers and Bible interpreters of the AELC, gave the main sermon. I also preached about holy places: "The Jews have their holy places: Sinai, Jordan, and Jerusalem. Muslims have Mecca, Medina, and Jerusalem. Hindus have the most: Srisailem, Kalahasthi, Draksharama (the three great lingams in Andhra Pradesh), Varanasi, Hardwar, Rishikish, Madurai, Tirupathi, and thousands of other pilgrimage places. So what do Christians have? We have not a place, but a *person*, the Savior Jesus Christ. He dwelt among us, served, died, and rose again to bring us life forever. It is his presence in every home, church, and human heart that makes common people and places holy. Others have Holy places of pilgrimages, which Hindus call

Devastanamulu, God's places. We have God's presence as his Holy Spirit abides with us. We are part of his body the Church. His holy place is with us and our heavenly home is with him. Let us rejoice."

We began our homeward drive on Monday at 5 a.m. with the hope of seeing wildlife. Going past the place where we had picked curry leaves, we rounded a corner and saw a magnificent eight-point sambur stag frozen like a statue in the headlights of our car. A sambur is as big as an elk. I was glad my rifle was in back, as I had no desire to shoot it. I had learned from Ruth that watching and leaving a beautiful trophy alive can be more satisfying than shooting it.

There were continuous rains in September while we were having mission council meetings in Guntur. We heard of awesome floods that had affected the upper Krishna River country, especially the Palnad, a distinct area of Guntur District where we had a congregation in every one of the 104 towns and villages. The radio kept us up-to-date. All roads into the area were flooded. Some bridges had been swept away. On the third day we heard that trucks could get through. People had no food; grain kept in shops had been soaked and spoiled; firewood needed for cooking was soaked. Ruth and I went to our Muslim baker and ordered a few thousand large buns the size of kaiser roles. He baked these for just the cost of the flour, and provided baskets for packing. We took the back seats out of our jeep station wagon and piled breadbaskets to roof level, filling the vehicle. Setting off, Solomon and I managed to churn through each mud-hole and stream with our four-wheel drive (which we fondly called water buffalo gear), going to village after village. Each hungry person received one bread roll. It was like feeding the 5000. To each one I said, "Take this bread, eat, and live. God loves you."

On the road we met migrant workers returning to their villages from the flooded-out chili harvest. They also ate. Finally at evening with half a basket of bread left, we found ourselves on the bank of the flooded Krishna. Upstream was the only bridge across the Krishna River for eighty miles either upstream to Srisailem or downstream to Vijayawada. We could see that four spans had been washed away by the raging Krishna as it came pouring through a V-shaped gap in the middle of the incomplete Nagarjunasagar Dam. Now that the river was lower and calmer, people stranded on our side were being ferried across the river in little round flat boats, six to a boat. We had just enough bread remaining to give one roll to each person waiting to cross the river. I was overcome and wept much that day. "Take this bread, eat, and live. God loves you." Muslims, Hindus, and Christians had all shared the bread baked by a caring Muslim, given out with a blessing by Christian hands.

Homeward bound, we stopped in Macherla at our Christian Public Health Center, which had been established by Myrtle Onsrud, our old friend from Milwaukee days. She had stored several tons of Lutheran World Relief bulgur wheat and cooking oil for a food-for-work program. In this emergency, the wheat was a Godsend! Her center, on higher ground, was a shelter for hundreds. She and her staff were feeding 1000 people a day with *upma* (a dish prepared with onions, oil and wheat), made with this bulgur wheat. We spent time with her in prayer and then shared *upma* with her and the refugees.

For the next five months Ruth and I were engaged in flood relief work in the Palnad area. I was happy to be able to visit more than sixty of the flood-damaged village congregations. We assessed damages and provided encouragement and financial aid for materials to repair and rebuild. Here we met and worked with some of God's finest and most devout people. We recalled the history of our mission. It was in the Palnad that Father Heyer found the warmest reception to the Gospel and was able to establish the strongest congregations more than 120 years earlier. Our church was able to help in the reconstruction of churches, and to rebuild five of the hardest hit villages with generous funds received from the Board of World Missions and Lutheran World Relief. Clarence Lomperis headed up this village reconstruction.

After experiencing all of these things we realized why God had led us to stay another year in Narasaraopet.

Great discussion with a Christian farmer friend

Picnic by a well, enroute to Tokapalle

Visiting a convert family in Yeleswaram eight years after Ruth and Bible woman first met them

Ruth at Ettipothula Falls near Nagarjunasagar

CHAPTER 12

RAMBLINGS IN SWITZERLAND, GERMANY, AND ONCE AGAIN TO MEHOOPANY CREEK

At the end of April 1965 we packed and headed for Kodaikanal to wait for the children to finish the school year in May. Then we set off for the States. First we went to Bombay, where we spent some time with Chuck and Char Gosselink, who were working for the United States Information Service. From there we flew to Basrah, Iraq, for a wonderful two-week visit with Ruth's parents, Christina and George. We had such good times with them, playing tennis (now with four teams), going on desert picnics, and attending memorable parties. Our children were excited and happy to be with Grandma and Grandpa again. We consumed enormous amounts of dates and *qubis*, that great Arab bread. From Basrah we flew to Baghdad, staying overnight in a fancy hotel, and then on to Zurich as the only passengers on the flight.

In Switzerland, we went by train to Zermat for four days. We wanted to hike around each day to see the Matterhorn, but the mountain was always in the clouds. We went on many walks, and on the third day took the cog-railway to Goernograt Glacier. From that high point one can usually get a magnificent view of the Matterhorn, but all we could see was fog and clouds. From there we hiked the six miles back home through alpine forests and meadows, and we sang a song I had made up, "What is the matter with the Matterhorn? Why does it hide its face in shame, and why did we come here on the train?" On our last day as I awakened at 5 a.m., I saw, through the window, the beautiful peak sparkling in the clear air, and I jumped out of bed to rouse the family. We hurried outside and walked around looking at the majestic summit until 7 a.m., when it disappeared as the clouds masked it again. What a sight it was!

From Zurich we flew to Frankfurt where we were welcomed by our distant Schmitthenner cousins. We stayed with them and the next day attended a Schmitthenner reunion in Heidelberg. It was held in the same hotel where my mother and dad had enjoyed a reunion with dad's German cousins in 1929, when I was just a year and a half old. We drank wine from the same silver reunion cup they had used thirty-six years earlier. As the cup made its rounds, during a moment of silence everyone heard Peter ask his mother, "Mom, can I have communion too?" Everyone loved that. And it was a kind of communion celebration for all of us. How enriched and blessed we were to share in this reunion!

We spent the summer at Bella Sylva, having very happy times. Remembering my aunt's advice, Ruth said, "Let's not go traveling around trying to see our friends and family. We'll invite everyone to visit us here." So we stayed put, invited friends, and they did come. Our children had a succession of playmates, including many cousins. Every afternoon we went to the swimming beach. Each of our children progressed in swimming so that they could swim to the beaver house and return, or to the dock and back, both of which were several hundred yards away. Fishing expeditions were very successful. I seemed to be cleaning sunfish, also called bluegills, and perch almost every day and we often had fried fish for brunch or supper. Some nights we would go cat-fishing near the beaver house and enjoyed beaver watching while we fished. We had tasty cookouts grilling with cherry wood coals, and we picked blueberries to eat in pies, on cereal, with hotcakes and in jam.

We had great hiking expeditions. Our children were old enough now to hike to "The Gorge" on lower Mehoopany Creek. We started out one bright day with some cousins and our neighbors, the Conant kids. We hiked the blue trail, crossing our lake outlet to an old logging railroad bed, and then went downhill to the old horse trail of lumbering days (perhaps even earlier Indian trail days). We heard the creek babbling louder as we descended to another old rail trail in the valley that followed the creek. This brought us to the ruins of an old fishing shack where dad had camped overnight for trout-fishing expeditions. Crossing Mehoopany Creek, we took the State Game Land road parallel to the creek, then a path to reach the stream as it entered the gorge.

The gorge is about 150 feet deep with very steep sides. The creek bed, wild and rugged, had potholes, rapids and a "shoot" where the whole creek gushes through a trough about thirty inches wide. That makes a great place to slide if the creek is low. Below the shoot is a beautiful wide pool ten feet deep in places. Shelves of rock on the north side can be climbed and used for diving from various heights. We found the pool to be freezing, but stimulating and challenging. We surveyed the pool, swimming underwater, to find good unobstructed depth underneath the diving rocks; and then we began diving and swimming against the current and water-sliding down the shoot.

I took out my kettle, made a fire, and began my tea ministry. We roasted hot dogs, told stories, and explored the ruins of the railroad bed built through the gorge on a foundation of huge hemlock logs. We could see the remaining logs, still lashed together with rusted steel cables. These had survived more than seventy-five years of the floods that roar with terrible force through this constricted gorge. Ruth and I rested for the haul home, drinking tea and watching our children and their friends swim and dive and slide with boundless energy.

In the fall of 1965 we moved to Upper Darby, a suburb of Philadelphia. I enrolled in a Master's program in Indian Studies at the University of Pennsylvania. Bill and Hans attended junior high, right across the street from our home. Chris entered sixth grade and Peter fourth. Bill and Hans played soccer. Bill took swimming lessons at the YMCA, while Hans learned to play the drums. Chris learned to sew. Pete became a baseball fan. I worked hard and finished my M.A. course requirements and planned my thesis, *Migrant Labor in Guntur and Godavari Districts*.

In June of 1966 things happened fast. I turned in my last term paper and wrote exams. We packed and sold our useless Nash Rambler. Our barrels and boxes were shipped to New York. We boarded the train, took off for New York and London, and then flew home to India.

CHAPTER 13

WALKING BY THE CANAL AT BHIMAVARAM, KODAI VACATION HIKES, FROM BERIJAM TO VEMBADI PEAK, AND SAFARIS

When we flew from New York to London in June 1966, we were a party of eight. David Lueders, Chris's class mate, and his younger sister Ellen, a classmate of Peter, had to return to Kodai School before their parents were ready to leave Wisconsin, so we offered to take them. We found London not very child-friendly. At one place Ruth led the way to board a bus, followed by six children, and I brought up the rear. She was asked by a frowning conductor, "Are all these going with you?" We felt like the Londoners could hardly tolerate children. How had the British Empire lasted so long?

My brother Fritz met us in London and took us to a bed-and-breakfast he had reserved for us. Fritz was at London University for a year with his family for post-doctorate studies. He and Alice spent three days giving us a personally guided tour of London, their favorite city. They knew the double-decker bus and underground routes and all the interesting places. We had a delightful time with them and our children enjoyed their cousins Ed (Augie) and Tom, with their London accents and taste for sour lime.

From London we flew to Delhi. While going through immigration there, I reached into my briefcase for our documents and my hand felt the goo of sticky glue. At the last minute before leaving our home, Ruth, always frugal and saving, had put a large container of Elmer's Glue upright in my briefcase. The air pressure had caused it to overflow into everything. I spent a half hour in the bathroom, along with a helpful attendant, wiping the glue off our passports, other documents, and the inside of my case. The ticket agent at Indian Airlines then made matters worse. "Sorry, there is no Schmitthenner name on our reservation list for the flight to Madras. You will have to wait until tomorrow."

I was insisting, "No sir, that is highly impossible!" We had four hours until the flight. I kept talking in a polite and friendly manner about the children, how tired they were, how our tickets were clearly marked, "reservation confirmed," and I also told him that we were poor missionaries. This I did to counter his claim that he was underpaid, and had a big family with ten children to educate. I knew he wanted me to pay something extra. My conversation with the ticket agent went on intermittently for three hours. It was like a game we both enjoyed. Finally, when I again approached him, he was more reasonable and said, "Good news, you can all fly together as far as Hyderabad. There, two of you will have to get down and wait. Only six seats are available from there."

"Yes, We'll take it. I have many friends in Hyderabad," I said. We would be in Andhra Pradesh, where we were known. We boarded the plane and had a pleasant flight. As we neared Hyderabad I said to Ruth, "If they force us, Bill and I can get down here and take the train to Madras and Kodai, but our tickets say 'Delhi-Madras, confirmed.' So none of us will get down here. Pretend you are asleep." The children were sleeping anyway, exhausted by the long flight from London. We stayed in our seats "sleeping" in Hyderabad. After an hour people began to board again as we dozed. We overheard the crew having a heated discussion. "We have two extra passengers, what can we do? Who is responsible for this mistake?" A stewardess said, "Let them take our seats, we will manage." Over the PA-system classical music, ragas and gentle drumming soon signaled to us that the flight was about to begin. The plane began to move and we were soon airborne. Ruth and I woke up and looked to see what the Krishna River crossing would be like. We were flying at about 18,000 feet. The air was clear.

What good fortune! We passed right over Srisailem and could see the 1500-foot deep gorge where the river makes a huge loop through the Nallamalai Range. The river flows east, turns due north for a mile, then east for half a mile, then due south for a mile, and then makes another right angle to flow east to the dam site. The whole peninsula is part of the *Devastanam*. We could see the entire temple complex, the dam site, and all the roads and workings. Flying over the desolate but beautiful Nallamalai range, we remembered Gundlabrameswaram.

From Madras we took the flight to Madurai for the first time. This time the children were wide-awake, and they enjoyed viewing Tamilnadu from the air. We could see the Palni Hills as we flew right over Kodai Road Station, the Sirru Malai range and hills near Madurai. From Madurai we took the bus to Kodaikanal. Our children were fully accepted and secure among a bus full of Indians, as they munched *i.j.* (*Indian snack food*). No one asked, "Are these going with you?"

We stayed in Woodhaven for just two days, put the children in boarding, and said our goodbyes. Ruth and I went together to Guntur, where our baggage and furniture were stored. After arranging for its shipment by lorry, we drove our assigned jeep station wagon to Bhimavaram, in West Godavari District.

Going first through the Krishna Delta, then the delta of West Godavari, we passed endless acres of irrigated rice fields, sugar cane, turmeric, vegetables, mango orchards, and coconut groves. An American agricultural expert, Mr. Bacon, who had worked in this area, told us that the soil in West Godavari was the richest he had seen anywhere in the world—better than Iowa. The delta had been organically farmed for fifteen hundred or more years, yet is as rich as ever. Now, with year round irrigation crops grow fast and abundantly all year-round in this most fertile area.

The people of Bhimavaram gave us a heartwarming welcome. Synod President K. Raja Rao, the Augustana Hospital staff, Pastor Raja Gopal, and other pastors came to greet us and offer help. We quickly settled in the grandest house on the mission field. It had been built by Rev. Dr. E. Neudoerffer, a very dominant and capable church builder and seminary professor. (On government maps the house is marked as *Bishop's Residence.*) The porch going halfway around the house was so spacious that the District Christian Workers' Meetings and retreats were held there for over 100 participants. This spacious bungalow was set in a garden of suppota, Australian pine, coconut, and mango trees. There was a green colored cement elephant fountain with water spraying from the upraised trunk in a lily pond built by Henry Moyer, who had also built our Yeleswaram house. Being near the main drainage canal there were also many other large old trees like the nidra ganneru, or Samanea Saman. *Nidra* in Telugu means *sleep.* The tree is so named because its small miniature fern-like leaves on a long stem fold up and *go to sleep* in the evening. The nidra ganneru trees have most beautiful and fragrant flowers. Some of the trees were four or more feet in diameter. Their branching crowns provided a haven for birds of many kinds. Never had we lived in such a garden.

Leila Van Deusen, our sixth-grade teacher during Kodai years, was the only other missionary in Bhimavaram at that time. She welcomed us with open arms and graciously entertained us with a series of dinners attended by various Christian and other leaders of Bhimavaram. How good it was to be her co-workers! After a term of teaching in Kodai School she had been called to serve as Dean of Women at Andhra Christian College, Guntur. Seven years later she began working with Bible women in West Godavari Synod. Leila lived in the Women's Hospital Compound across town. As she was now a senior friend and advisor, we were no longer permitted to call her Miss VanDeusen or Aunt Leila, but just Leila. Occasionally Ruth and I would accompany her when she visited Bible women.

We settled into our work. Ruth took an active part in the Streela Samaj or Women's Group Ministry, going to many places with women leaders who were college and high school teachers, medical workers, pastors' wives, and Bible women. Never had Ruth worked with such talented, well-educated, devout, and committed women. She consistently refused to be an officer, but was a most supportive co-worker to all who had responsibilities.

My work was with the synod president and the evangelistic pastor. We visited evangelists and Bible women, and the families to whom they witnessed. We helped plan church worker retreats, attended one evangelistic camp in each of the three fields of the synod every month, and spent time settling disputes in congregations or among workers. The congregations in West Godavari had zeal, fine traditions of worship, and the highest standards of church life. In our five AELC synods one third of the pastors were from West Godavari. There was a saying in the church, "If a pastor fresh from seminary is assigned to a West Godavari parish, he will become a good pastor. If an inept or bad pastor is assigned to this synod, he will be corrected and will learn to work hard and faithfully. If a good, capable pastor comes here from another synod he will blossom and become an excellent pastor." In my years of experience with this synod this proved to be true.

One afternoon Ruth got up from her siesta, went to the window on the canal side which was shaded by the nidra ganneru tree, turned and softly called to me, "Sam, come here quietly; parakeets are building a nest." I joined her, watching through the screen as a pair of rose-ringed parakeets, working by turn, excavated their new home. The male would chisel out chips of wood from the side of a half rotten branch, then the female would throw out the loose chips. As we too were settling into our new nest, we identified with these new neighbors of ours and enjoyed watching them each day.

From our house there was only one place we could walk that was not in the town. Our home shared the compound with the Lutheran High School, the boys' hostel, Moyer Memorial chapel, and teacher residences. We would walk through the high school grounds to the far gate, then climb the canal bank and walk along the canal away from the busy town. The canal bank was wide enough for two-way bullock cart traffic. We'd walk a mile or two, watching fishermen fling nets from the shore or from their boats. Many of the fishermen caught shrimp. Tiger shrimp, the best variety with red and whitish stripes, were great in curry made with *gongora* (sour sorrel).

The bird-life we saw on these walks was incredible. When our children came down from Kodaikanal School they took an active interest in birdwatching. In the winter of 1968 Chris made a bird list which I pasted in my Salim Ali book. She had counted thirty-nine varieties of birds seen on these walks and around the garden. Those of the canal environment included varieties of kingfishers, jacanas, seagulls, redwattled lapwings, stilts, little stints, avocets, sandpipers, river terns, cotton teals, two varieties of egrets, gray herons, fishing eagles, two varieties of hawks, three varieties of wagtails (gray, yellow, and white), parakeets, bee-eaters, drongos, and blue rollers, doves, jungle and ordinary crows. Bill took great photos of canal scenes, sail barges, fishermen casting their nets from their skiffs, of bullock carts and majestic old trees.

Many afternoons we played tennis with high school teachers, Raja Manoharam and Dr. Jeevaratnam, a retired doctor, and with the three teams from our family. An old tennis court in front of the house had been restored with a lorry load of good clay and a new net before our children had come down from Kodai.

One of our pastors, Aluri Babu Rao, asked me to survey his entire parish of sixteen village congregations. We had learned much about parish surveying in Narasaraopet. Refining that process, I trained him and Joseph, the evangelistic pastor, and we made a comprehensive survey of Yendagandi Parish. Each of the sixteen congregations had a committed teacher or a lay leader who would visit the sick, conduct funerals and lead Sunday worship, except when the pastor came on a particular Sunday to give communion. During the summer Pastor Babu Rao would hold a weeklong school for them. With expert Bible teachers and other pastors' help they went over lessons and preaching plans and had spiritually renewing worship experiences. In a way, each village had its local pastor in residence and Pastor Babu Rao was the teacher-pastor who administered the sacraments. I wrote a paper about this remarkable ministry at Yendagandi parish that was published by Andhra Christian Theological Seminary, Hyderabad, in a booklet titled *New Types of Ministry*. In West Godavari, as in other synods, I learned and received far more than I could teach or give.

Ruth and I would take our canal walk even in the hot, sultry months, when the air was so still that not a leaf moved. The humidity was at times frightful and most debilitating. But we felt we had to walk. We needed the exercise and the time together in the countryside to talk and relax. We let our minds ramble as we enjoyed together the same scenes and beautiful sunsets. Our Bhimavaram years were more relaxed than our Narasaraopet years, as my duties without the stress of the treasurer's responsibility were less demanding and less time was spent in travel in this compact synod. Between our garden and the canal walks, even the worst humidity was bearable. Life was pleasant, our friends gracious, and the church solid and faithful.

* * *

Every May vacation we went camping with our growing children in Kodai. For several years in a row we had camped at Berijam Lake beyond the usual camping places, near the second dam at the northwest corner of the lake. During World War II an extensive pyrethrum plantation had been undertaken by the Forest Department. The land around the roadside of Berijam Lake had been terraced and hundreds of acres planted with beautiful large Pyrethrum daisies used in the manufacture of badly needed insecticides. After the war the Forest Department planted wattle, an Australian tree with good tannin bark, on the terraces. This all became an ideal spot for tenting and sitting around campfires.

Camping at Berijam was so much fun. We swam every morning and afternoon. As all our children had learned to swim well at Bella Sylva, they swam with confidence and observed rules of safety. We also had good times fishing for carp. From the time I was a boy we had used the old dugout long canoe made from a single tree trunk ages ago. This was beginning to leak at one end. We patched it with clay dug from cliffs near the boathouse and loaded the boat so that more weight was in the rear end, with the leaky end higher in the water. But each year the leakage increased. So from 1968 on we brought along and used our inflatable rubber raft. We had tried it out on the canal by our house in Bhimavaram. It was great fun and made exploring the other side of Berijam possible. However, when the wind blew hard we could not row against it in the inflated sail-like boat.

From our camp we could look across the end of the lake and see Vembadi Peak rising all the way from lake level. The peak dominated that middle part of the Palnis. Our family decided to climb Vembadi. This was fifteen years after our second attempt, when Ruth had been carrying Hans. After breakfast we crossed the northern dam of Berijam and slowly climbed the mountain. The distance was not very great, but I imagine we climbed for more than 2500 feet. When the steepness got to us and we ran out of breath, Ruth and I zigzagged. The children with their young muscles, light bodies, and good lungs just kept going straight up, arriving on top long before we did. Several times Ruth and I paused for breath, looked at each other, and smiled, remembering our first attempt from the other side, at age sixteen. We talked about the second trip. The baby Ruth carried then was now a boisterous youth, full of energy, already on top waiting for us "slow pokes." Life for us had been full of rich blessings. We arrived on top to be welcomed by our children, share lunch with them, and enjoy a delicious breeze and magnificent views from the 8207-foot peak. To the east we could see Gundar Valley, the great eucalyptus forest, and the observatory. To the west we viewed all of the Berijam area and the more distant Vanderavu ridge. Finally, after years of life and love, we had made this destination a reality, and we shared this time with our children. God is great and God is good!

We had other great camps at Vanderavu and in the pines by Niner's Knoll, a small stand of pine near the road between Doctor's Delight and Green Hut. We also camped in forest bungalows at Poombari and Mariyan Shola. One May we camped at Mariyan Shola with Ruth's brother Chuck, his wife Char, and their sons, Jay and Rob. The forest bungalow we had rented had no beds, so we slept in our sleeping bags on mats. Each night we enjoyed a fire in the fireplace, roasted marshmallows, told stories, and sang. Ruth was our family song leader and knew all the children's songs. Whenever we would go for a car trip as a family, Ruth would have the children singing a good part of the time.

One morning at Mariyan Shola, little Jay woke up while it was still dark to hear the birds beginning to sing. Crawling up onto his father's stomach, he began singing in a loud clear voice, "God has created a new day, silver and green and gold. Live that the sunset may find us worthy his gifts to behold."

"Jay, shhh, go back to sleep!" Chuck kept saying, but his clear song was repeated again and again until we all got up. We went for a dry hunt as dawn was breaking and walked right up to a herd of bison grazing close to the cabin. Thanks to Jay we all had that thrill!

During our Bhimavaram years we had some great safaris with our children. One May we took a ten-day journey, crowding into an Ambassador (India's ubiquitous car, modeled from the old British Morris Eight car). First we went to Periyar game preserve, and stayed in Aranya Nivas (forest dwelling place), a lovely guesthouse at Tekkadi, (place of teak). At dawn we took a launch around the lake to see wildlife. Unfortunately, one of the tourists with us had a radio turned up and refused to turn it off, and we saw only one lone bison and several pigs in the distance.

Next we drove to Kanya Kumari the southern tip of India where the Indian Ocean, Bay of Bengal, and Arabian Sea meet. For Hindus this is a most holy place. Then we journeyed to visit the old wooden palaces of the ancient Travancore Rajahs at *Padmanavapuram*, where we saw exquisite woodcarvings. *Padmanavapuram* means *city of the lotus growing out of the naval of Krishna*, "creation," a theme often depicted in Indian art. We visited the modern city of Trivandrum, the Malabar Coast, the coconut gardens of Kerala's backwaters and then spent two days in Cochin. We visited old Dutch buildings from spice trading days, which enthralled Ruth, proud of her Holland Dutch heritage. We spent precious time in Cochin's four hundred and fifty-year-old Jewish synagogue. Driving back to Kodai through the Cardamom hills, we met seven wild elephants blocking the road just 100 feet ahead of the car. We picked up two men walking in front of us, who were afraid of the elephants. Squeezing five people into the back seat, we waited patiently for the elephants to move off and then drove the two men to their village. After that we ascended a *ghat* road to the High Range beautiful tea gardens around Munnar. From there we drove past the cable car's Top Station to the pass above Vanderavu, the highest road in South India, where we had a picnic. After dark we set out going past Berijam, arriving back at our Kodai home, Woodhaven by 10 p.m. It was a beautiful and memorable experience for our family to share in seeing the wonders of Kerala, India's most progressive, highly educated state, with its large influential Christian presence. Roughly 25 percent of Kerala's population is Christian. Churches dot the Kerala hillsides.

The following year we motored to Kotagiri in the Nilgiris to see the venerable Dr. E. Neudoerffer, long retired and living in his home, "The Roses," at Kotagiri. We told him how we enjoyed living in the house he had built in Bhimavaram, and working in the church he had helped to build up and guide from the time he began his India ministry in 1900. Talking with him was like viewing sixty-eight years of church history embodied in one great man.

Then we drove to Bandipoor game reserve in Karnataka, the old Mysore Native State. Staying in the forest guesthouse, we saw hundreds of spotted deer, *chital*, that evening. At dawn, we went in a van with a ranger and had many exciting close encounters with bison, wild elephant, sambur, peacock, jungle fowl, and *chital*. We climbed on elephants for a jolly ride through a section of jungle, seeing more deer. From Bandipur we visited the Maharajah's palaces in Mysore City, savoring the splendor of ancient India.

On the way home we visited the Siringapatam battlefield where the great Muslim Ruler, Tipu Sultan, the "Tiger of Mysore," was finally defeated and killed by the British. On the final morning we visited a bird sanctuary on a small river that was particularly delightful. Never had we seen so many kinds of water birds nesting, packed so close together. We were glad that India has many wild life and bird sanctuaries. Finally, we came back to Kodai. These were times of bonding, growing to appreciate our teen-agers, and experiencing many good things with them.

Vacation at Berijam Lake in the Kodai Hills

Bill at Berijam with the ancient dugout canoe and our inflatable raft

Delighting in wild flowers

Safari – "jolly ride" with elephant at Bandipur National Park

CHAPTER 14

A WATER RAMBLE ON COLLERU LAKES, A NEW HOME IN GUNTUR, AND KODAI GRADUATION

January of 1969 would unexpectedly be the last time our whole family was together in Bhimavaram. Before the children went back to Kodai School, we had a water ramble with them, inviting our friends, the Hagstads, and a Canadian Baptist missionary who arranged the rental launch for us.

Looking at a map of coastal Andhra Pradesh, one can see how the deltas of the Krishna and Godavari rivers have merged, encircling a body of water that is now an inland sea, named Kolleru Lakes, about 25 miles long and 10 to 12 miles wide. The size of the lakes vary greatly. During the monsoon it becomes one lake flooding a large area. During the dry season it shrinks way down, becoming lakes. The geography and ecology of the lakes are fascinating and unique. The Kolleru civilization is, to me, the best example of people adjusting and living in harmony with their environment while prospering, and preserving the habitat that sustains them.

On the drive past the lakes the island villages appear to be huge ships or barges, seeming to float in the distance. Each village is built upon a manmade mound of soil that was built up during the dry season by mass labor centuries ago. The people of the Kolleru live by fishing, growing rice, and raising ducks and water buffalo. They make half mile long woven fiber fish traps using the reeds and swamp vines available. The Kolleru fishermen paddle around in very narrow 18-inch wide canoes made of hollowed out palmyra trees, which grow abundantly along the shore. As we plied through the waters we passed fishermen in their easily turned-over craft.

Standing on one foot and paddling with the other, they would throw out their dragnets. In the Krishna-Godavari Delta area if one has good balance they call it "Kolleru balance." Each day from Kaikalur rail station many hundreds of live fish are shipped in water containers to Calcutta.

The village women and children collect snails. The foot of the snail makes good curry. The inedible parts are food for their large flocks of ducks. In each village we saw high mounds of snail shells. These are burned in the dry season with rice husk to make *shunnam*, a fine slaked lime used for whitewash. Duck eggs are shipped by the thousands to Calcutta and Madras.

Ducks also find food in the harvested rice fields. Water buffalo slosh around all day, often with just their heads showing, eating a delightful banquet of aquatic plants. The villagers live off the milk and yogurt, or make *ghee* which brings a good price. They also weave baskets and make ingenious rattraps. The valuable palmyra trees growing around the lake provide them with their canoes, leaves for roofing, material for mat and basket making, fiber for brushes and construction rope, and *toddy*, a healthy drink which ferments in a few hours (which my mother had used as yeast). *Manjulu*, a succulent snack from the green palmyra seed, and *taggulu*—roasted, tasty, tender, carrot-size roots of the palm nuts (which are planted in sand plots for this purpose), are additional blessings this tree brings to the people of Kolleru and Andhra Pradesh.

Kolleru Lakes remain fresh, as they are fed by a number of streams. But there is only one outlet, the *Upputeru* (Salt River) which flows to the sea. The salty tide coming up the Upputeru is blocked from entering the lakes by a masonry spillway at the road crossing. Varieties of fish and shrimp swim up the outlet from the ocean to spawn in Kolleru, crawling or jumping over the spillway or by swiming over the flowing outlet during the monsoon rains.

As water recedes in the dry season the drained fields are planted with a variety of long stemmed rice that was specially developed to grow in high water. Deeper channels around the villages and fields provide fresh water for irrigation. Kolleru also has a thriving brick industry. Each year some of the channels are desilted, and the mud is used to make bricks which are fired with rice husk.

If a village needs to be built up or expanded, all available laborers will form a remarkable earth-moving chain. Earth diggers fill baskets which are passed from hand to hand without any steps between. While full baskets are passed up to the village site, empty ones are passed back in perfect rhythm. This human conveyor belt operation is the age-old way of building up massive fort walls and village sites in low-lying delta areas.

This is a sanctuary and home of the spot billed pelican, which nest in the high palmyra trees. The lake abounds with many varieties of duck and aquatic bird-life. In my Salim Ali book I listed 30 varieties which we saw on the lakes. But that superb book could never prepare us for the large number of great flocks which we saw all day long. I have often thought this jewel of a lake, with teeming bird-life and great ecology, would make a perfect National Geographic documentary.

Ruth and I enjoyed this last outing with our children and friends before they went back to school in January of 1969. Again, it was hard saying goodbye. In the five months since we had last seen the children they had changed so much, and had some ideas and ways that bothered and some-times frightened us. Some days we found it hard to communicate. The boys would say, "Oh Mom, Dad, don't be so paranoid." After hearing that expression many times I finally said, "Yes, we are paranoid. Your mother is annoyed; so am I, we are a *pair annoyed.*" Well, we learned to lighten up, listen, remember our teenage days, and try to understand. We also realized that their peers—fresh from the States where the 60's teen revolution was going on—put pressures and ideas on our children that we had never had to deal with. Yet, God is good, and we knew He would watch over and lead them safely through life.

Then abruptly a great change came to our lives. At the convention of the AELC in May 1969 I was elected to be the president of the church. That meant saying goodbye to our friends in Bhimavaram and moving to Guntur to occupy the church president's residence. I went to Kodai to spend several weeks with the children and Ruth, who were somewhat shocked by all of this. We all were! My missionary friends were—it was a complete surprise. On June 1, I flew from Madras to Vijayawada, took a taxi to Guntur, and received the office from outgoing president Rev. Kalapudi Devasahayam.

When Ruth put the children in Kodai School boarding and came down to the plains we went Bhimavaram, said goodbye to all our friends, packed up and moved our things by *lorry* (truck) to our new home Guntur.

The President's house was not huge with high ceilings and great porches meant for workers' meetings like the five old colonial type mission bungalows we had lived in before. It was like a well-planned Indian upper-class suburban home, with smaller but quite adequate rooms. There was no air conditioning, but every room except the bathroom had overhead fans. Downstairs was a spacious front porch with cane chairs and a large fan where we could meet people. In front of the porch was an old peepul tree which provided great shade and was home to many birds including the *Kovela* (cuckoo). Beyond the reception porch there was a dining room, and on either side bedrooms with an attached bath. A kitchen and back porch—where we stored food and washed dishes—completed the downstairs.

Upstairs was a bedroom with bathroom, a sleeping porch shaded by the peepul tree in front of the house, and an upstairs living room that could be used as a bedroom. We had plenty of room for our children and visitors as well. After spending the first night in our new home, we woke up to the song of the kovela, remembering the cuckoos of Peddapuram and immediately felt at home and at peace.

We had only one more vacation time, with all our children, in Guntur at the end of 1969. Bill and Hans spent the earlier part of their vacation traveling with friends to North India to see a number of the fabulous sites of this ancient and fascinating land. By the time they returned we were experiencing our first Christmas season in Guntur. Each Christian institution in this most Lutheran of all Indian cities had its own Christmas "function." As the new president I was obligated to preside and give the main message, and Ruth, as 'first lady' of the church, would give out prizes to meritorious students, or gifts to staff or to the poor. So our whole family attended programs at Andhra Christian College, three men's hostels, a girl's dormitory, two Lutheran high schools, Kugler Hospital and Kugler School of Nursing, the Boys' Industrial Training School, Lotsch Library, and the Synod Pastors' Christmas. These were our "twelve days of Christmas" *before* Christmas Eve. The programs were very good, with great dramas, pageants, singing, and dancing. Our children were good sports and went to all of these with us, enjoying many items of the programs. But after a while it became too much for all of us, as these programs took up much of our family time. The festivals began in late afternoon and lasted for two to three hours, after which rich, curry and rice meals were served at 8 p.m.

Christmas Day was very long and strenuous for me. The night before we had been kept awake by carolers who came in band after band to bring the good news to the new president and his family. The children had a special kind of rhythmic dance song called a *Gearro*. These were chanted in rhyming verses, with a leader who would periodically shout out, "Cherra Hai, Atcha Hai!" then say a line of the Christmas story in Telugu rap style that was answered by the other children as they hopped and danced. It was noisy, fun, and dramatic with meaningful verses. Each group of carolers carried its own large star made of bamboo frame and colored paper with a real lighted candle inside. Things would not quiet down until after 3 a.m. Christmas morning.

At 6 a.m. I always attended and preached at the English Sunrise service. After breakfast I would visit four or five village congregations in some parish that was undergoing a pastoral vacancy, preaching in Telugu and rejoicing with God's people. I would arrive home by 11 p.m. or sometime past midnight.

On December 26 we would celebrate our family Christmas. That was also Ruth's birthday, so this had been a tradition from our Yeleswaram days and continued to be our way of celebrating Christmas together, with no schedules or obligations. It was a precious time of peace, when Ruth would delight in celebrating her birthday while enjoying family Christmas and our Christmas dinner with a few friends. Even in India we always had a turkey! Our cook, Prakasam, was an expert at raising turkeys, and we always bought his best one.

Several days after Christmas we would drive to our mission retreat at Vadarevu on the Bay of Bengal, where we celebrated New Year's Eve and New Year's Day together. That was a most enjoyable time. All the Lutheran missionary families and singles came. Our children spent most of the time on the beach having a good time with their friends. But this time the two oldest were sad, knowing this would be their last mission retreat at their favorite beach and that even if they ever could see Vadarevu again it would not be with this missionary family. It is hard to say goodbye to such special people and places.

Before the children went back to school I took Bill and Hans rubber rafting on the Krishna River through pretty wild country.

The first evening while going down some rough rapids, our boat bottom was torn and we started shipping water. At the end of the rapids we camped on a sand bar, building a big drift wood fire to dry out everything We went to sleep listening to the river and the night-jar bird. The next morning I walked half a mile to a village where there was a Christian schoolteacher I knew. He sent a rescue party to help us carry everything to the village, gave us an early lunch of *sambar*, a spicy vegetable soup and rice, and arranged for a bullock cart to take us with our baggage eight miles to the pastor's house at Dachapalle on the main road. From there I walked to the bus station. Boarding the bus, I realized my wallet was in the car, but a passenger who knew me bought me a ticket to Bellam Konda. From there I walked to a nearby high school, where I met the headmaster. Explaining that my van was at Mallepalle on the river, seven miles away, I asked him if I could please borrow a bicycle from one of the staff. "Oh yes, I will arrange it, but first tell me your story while you have a cup of tea," he said with such friendly interest. After relating the story of our adventure and sipping two cups of tea, I pedaled to Mallepalle to meet Kotiah, our faithful driver. There we enjoyed a vegetarian dinner in the home of the Brahmin *munsif* (head officer of the village). Returning by car to Bellam Konda, we dropped off the cycle, thanked the headmaster, and drove to Dachapalle to pick up Hans and Bill and our gear. Where else in the world could one find more trusting, helpful, and hospitable people?

Three days later Bill and Hans said good-bye to their new friends in Guntur, as well as our cook Prakasam and his wife Paranjyothi, who had been part of our household for their entire lives, and they returned for their final term of school at Kodaikanal along with Chris, then in tenth grade, and Peter, in eighth grade.

In May of 1970 I turned over my office to the vice-president, Dr. G. Devasahayam, a professor in our seminary, who would be in charge during my three months leave. I went to join the family in Kodai.

Bill and Hans graduated early in May. That was a great event for the whole family. Ruth and I got quite emotional thinking of Bill and Hans, now ready to face the world, and of our own graduation 26 years previously. After their graduation we had no time for hiking. We immediately packed up to commence our first journey flying east from Madras by way of Singapore, Thailand, Hong Kong, the across the Pacific to Japan, to Hana, on Maui, and finally to Tucson, Arizona, to be with Ruth's parents.

The Peepul Leaf

A peepul tree reminds me of my favorite people, who are beautiful, filled with spirit, with hope, and with promise. It is one of the great fig trees of India, ficus religious. Huge ancient peepul trees—up to eight feet in diameter—are often found on temple grounds and at village gathering places. The beautiful leaves quaver and tremble at the slightest wind, and they reminded early visitors from the Mid East and West of the quaking aspen or poplar tree. The name *peepul* is thought to be derived from the word *poplar*. When the wind blows through the peepul tree it sounds like rain, hence the name *rain tree*.

What is this leaf?

A touch of God's creation
A tiny spot of shade that cools the earth
A rustle in the wind that whispers rain
A marvel workshop where solar light turns into figs for food
A home and joy to birds of every kind
A living green that trembles as it speaks of life
A minute air conditioner giving water from the earth to sky

A structure, beautiful, delicate, yet strong
That works in all these ways—yet short its life
It withers, dies and falls, and losing self
Becomes a home for grubs and ants
And then becomes the food for one more leaf
To live and work and bless this earth
A perfect detail of God's glorious plan

Family in Kodaikanal – May 1969

CHAPTER 15

JOURNEYS THROUGH EAST ASIA, MAUI, TUCSON TO PENNSYLVANIA. THEN BACK TO INDIA AND VADAREVU ON THE BAY OF BENGAL

One day in 1966, Ruth had come to me and said, "Sam, guess what? Mom and Dad have decided to buy a house in Tucson, Arizona. They say it's wonderful there. They won't have to shovel snow, there is a Reformed Church of America within easy walking distance, and they love being able to drive out into the desert. It reminds them so much of Iraq. But, Sam, it's so far away from all of their children. What are we going to do?"

"Ruth," I said, "they need a place where they can be comfortable and happy. We'll just visit them as often as we can. Arizona sounds like fun with so many interesting places there. We'll make the best of it." The words I spoke then were to be tested soon. We would be "making the best of it" on our first visit to their Tucson home, our destination as we began our journey east.

Flying first to Singapore, we stayed with Lutheran missionaries, John and Betty Lou Nelson. Betty Lou was a Wood girl, a big sister to my sister Molly. They gave us a good view of their progressive church building and ministry. What impressed us most was the Bethel Bible Series training program they had given to many successive groups of laypersons. It was the best course I had ever experienced for teaching the concepts of the Bible and applying them to every phase of personal and church life. It had been very effective for Bible learning, ministry, and intentional evangelism, and had borne much fruit in the church of Singapore. We had a noisy time with the Nelsons; our four children and their six got along boisterously.

Next we went to Thailand and enjoyed cruising along the river in Bangkok and visiting famous Buddhist pagodas. Our last evening there we enjoyed a traditional full-course Thai dinner, followed by the Thai version of the Indian epic, the *Ramayana*, presented as a dance drama. Next we flew to Hong Kong to visit missionary friends and to explore the "ladder" streets.

From there we flew to Kyoto, Japan, to visit the World's Fair, Expo 70, and see the old classical buildings and parks in the ancient capital of Japan. We stayed in Kyoto with a Japanese pastor's family, enjoyed their simple lifestyle, and became enthusiastic consumers of Japanese food.

We were impressed at how progressive Japan was. One day we went to a little hole-in-the-wall shop to have my watch repaired. In broken English the shopkeeper asked in amazement, "Why you buy Swiss watch? They no good!" He repaired my watch, then set it in a small machine that printed out the rhythm, something like an electro-cardiograph. He placed his watch in the machine, and we could see a more steady printout pattern. "See, next time you buy Japanese watch," the shopkeeper said. Our taxis were powered by methane gas from cylinders stored in the trunk. It would be 15 years before Los Angeles began using methane to power buses for cleaner air.

From there we went to Hana—located on the island of Maui—to be with my mother's youngest sister, Aunt Rebecca. There we spent ten days enjoying wonderful warm swimming, sightseeing, viewing the island through the eyes of one who loved and knew heavenly Hana more than anyone. Rebecca had made great arrangements for us. Her congregation in Hana, the Wanalalua Congregational Church, was between pastors, so I was asked to serve them for the few days we were there. We lived in the furnished parsonage with a fridge stocked with food and fresh fruit and had the privilege of using of the pastor's car. I led service and preached on two Sundays and later in the week presided over a luau in honor of a child I had baptized.

Our next flight took us to Los Angeles and the home of Aunt Mina Auringer, Grandma Christina's younger sister. She took us to Disneyland and made us feel at home in America. The next stop was Tucson to be with the senior Gosselinks. The children were especially glad to see their grandparents again.

George and Christina took us for a scenic drive up Mount Lemon, the 9000-foot peak that dominates the Tucson area. We drove from desert on the plains, through tall arms-stretched saguaro cactus, juniper, and scrub oak forest, with mountain ash and sycamore by the streams. Driving higher, we passed through different layers of habitat, until we came to an area of ponderosa pines, then finally to towering Douglas fir and sugar pine forest on the upper slopes which received the most rain and snow. George knew where the best picnic places and hiking trails were.

Jenny and Carl Phelps, former principal of Kodaikanal School, had also retired in Tucson. We also met Emily and Spencer Hatch, the parents of Nancy, our classmate from Kodai School days. They, too, had retired to Tucson. Ruth and I reminisced about the dancing classes and tasty teas Emily and Nancy had held for us when we were in seventh-eighth grade at Kodai School.

With the senior Gosselinks we did not go on hikes or extensive rambles. We needed to hike, so one day Bill, Hans, Peter and I decided to go to the Grand Canyon. Driving there in Gramp's car, we camped out on the rim. Starting at early dawn, we spent the day hiking down the Kaibab Trail to the Colorado River, on the canyon floor. Taking our time, we snapped many photos in the changing light and reached the Bright Angel Creek and Ranch by 9:30 a.m. There we rested and enjoyed wading and lying in the stream. The long climb of over 5000 feet in only 9 miles was quite taxing, but the boys did it easily. "Dad, it's just like going down to Tope and climbing back to Kodai in one day."

Our next stop was Pennsylvania. We happily settled in the mission house in Gettysburg at 108 Springs Avenue, near the seminary. From there we had good visits with Aunts Katie, Dot, and Elizabeth in nearby Chambersburg. Late in June we headed for Bella Sylva, where we were happy to see my brothers, and sister, nieces, and nephews and enjoy good family times. We had afternoon swims each day in the lake, tribal picnics and camp fires, and went on several of our favorite hikes.

By mid-July I had to take Peter and Chris with me back to Kodai School. Ruth had planned to stay with Bill and Hans until their colleges opened. Saying goodbye to Hans and Bill was very hard!

Chris, Peter, and I flew to Paris, where we had two days of great rambles and superb food. From there we flew into Madras, took train to Kodai Road and the bus up the Ghat to Kodai. Pete and Chris were happy to see their old friends. They immediately settled down to work, as they had missed a few days of school. I returned to the president's work in Guntur. Ruth stayed in the States until the end of August and then came to join me. When I saw her getting off the plane in Madras she was carrying a five-foot-long styrofoam body surfboard. Wow! She knew I had wanted one for the beach at Vadarevu. She had gone to the trouble of lugging it around, changing planes three times in twenty-four hours, just to bring me something special. She was the something special I needed, and I was overjoyed to see her again. We settled in for a longer term in Guntur.

Work was most demanding, and the hours long. People would come to see me from six in the morning till late in the evening. I tried to give people equal time, whether they were slum or village dwellers or "important" people. Leaving town was the only way I could have a day off.

Ruth also needed a break. She had become more and more involved in many aspects of church work. She was in charge of distribution of Church World Service medical supplies for the seven hospitals of the church. She had opened a church guesthouse, remodeling an old missionary residence, furnishing it, and working out systems of administration and maintenance. For a time she was also in charge of Lotsch Library, and she served on planning and program committees for the *Streela Samaj*, or women's work of the church, attending many of their meetings, Bible studies and rallies. Besides this she did a great deal of listening and counseling, especially with the women of the church.

When we could manage a much-needed day off I would reserve the church guesthouse at Vadarevu, by the sea. When possible we would go there for two nights and a day to relax. I could catch the six-to-eight foot waves with the surfboard Ruth had brought me, and surf in all the way to the beach. We enjoyed fresh seafood dinners of sea bass, herring, shrimp, or catfish, which we bought from the fishermen when their sail powered catamarans landed on the beach in the evening. *Catamaran* is a Tamil word, meaning *tied logs*. Jesudas, the guesthouse watchman, was an excellent seafood cook. One day, fishermen friends brought us a huge king crab. We bought it for two rupees (twenty-five cents). With buttered parsley potatoes, sliced tomatoes, and pepper-lemon-butter sauce we had a crab feast using two 2 pliers from the car to crack the claws. What a way to end the day!

Every year over New Year's Day we gathered for our mission retreat at Vadarevu, living rugged in tents and blockhouses with camp cots. There was always a special speaker from outside our church for Bible study and one of our own missionaries for a series of devotions. One year Bishop Leslie Newbegin was our guest speaker. Hymn singing, communion service, and several fun nights with bonfires of driftwood we had gathered made these retreats very special.

We sometimes planned an afternoon off to visit historic Motupalli. We would drive in jeeps and trailers eight miles south along the beach. From there we would walk half a mile inland to the village of Motupalli. On the shore side of the village stood an ancient temple with a large upright inscription stone written in archaic Telugu which tells about Marco Polo landing there and making trade agreements with the Kakatiyya Queen, Rudramma Devi. She had controlled that area of the coast from her inland capital city, Warangal. The very last time we visited this temple the inscription stone was missing. The watchman told us that treasure hunters had dug around and under the massive pillar causing it to topple. The priest had reported this to the police, who informed the Department of Archeology of Andhra Pradesh. They moved this valuable historic stone to the State Salar Jung Museum, Hyderabad, where it is now on display.

Ruth and I had many walks and refreshing swims at Vadarevu, sometimes by moonlight. Swimming at night was fascinating because the plankton in the water gave a phosphorescent glow when disturbed. We would light up like Christmas trees as we swam along. Our rambles on the beach enabled us to relax and listen to each other, and helped to renew us for the demanding ministry of church administration in Guntur.

Whenever there was a retreat in Vadarevu, the pastors and evangelists and Bible women would spend some time in the nearby fishing village, and the fisherfolk in turn would often come to listen and learn at our retreats. After a number of years many of the fisherfolk caste accepted Christ. I have notes in my Telugu Bible that on New Year's Day in 1974, I baptized 25 fisherfolk in this village.

From that day until now the congregation has grown and flourished.

Vadarevu Beach

Prepared and ready for mid-life crisis

CHAPTER 16

CRUISING DOWN TO TOPE, AND MEETING THE DEITY OF VELLAGAVI

In 1973, a year before Peter graduated, his brothers Bill and Hans, visited us from the States after several years of college. We met them in Kodai as we wanted to have time to enjoy our visit with them during our vacation. It was a joy it was to meet them as adults and to be lifted by their enthusiasm and tremendous energy. Peter was happy to have his brothers back. His friends spent lots of time visiting in our home at Woodhaven because of Pete and his brothers, and because "Aunt Ruth" was their favorite and the only barber they could trust.

We missed having Chris with us. She had graduated in May 1972. I had gone up early to Kodai to be there for her final concert—she was one of the best pianists in Kodai. But her mother was upset when she came onto the stage. Ruth whispered to me, "Sam, she's in her bare feet! How could she do this?" Chris was "making a statement," but she did play very well. Her graduation was memorable. She had been accepted by Oberlin College, and soon it was time for her to go. We went with her to Madras and saw her off on the plane. She traveled via the Philippines to Tucson to be met by her grandparents and by Bill and Hans, who had driven from Kansas City to meet her.

Ruth enjoyed cooking the boys' favorite things and planning things to do together. One day, after breakfast she said, "Sam, let's all hike down to Tope. You know, I've never been there and have always wanted to go." The boys and I were dumbfounded. How was it possible that in all her Kodai years she'd never been on this favorite ramble of our boys. Ruth said, "We could hike down, have a van meet us at Tope. We agreed with enthusiasm to hike the next day.

Next morning we started out. Going down from 7000 feet to 1000 feet elevation over a nine mile trail may seem to be an easy coast, but is actually very difficult. It is hard on the feet, hard on the knees, and hard on the thighs. Toes develop bad blisters; knees turn to jelly, and thigh muscles constantly grow sore. But mentally we had a great time going down. The Coolie Ghat trail had been the lifeline over which all Kodai-bound traffic flowed before the Ghat Road was completed. Afterward it has been used only by cattle herders, forest-produce gatherers, and hikers. The original trail had many switchbacks. Through the years hikers had developed numerous shortcuts. After World War II an electric pole line had been installed from Periyakulam to Kodaikanal right up the trail ridge, crossing the switchbacks. Our children scampered down the very steep "pole trail." Ruth and I used as many of the zigzags as possible, favoring our feet and legs. Some sections near moist seeps were so densely overgrown that we had to retreat and use some of the shortcuts after all.

There were many good views. As we descended the trail we could view Coaker's Walk, Priest's Walk, Fern Cliff, Eagle's Cliff, the Plains, Vellagavi, and Pambar Falls—which was fairly full and beautiful to behold. Even during our first rambles to Pambar Falls and Priest's Walk, Ruth and I had talked of hiking to Tope. Now, thirty years later, we enjoyed this with our grown children. The fulfillment of hopes and dreams sometimes takes a long, long time.

Finally, we reached Tope. *Tope* means *a grove of trees*. This spot had provided accommodation where expeditions had assembled before the onward climb to the cool Kodai hills. Travelers would come by train to Madurai or to the Kodai Road rail station, then travel more than thirty miles from late afternoon through the night by bullock cart with relays of fresh oxen until they arrived at Tope. They then rested in the shade while luggage was transferred to pack animals or coolies and arrangements were made for sedan chairs for the ascent. The stream flowing by there was none other than Pambar Stream, now strengthened by other merging streams from forest *sholas* on the lower Palni slopes. This stream provided a good pool for swimming, and above the pool was a superb water slide. As it was nearing noon on the hot plains in mid-summer and we were grimy from hiking, we really needed a swim! We all had sewn patches on the seats of our swimsuits, as we knew the rockslide could quickly reduce a swimsuit to rags. What fun we had! Hans showed us where, during an overnight high school camping trip, he had rescued one of his classmates who had been caught in the whirlpool below the water slide during high water.

After lunch and another swim we boarded the van that had come from Kodai to meet us, and drove to Madurai. We visited the Madurai Meenakshi Temple, the greatest temple in South India. We delighted most of all in the life-size stone carvings of the marriage of Lord Siva with Meenakshi, the Madurai name for Siva's consort Parvathi. Meenakshi means "fish-eyed one." Looking from eye level at the superb sculpture, Meenakshi appears to be demure with properly modest downcast eyes. But when you sit and look from a lower angle you note that she is smiling. In Indian art, goddesses and beautiful women are depicted with fish-shaped eyes, the fish head being near the nose and its tail coming from the corners. Nothing is as beautiful as a fish under water making a quick turn. Ruth knew this, yet never appreciated being called, "Oh beautiful fish-eyed one!" She preferred "Oh beautiful hazel-eyed one."

The next day Ruth and I were so stiff we could hardly walk. We could go up steps all right but could only descend stairs by walking backwards. Our teen-aged children were sore, but not as sore as we were. Climbing the Coolie Ghat is harder on the heart and lungs, but far easier on feet, knees, and thighs.

After our Kodai days with Bill, Hans, and Peter, Ruth and I returned to Guntur, and Peter entered boarding to begin his senior high school year. The two older boys went on other trips with friends and then came to Guntur for a brief time. We gave them a good send off, and they returned to the States to college and work. We were grateful for the mission policy that made it possible for children to have a special visit with their parents during their college years.

During the last years Peter was in Kodai School, Ruth had been a member of the Kodaikanal School Council. For that most critical period of the school's future, the council—with Ruth's enthusiastic support—made a momentous decision to enhance the mission and vision of the school. They purposed to convert Kodaikanal School, which had been administered by mission boards, to be an autonomous, multi-cultural, Christian international school. Their hard work and wider vision made possible the implementation of what is now known as Kodaikanal International School, or KIS. Peter's class of 1974 was the first to graduate from this new school.

Preparation for Peter's graduation and the graduation night party involved a lot of planning. I had been asked to serve as M.C., so I secretly met with Peter's class and had them work out a drama where they pretended to be their parents planning this last great party for their "babies." They carried it off splendidly! During the previous winter at Vadarevu beach, George Penner and I had made a slide presentation of Peter and two of his friends, creating a new legend of two fishermen friends, one Tamilian and the other Telugu, at the beginning of time on the Coromandal coast. The two had quarreled but were reconciled to trust each other by a benevolent god, Dharma Swami, played by Peter. Our slide story was a hit and a complete surprise for all. After Peter's memorable graduation we flew with him to the States for just two months. We had all the children with us at Bella Sylva for a short time, then took Peter to Clark University in Worcester, Massachusetts, and returned to India at the end of August.

* * *

Chris came from the States to visit us in 1976. She had one more year to go for her B.S. in Nursing Studies at Keuka College in New York, and had wanted to have overseas nursing as one of her credit courses. She worked at Kugler Hospital in Guntur, revived her Telugu and enjoyed serving and learning with the wonderful nurses of Kugler, especially in the community health camps they conducted in the slums of Guntur.

In May we went to Kodai for vacation. Neither Ruth nor Chris had ever been to Vellagavi, the village halfway to the plains that Ruth and I had gazed upon and talked of visiting even when we were in high school. Now we would see it with Chris. We started off early in the morning with our lunch, plenty of water, and a quart flask of hot tea. We stopped for the view from Dolphin's Nose. Then we began the long, zigzag descent to Vellagavi. Crossing a saddle, going uphill for a bit and then down again, we passed through a *shola* where cardamom and coffee were being cultivated in the shade. Ruth and Chris appreciated how the villagers could make a good living growing coffee and spices while preserving the natural *shola*.

As we hiked I told them about my hike to Vellagavi in 1956 with Jack Peery, a senior missionary friend, who was then sixty years old. When Jack and I had drawn near to the village we had noticed two small, one-room shrines. The first was whitewashed. To the side of it was a newer second temple built of cut stone. We had looked inside the first temple and had seen the deity, a light-faced pink-cheeked Englishman wearing a *topee* or pith helmet. He was garbed in an olive hunting shirt and shorts with long stockings and boots. In his hand was a gun (*ayyudha*, meaning weapon) and at his feet was a white black-spotted hunting dog. Most Indian deities have a *vahanam* or animal vehicle: Siva rides a bull; Ganesh has a rat at his feet; Saraswathi, godess of music, rides on a peacock; Durga rides on a tiger. So this deity had his hunting dog.

Uncle Jack, who had visited this place before, had narrated this story:

> Many years ago the villagers here were being bothered by a marauding ti-ger which killed and ate many of their cattle and goats. A report was sent to the collector at Madurai. One of his officers came up to Vellagavi with his weapons and a hunting dog, and was able to shoot the tiger. Sometime later when a leopard began to carry off their goats they again sent a mes-sage for help to Madurai. The same officer returned and, with the help of his dog, tracked the leopard to its lair and killed it. The villagers ac-knowledged this hunter as an avatar or incarnation of God who had saved the innocent village people from these cruel ravaging animals which had caused them so much loss and fear. Therefore, they built this temple and have worshiped the hunter reverently ever since.

Ruth, Chris, and I came to where we could see both temples. Go-ing to the hunter's temple we looked in through the bars of the closed door. We saw the same figure, but his visage had changed. He now had a brown complexion, a fierce Tamilian deity-type mus-tache, and a shawl around his shoulders. Though his visage had been Indianized, the pith helmet, hunting boots and shorts, gun and dog were still there.

We walked around the village, meeting friendly people. Here and there people were drying coffee beans on large flat rocks. We saw piles of limes and hill bananas they had harvested from their or-chards and would carry up to Kodai by head load the next morn-ing. The villagers graciously gave us bananas to eat. They were small, but sweet and tasty.

As we hiked up the steep trail, we talked about how the god had changed. Ruth liked the legend of the English God of Vellagavi. We rested every fifteen minutes, drinking hot tea and water at alternate stops. As we climbed over 3000 feet to reach Kodai, Chris ran ahead to appear suddenly from various places of ambush: boulders, tall clumps of lemon grass and, once, from up in a rhododendron tree on a zigzag above us. Her youthful energy and antics helped us make it up the hill.

Half way up, as we rested, taking in the view of the village with the plains in the background, I told Ruth and Chris how her father Gosselink, Mr. George and I had gone down to Vellagavi together when he was 62 years old. He had never been to the village and had greatly enjoyed the hike. On the way back to Kodai he kept right on climbing at a steady pace for quite a long period, as I did. Finally, we looked at each other and stopped.

"I didn't want to slow you down and was trying to keep up," he said. To which I answered, "I was waiting for my senior father to stop, and wondered how long I could keep up." We laughed, rested, drank water, and proceeded more sensibly, stopping frequently for rest, enjoying each other's company and the views, and ended up having tea at the Gosselink vacation cottage.

When Ruth, Chris and I arrived home, happy, tired, still talking and wondering about the changing god. We each had *periya snanam* (big bath) followed by Gosselink-style tea.

* * *

Through the years I wondered about this beneficent village deity. Who was this Englishman? What else had he done? What traditions and stories would the villagers now tell about him?

Many years later, after Ruth had passed on, I set out on April 8, 1997, to fulfill my desire to have one more visit to Vellagavi. With me was Muniyandi, a Tamilian who also knew some Telugu and English. Starting from Kodai at 6:30 a.m., we easily made it to Vellagavi by 9:30 after a stop at Dolphin's Nose. We met a number of people at the edge of the village, including the priest. But he would not open the temple for us. Among the crowd were many friendly, hospitable people. In one house we were given homegrown coffee with milk, in another, the juice of local limes, and in a third, *dosai,* a crepe-like pancake made with lentil flour. We had interesting conversations and learned much about this village of 1000 valiant people. We visited all four of their temples and their volleyball court, their pride and joy.

A village health worker, Vetravel, told us that at present there is no one with a serious illness in Vellagavi. The Kodai School doctor, Bruce DeJong, informed me that this may be true now, but that four of the residents recently had died of heart attacks. With all the climbing that daily life necessitates, the villagers must be healthy and hardy or they pass on quickly. We found them to be friendly and joyful people, and we delighted in their company. They are very much connected to the outside world. Forty-eight children were attending the local two-teacher village school. A number of their youth were studying in residential secondary schools in Kodaikanal or Periyakulam, and ten college graduates were living in the village. The day we arrived a festival was going on. A number of relatives had come from other villages, including Vilpatti and Periyakulam.

After spending more than two hours getting to know a number of people, we asked them to tell us about the god in the first temple. The priest, a Chettiar (a Telugu tribe), a sixty-year-old elder, a villager who had worked in Hyderabad and knew Telugu, and others all joined in telling the story first in Tamil, then in Telugu, with a few English words thrown in. A lot of discussion accompanied the telling of the following interesting story about the god of this temple, now called the Poombarandi *Koil:*

> *Many, many years ago there lived in Vellagavi a lad named Poombarandi, who was a great hunter, even as a boy. He used to shoot birds with a bow and blunted arrows. One day while hunting, when he was eight years old, he met an Englishman who was trekking in the area. The hiker watched him skillfully shoot several birds.*
>
> *Then he challenged him, "Little boy, see if you can hit my finger from where you are standing," and he held up his left index finger. Poombarandi drew his bow and shot, from 70 feet away, breaking the Englishman's finger. Though in pain, the Englishman was delighted with this talented, personable boy. So he went to Vellagavi, met his parents and gave his name, Levinge Dorai, to the boy.*
>
> *He blessed him and said, "You will be a hero and a blessing to this village, your name will henceforth be Levinge Poombarandi."*

They had two different endings to this story. The first was:

Levinge Poombarandi was a great blessing to the village. People consulted him about everything. He was very devout (bakthi) and helpful to everyone. From somewhere, probably his English benefactor, he procured a gun and would hunt with it and help feed the village. Out hunting one day his gun went off accidentally, and he was shot in the thigh. He knew he could not make it back to the village and as he lay dying he willed his spirit to appear to his brother. After his death, his spirit appeared to the brother and gave instructions that the people of Vellagavi should build a shrine for him. This they obediently and gladly did and the temple was dedicated to Poombarandi Levinge Dorai, to honor the great hunter.

Poombarandi's sixty-year-old grandson gave his version:

Poombarandi lived to be sixty years old. He was a blessed person who loved God. The village was always very happy with him as their hero and benefactor. He finally died from fever. His brother had a vision of him a few days later and the spirit said, "Build a temple in my name, Poombarandi and Levinge Dorai." So the temple was built to honor both of these heroes.

After hearing, discussing, and finalizing these stories, and realizing that the two different endings were not to be compromised, we were ready to go. But first we visited the Poombarandi Levinge Dorai temple again. Looking in through the bars at the deity we saw that Poombarandi Levingi Dorai now had a turban over his pith helmet, a beautiful gold embroidered *kandava*, a stole-like scarf of honor around his neck, big white eyes, brown skin, and the same fierce Dravidian deity-style mustache. He was still wearing olive drab hunting shorts, still had a gun, *ayyudha*, in his hand, but now there were two dogs, the original Dalmatian on one side, and a brown village dog on the other. What great transport—a two-wheeler *vahanam* vehicle! Villagers worship Poombarandi every Sunday. The other name for the temple is the *Vairam* (hero) Temple. The villagers told us they had heard both temples were 300 years old. None of the villagers mentioned an Englishman shooting marauding tigers or leopards. At a third temple at the center of the village we saw a carved pillar depicting a hunter shooting a leopard-like animal springing down upon him. No one of our informants knew the story depicted. Their present oral tradition does not seem to include the old Uncle Jack story of the hunter saving the village.

A week after the trek to Vellagavi a young Australian doing research about English Hill Stations informed me that Sir Veer Henry Levinge had served as collector of Madura from 1860 to

1867. Later my son, Peter, looked up the records of Sir Levinge in the British Library in London. Sir Levinge was the 8th Baronet, Knockdrin Castle, in the country of Westmouth, Ireland. He had joined the civil service in Madras as a writer at age twenty and later served as collector at Madurai until his retirement April 8, 1867. He never married. In 1863 he built the *bund* forming the lake at Kodai-kanal and financed many public works around Kodai. He retired to Kodaikanal in 1867 and lived there until 1884, making his residence in Pambar House, which became the social center of the community. There, he planted varieties of tea from every province of China. This tea garden, the only one in the Palnis, was still there. I went to see Pambar House and the tea plantation. The tea bushes had been carefully pruned, and the tea was being harvested as I visited. The tea garden is on the southeast slope between Pambar House and Levinge Stream, the English name for Pambar Stream (Tamil), was named for this original hunter-god of Vellagavi, who passed away in March 1885 in Madras at age 65.

CHAPTER 17

A RAMBLE OF PRAISE TO KONDAVEEDU AND SERIOUS HIKES TO KUKKAL AND VANDERAVOO

After our children had all gone to the States, Ruth and I continued to come to the Kondaveedu Fort, sometimes with friends. It was close to Guntur and the perfect outing when we needed a break from busy Guntur life. Often on these hill rambles we enjoyed seeing schoolchildren with their teachers on guided educational excursions.

We began to notice how, since our first visit, the fort walls around the village were being dismantled for their wonderful, 'cut-sized,' granite-like stones. It pained me to see this historical monument being obliterated, so I wrote a proposal to our District Collector, the chief government officer in our large district (equivalent to about eight counties in Pennsylvania.) I pointed out what a valuable asset this fort was and how popular educational field trips to the fort were for schoolteachers and students. I suggested that it be made into an historic monument park to provide for protection, for historical and archeological research, and for interpretation of this interesting and valuable historic site. The collector was very interested, but his abrupt transfer ended this effort.

One year in the mid 1970s we were visited by the Lutheran Youth Encounter team Rainbow of Promise. Eight dedicated young people, most of whom were part way through St. Olaf's and other Midwest colleges, came on a mission of song and witness to the young people of the Andhra Evangelical Lutheran Church. They stayed with us in Guntur, giving concerts there and in surrounding towns for more than three weeks. How Ruth and I re-

joiced at having them! We missed our children, who were all studying in the States, and so the ministry of the Rainbow Team was
most meaningful to us. They sang with radiant joy and faith and
inspired many. They were so greatly loved and appreciated that our
church requested for Rainbow Teams to return every year. Since
that time they have been ministering among the Lutheran Churches
in India and at Kodai School every other year.

Ruth said after she talked it over with me, "You Rainbows have
been working so hard. Tomorrow is your day off for your retreat.
Let us take you on a picnic to a hill fort. You can have your team
devotions up in the hills." They agreed.

What a wonderful day we had with them at Kondaveedu! The day
was beautiful with a cool breeze, and the bird life wonderful. After
we had been climbing quite awhile, Carmine, who later became a
missionary in Nepal, began to sing *Lead Me to the Rock That Is Higher
Than I.*" Then all joined in singing Psalm 61, as we climbed higher
and higher.

> Hear my cry, O God, listen to my prayer. From the end of
> the earth I call to thee when my heart is faint.
> Lead me to the rock that is higher than I
> For Thou art my strong tower against the enemy (RSV).

That was a precious moment for Ruth and me. We had been feeling the strain of church leadership, opposition politics, and many
heavy church burdens, and we were lonely without our children.
The Rainbows lifted our spirits and put a song back into our hearts
again. I wrote in my Bible that night by Psalm 61, "The Rainbows,
climbing Kondaveedu." During their devotions at Kondaveedu we
joined with them saying Psalm 121, "I lift up my eyes to the hills
from whence does my help come. My help comes from the Lord
who made heaven and earth" (RSV).

From our upstairs west window in Guntur, we could see the
Kondaveedu range. Often a glance to the hills on a busy day would
bring to us the memory of the promise and joy the Rainbows had
given to us and renewed trust and hope in the "Rock that is higher
than I."

* * *

That summer in Kodai, as we breakfasted in our newly assigned cottage, Rockford, Ruth gave me a special look and asked, "Sam, I know you and Ed are planning a hunting trip to Kukkal Cave. How would you like to take Joan and me with you?" Her question caught me by surprise. Then she said, "You know, I've never been to the Cave." Suddenly I realized how loving she had been about my occasional hunting trips. She always encouraged me to go have fun hunting, and had waited patiently for me to return, often a day late. Then she would listen to my stories of near misses, or how I had shot down a small tree in front of a deer that ran off.

"All right, Ruth," I said, "we invite you and Joan to join us on a 'hunting-moon' to Kukkal Cave."

Ruth rewarded me with a very bright hazel-eyed smile. We made plans, deciding to take Perumal, our usual safari guide. Perumal went by bus a day ahead to arrange for two hill tribal men he knew in Kukkal village to help carry all the stuff we'd need. We borrowed a jeep and, early the next morning, drove out to Kukkal village, parking at the forest bungalow. Perumal and his two tribal friends were waiting for us. We loaded up and prepared to run the gauntlet of the nearby leech *shola*. This rain forest extends from near the bungalow for about a mile and a half up the hill to Kukkal Rock. The tribal men rubbed their bare feet and legs with certain forest leaves and with cut cloves of garlic to stave off leeches. We rubbed garlic on our hiking shoes. Then off we went.

We had to hurry, puffing uphill all the way, because on every leaf and shrub on or by the path there are inch and a half long leeches, standing and swaying at the ready, trying to get a hold on a foot or pant leg. I had cut leafy wattle branches, which we used to brush leeches off each other's shoes and pants. The tribals and Perumal went on ahead at a fast clip. Ruth walked in front of me setting the pace, and I kept brushing leeches off her. Once she turned and with a twinkle in her hazel eyes asked, "Aren't you switching me a little too high? Surely the leeches are not up that high yet." Yes, we had fun. In spite of the garlic and constant switching, however, some leeches managed to get on. In the *shola* we saw black Nilgiri langurs jumping around and heard them whooping. Then nearby a barking deer sounded its warning bark. In the distance we heard bison crashing through the undergrowth. This *shola* has huge, old trees. Some of these live for up to 500 years. Several trees that had fallen across the path were too large to clear away so the trail went around them. One feels very uneasy in this primitive, wild, and leech-dominated place. Surging adrenalin helped us climb fast! How do deer, bison, and monkeys manage with all the leeches?

Arriving at the grasslands at the top of the *shola* where there were no longer any leeches, we asked Perumal and the men to continue on to the temple. Then we examined ourselves, taking off our shoes, socks, and trousers. We found leeches on our ankles and shins which had gone right through the weave of our socks. One was attached to Ruth's leg, and one was on Ed's derriere. With salt we easily removed them but could not stop the bleeding, as leeches quickly inject an anticoagulant into the bloodstream before sucking blood.

We climbed to the small solid stone temple crowning the highest point to enjoy the view of Kukkal Valley below, the village and cliffs to the east and Manjampatti Valley and beyond it the higher hills of Kerala State to the west. It was a clear day so we could see all the way to the Gundar eucalyptus *shola* near Kodaikanal, the Vanderavu Ridge, the highest and most western part of the Palnis, and, far to the west-northwest, the cloud-covered Niligiri Range. What a treat!

The Kukkal Rock temple had been built either by the Maharaja of Pudakottai or his sons, who were great sportsmen. They had shot bison and several tigers nearby. They also had built a stone swing for the goddess Parvathi to swing out over the cliff. From there Ed pointed out to Ruth and Joan the large overhanging rock which we call Kukkal Cave, about two miles below in the valley to the north of us. As we descended toward the cave I showed Ruth and Joan where I had shot a large but gaunt, wounded, trophy-horned bison the year before. Dave Lindell, one of our missionary friends, had photographed the mercy killing; the bull had been so weakened from wounds and starvation it couldn't hold up its head. Ed showed the place where, with Jim Bergquist and Dave, we had crept up on a bison herd and then yelled to stampede them. To our surprise several more bison had bedded down in the deep grass above us. When they stampeded too, right past us, much adrenaline rushed through our veins.

Using binoculars we checked all the slopes below, seeing no sign of bison. Then I heard Ed say, "Oh no!" He pointed to a new grass-thatched hut way down the valley, about a half-mile from the cave and said, "*Ayyoo*, it'll never be the same again."

We hiked down into the bottom of the valley coming to where the path splits. The cave trail branches left there through shoulder-high grass. The path is easy to miss. The other path goes straight up the next hill to Samykanal, the foothills below Kukkal area, and leads eventually to the plains. As we neared the cave I said to Ruth, "Look straight up the hill above us. See that narrow ridge of grass clumps halfway up that rock face? That's where Bill, Hans, and I saw the herd of ibex (Nilgiri Thar) when we camped here in 1969. The boys spotted them first. We looked through binoculars and my riflescope to see a ram, four ewes, and three kids crossing the cliff. They were playing along the ledge. I could have shot the saddle-back, but couldn't dream of it. Thar are rare and beautiful to watch! It was a privilege just to see them."

Our path led us to the cave and we quickly settled in. There is enough room under the overhanging rock for twelve or more people to camp. We cut fresh bracken to use as padding under our sleeping bags. The two tribal men and Perumal climbed down a rough path for a few hundred feet to fetch water from a stream below. Then they gathered dry firewood. The cave was dry, and a warm breeze came from the hotter Manjampatti Valley below. As we four ate our lunch, the other three men cooked up a good onion, chili, dahl, and eggplant curry. They told us they expected hunters' meat the next day. Ed suddenly pointed, "Look, across the valley, a lone bison bull." There it was, grazing peacefully about 300 yards from the cave. I was happy that Ruth had the chance to see the bison. Actually, the Indian bison is neither a true bison nor a wild buffalo. The Hindi word *gaur*, a loan word in the English dictionary, means wild ox, and the Tamil name *katumadu* means *forest ox*. Gaurs, over six feet at shoulder level, look like extra large cattle and are black except for white legs. We viewed the wild ox for a long time through binoculars. What a treat!

After lunch and some rest I said to Ruth, "Now I have a special surprise." I led her around outside to the top of our overhanging rock. There grew great clumps of lavender rock orchids, wildly in bloom. Her hazel eyes glowed with delight.

"But Sam," she said, "we're not getting these yet in Kodai from the orchid man. How come they bloom so early here?"

"Ruth, here it's two thousand feet lower than near Kodai where I picked orchids for you. Here it's warmer and it rains more often. Aren't these the greatest?" I picked three blooms, touched them to her face, and put them in her hand. Our family had always loved orchids. Coming back from hikes we sometimes brought back blooming orchid plants and planted them in the rocks near Cotta House or on an old stump at Woodhaven. There they grew and blossomed.

After tea Ed, Joan, Ruth, and I took the trail going down the ridge toward Manjampatti for about a mile, going slowly as we looked and listened for game. Sounds of breaking branches came from the little valley below. Soon we saw five or six elephants foraging and pulling down occasional branches. We watched them until the sun began to set behind the Manjampatti hills, then we walked back up to the cave. After a supper of rice and corned beef hash, we built up the fire and told stories. Perumal told stories of great hunts he had been on in the past with Joel *Dora* Mayer and others. He sang songs in Tamil and then said, "Tomorrow, Master Ed and Master Sam, I am hoping we will see lot of hanimals and get too much good meat." Then he asked us to plan for a hunt in Manjampatti before the monsoon came and requested that we give him an advance of 100 rupees to make "all good harrangments for porters from the village of Killonavay."

Perumal was a mixed blessing. He had great contacts with hill people of Killonavay, Kukkal, and other places, and worked hard to arrange hunting trips and find "hanimals." But for the rest of the year he was a persistent pest. He'd come around for an advance to buy seed potatoes or for a new ax so he could earn money cutting firewood. We did buy one for him and hired him to cut up a cord of *eucy* wood. A one-day task for our usual woodcutter took him three days. Then the ax was stolen. Every year he came up with different ingenious plans to make money.

Once every twelve years the strobylanthus flowers bloom profusely throughout the Palni Hills. This twelve-year *pushkaram* sequence and the *koranchi pu* are sacred for Hindus. On a Kodai hilltop is the Koranchi Pu Temple. In such an auspicious year Perumal did very well selling "Holy," health-giving strobylanthus honey to pilgrims, tourists, and missionaries for twice the normal price of honey. This unusual plant covers the hills with its nectar-laden blue blossoms every twelve years, and gives the bees (and Perumal) the best years of their lives.

Invariably, within five minutes of my arrival at our Woodhaven Cottage in Kodaikanal, there would be loud knocking on the door and loud calling, "Master Sam!" Perumal had found me! "I have been waiting for you with empty pockets. When will we be going to Manjampatti? Master Sam, without you I have been suffering like anything! Please give me 100 rupees advance for Manjampatti trip so I can buy rice for my family." Yes, it was this man that we had brought along on our Kukkal *huntingmoon.*

Ed and Joan had their designated sleeping area. Ruth and I had a lower smooth area among the rocks. Before we hit the sack I asked, "Ed, should we tell the girls about the night Dave Lindell and Jim Berquist camped here with us?"

"No, tell them in the morning," he said. We built up the campfire and had several logs to add during the night to keep the bears away. Then we hit the sack.

By the time we woke up, Perumal and the men had coffee ready—their style, with *jaggery,* crude brown sugar, and powdered milk. Then, over a pancake breakfast we told our wives that when Jim and Dave were with us the first night in the cave, we were awakened in terror by Jim Bergquist screaming. Ed and I had jumped up with flashlights and rifles ready. We had seen bear dung the day before at the edge of the cave and thought one was attacking Jim. But there was only Jim thrashing around in his sleeping bag. He stopped hollering and said sheepishly, "There was a rat in my sleeping bag!"

After breakfast Ed and Joan hunted down the ridge again. Ruth and I climbed up the Samykanal way to see what was on the other side, hoping to spot thar, but we had missed the best time, dawn. For our strenuous climb we were rewarded by superb vistas. We walked a long distance enjoying the grasslands, then forest. We had hoped to spot a white gaur. Five years previously, Ed and I had seen an albino calf, and I had read about the rare albino bison of Manjampatti in *The Hornbill,* a conservationist magazine published in Bombay. I always looked for these, but we didn't see any gaur that morning. We returned to the cave for a late lunch and were again reminded that the men wanted meat curry.

Ruth and I went in late afternoon down the same ridge we had been on the previous evening. This time we didn't see any elephants. We first heard the chatter and then saw a Malabar squirrel jumping in the treetops. Jungle cocks crowed in the valley below. Then, to our amazement, we heard roaring and bellowing in a nearby valley to the northwest of our ridge. It sounded fierce, fearful, and desperate. "What is happening?" Ruth asked.

"I'm not sure, Ruth," I said. "I've never heard anything like this before. It sounds to me like a bison and a tiger are having a fight." After five or six minutes it was suddenly very quiet. The place of action was over half a mile away, in a deep valley *shola* and the sun would soon set. We thought it best to head back to our cave. We shared with Ed, Joan, and the men what we had heard. Ed and I really wanted to check out what had happened there the next morning, but we were scheduled to head for home after breakfast. So that remained an unsolved mystery.

During the 1960s when I visited the cave quite often, I had left a logbook, pens, and pencils in a tin box on a rock with instructions that every visitor should sign in and write of their experiences and sightings. Al Fishman, an old-time veteran Baptist missionary and "cave man," gave me the idea. To my disappointment, this time the tin box and the logbook were missing.

Early in the morning we were awakened by Perumal moaning and saying, "*Ayyoo*, Master Sam, Master Ed, I am dying and will not see my family again!" He was having chills, and fever, and felt miserable. We fed him coffee and oatmeal, and gave him aspirin, assuring him we would not desert him but would get him home somehow. The tribesmen were not so sympathetic. They knew they would have to carry his share of the camp stuff, too, and that Perumal's sickness would cause much delay.

After packing and redistributing the loads, we started off at a slow but steady climb. By 10:30 we managed to ascend to the temple in spite of being slowed by Perumal who was moaning as he dragged himself up the mountain. Then a cloud came up and we were able to cool off in the mist. We made fast time going down through the leech *shola*. Even Perumal now perked up and hiked with good speed. He certainly didn't want the leeches to claim him. At the jeep we said goodbye and settled with our two helpful porters.

By the time we were in the jeep driving home Perumal felt somewhat better. We decided to go home by way of Berijam Lake, where we had a most refreshing swim. As we then drove to Kodai,

Perumal—now feeling fine—began singing Tamil songs and telling stories. He sang a song about Jim Bergquist and his midnight visitor punning with the words *ellugu banthi* and *yeluka banthi*. In Telugu *Ellugu banthi* means *bear*, *yeluka* means *rat*.

As we passed the Holiday Home he said, "What is this? These stourists spending lot of money, coming all the way to Kodai, and they spend the whole day home. Wholiday home!" I couldn't believe that Perumal, who was nearly dying before breakfast, was now singing and punning in Telugu and English without a care in the world. So ended our *huntingmoon*, an adventure Ruth and I would never forget.

* * *

In 1980, Peter, our youngest, came out for a visit after he had completed his B.A. in Geography at Clark University in Worcester, Massachusetts. He came with Pam, his serious girlfriend, who had studied with him at Clark. We had a great visit with them. They were able to do many things with us around Guntur, Rajahmundry, and Kodai. One day while on a journey our driver, Kotiah, suddenly pulled over, parked on the roadside, pulled out a garland of flowers from the glove compartment, and proudly tied it to the hood of the ambassador car. Then he grandly announced that the car had completed 100,000 kilometers and asked me to offer a prayer of thanksgiving for safe journeys, which I did thankfully. By that time the engine had been re-bored twice and we had broken 3 rear axles, but it kept going on those horrible roads for yet another 100,000 kilometers.

While visiting Rajahmundry we were invited to the Colony of Mercy, where Peter's good friend Steven, son of our cook Prakasam, was working as a clerk. Steven and the lady in charge had arranged a surprise engagement party for Peter and Pam. They dressed Pam up in a *sari*, rubbed her feet with tumeric, and sat her down next to Peter for the singing of wedding hymns and prayers. We had a celebration meal with special coconut rice. Coconuts were broken, and Peter and Pam were sprinkled with rice to make their marriage fruitful. When we left the orphanage girls and boys lined the road singing and wishing them a happy married life. Now, as they express it in Andhra Pradesh, Pam was officially Peter's "would-be." As we drove off our driver, Kotiah, who had known of this plan and was perhaps behind it all, chuckled and said, "Peter Babu, now you are 95 percent. ha, ha, ha!"

Our Kodai experience with Pete and Pam was wonderful. Peter took delight in showing Pam around Kodai and the school. We planned to show Pam the stunningly beautiful cliff trail from Mariyan Shola to Vanderavu. To accomplish this in one day, we hired a jeep with the owner, Mr. Vincent, driving. On the way to Vanderavu we showed Mr. Vincent where he should go to wait for us, by a small waterfall, beside the Berijam to Vanderavu Road. Then he drove us to the top of Vanderavu Ridge to where the road descends westward to Top Station in Kerala. From this 8000-foot high ridge we set off on the old 80-mile-round pony trail. This trail had been well maintained during the British Raj hiking years, long before the Berijam-Mariyan Shola-Vanderavu to Top Station road was constructed. It even had mile and furlong stones, and went for a few miles right along cliffs. We had been on sections of this trail when we had camped at Mariyan Shola.

After going more than a mile or so we ran into difficulties. The forest department had recently planted huge areas of native grasslands with wattle trees. This prolific tree is most useful, as the bark is full of tannin. Once a wattle plantation is mature it can be cut and sprouts vegetatively, so the forest requires no maintenance other than fire prevention. Terraces had been dug out and tree seedlings planted right across where the trail had been, obliterating it. We had to guess how to go, so naturally headed toward the cliffs. To make matters worse it became cloudy, and we could no longer see landmarks. After some time we found a trail and climbed a peak, hoping to get our bearings. It didn't help. Between us and the next high ridge were very deep ravines and dense *sholas*. Retracing our steps, we came to another faint trail and thought it would bring us out where we could find the ridge we needed. Then we saw a big herd of gaur on the path right in front of us and were able to stalk quite close to the herd and take photos. This was a new experience for Pam and a thrill for all of us. After a while I gave my tribal yodel yell and caused the herd to stampede toward the ravine, where they disappeared. For a while we were jubilant, but then realized our joy at seeing the bison was not helping us solve our problem. Where was the cliff trail? After wandering around some more in the clouds, we found we could not even retrace our steps. Then we came out on another hilltop crowned with a rugged wooden cross! There we found a well-used path. Being desperate and just wanting to find some sign of civilization, we followed this new path until we came to an old, badly deteriorated paved road. Only then did I realize that we had found the road going down to Top Station from Vanderavu. We were far west of the place where Vincent had dropped us. It was past 3:30 p.m. Hiking uphill as fast as we could we arrived at the top where the jeep had left us. We were still miles from the place where Vincent would be waiting. Then it began to rain. Peter would have been the one to go for help, but he had a very bad cold and pain in his chest. Ruth thought I should go since I was familiar with the road. I left immediately without my knapsack, taking all the shortcuts, trotting downhill, proceeding as fast as possible to meet Mr. Vincent and the jeep. Meanwhile, the others decided to walk toward Mariyan Shola to keep warm, staying on the road. It was often slippery going down the shortcuts, and I kept skidding but made good time. It was getting dark when I saw the jeep. Vincent had let down the tailgate and was brewing tea on a rock fireplace he had made under its shelter. I was exhausted and wet and so grateful for the tea he offered. He had been most concerned and told me, "I have been terribly worried, and had decided that after it became dark I would drive to Kodaikanal, report to the school principal and have him organize a search party. What happened?"

I told him how the trail had been spoiled and about the fog that had made it necessary for us to return to where he had left us. We drove toward Vanderavu meeting the others after several miles. Vincent brewed more tea for us. Thus revived, we drove home, thankful for Vincent's patience and good sense. "No one must ever hear of this. We Schmitthenners never get lost. *Ayyo*, how can we bear this?" said Peter, our geographer and cartographer. I remembered an old proverb, "We are not lost! Only the path has gone astray."

CHAPTER 18

WALKING WITH THOSE WHO SUFFERED IN VILLAGES HIT BY CYCLONE, MEETING MOTHER TERESA AND LEAVING INDIA

The last few years in Guntur were demanding, challenging, arduous, and blessed. We had our worst cyclone ever on November 19, 1977. Thousands were killed by flooding and collapsing houses. On the coast sixty miles from Guntur whole villages and as many as 20,000 people were swept away by a massive sea surge that came sixteen kilometers inland over the flat Krishna River Delta. The surge destroyed villages and ruined thousands of acres of fertile rice land at harvest time. Most of the rice crop was destroyed.

Our Lutheran church at Komili collapsed, killing sixty-five people and wounding scores of others who had sought shelter in this 'most permanent building' in the village. The devastation was unbelievable! The cyclone took the roofs off of nearly 100 church buildings, destroying many of them. Thousands of homes were devastated. Many thousands were left homeless. I handed over routine church work to the vice-president, and for five months concentrated on cyclone relief work.

It took a long time to clear the roads of fallen trees, many of which were huge banyan and nidraganneru trees. It was four days before I could reach Komili to visit, pray with, and comfort the survivors. We visited the cemetery in which all those killed in the church collapse had been buried in a mass grave by the young men of a nearby village who had come the next morning as they heard the sad news. We promised to help the people of Komili rebuild the church using reinforced concrete so that it could be used as a safe cyclone shelter in the future, and assured them theirs would be the first village where we would have a house-rebuilding project. We took several injured persons missed by the government emergency medical team to Kugler hospital, our church institution in Guntur.

One month later, Ruth and I decided to spend Christmas Day at Komili. The head of Heyer Hall dormitory at Andhra Christian College, heard of our plans and he promised to arrange for a meal to feed the whole village. The students and staff of the college raised funds for this Christmas project. The college team went there on Christmas Eve with pots and pans and all the food, camping there for the night.

Ruth and I started for Komili after the dawn Christmas English service at St. Matthew's Church. We arrived at about 9:30 and went around to each house. Sparse houses made of bamboo and thatch had been constructed hastily after the cyclone to provide temporary shelter. Though it was just a little over a month since their terrible losses, the village people were eagerly preparing for the Christmas festival. They had erected a *pandal* (bamboo and palmyra leaf shelter) where we would be having a worship service.

At noontime the whole village sat down on mats to eat the special meal together. Hindus and higher caste people also came to share in the comfort and joy of the occasion. The meal began with a sweet rice pudding, then proceeded into a vegetarian curry for the higher caste Hindus and mutton curry for the rest, with rice the staff of life. This meal—prepared and served by the cooks and staff members of Andhra Christian College—was truly a love feast that enhanced the fellowship and joy of the whole village.

All gathered for the Christmas festival under the shade of the *pandal*. The damaged wooden altar from the destroyed church had been repaired. We were astounded to see the altar cloth was a beautiful Lutheran World Relief quilt. Each family in Komili had been given a quilt on our second visit; one family had given their quilt to be the altar cloth. The service proceeded with children and youth singing special songs and saying memory verses. Several children were baptized, reminding us that life goes on and that we live out our baptism until our final call. One old man asked permission to speak. He said, "You know, we have wept and asked questions and wondered why we survived and others were taken. As far as I know and can understand the Lord took the best and most blessed men, women and children, and now they are happy with him. The rest of us were not ready, and we need to learn how to live in love and to follow our Lord more faithfully."

The offerings that were given that Christmas Day by the survivors who had lost homes and loved ones were greater than those given the previous year. We shared in Holy Communion. The Lord Jesus was truly present with us on that day in Word and with his body and blood! At the time of bringing in the offering, trays of a snack food mixture made of roasted lentils (*dahl*), brown sugar (*bellum*) chunks, bananas, and raisins had been brought in and blessed. After the final benediction, elders stood at various places with these trays. They asked everyone to share in the *prasadam*. It is an ancient Indian custom that food presented to the Lord should later be shared with those who have worshiped. Everyone shared taking a handful of the *prasadam*. Later, while driving home Ruth and I reflected on this. We had shared food with the people of Komili three times, first in a memorial love feast with the whole village, then in the supper of our Lord of bread and wine and, finally in *prasadam*, partaking of what was given in thanks to the Lord and returned with a blessing. Each one of these sharings of food brought great healing, comfort, and joy. Truly the people of Komili were blessed people. They had kept their faith and have grown to embrace a greater hope as the Lord had brought them through adversity.

* * *

Several months after the cyclone we received word that Mother Teresa was interested in finding a place where the Missionaries of Charity could work in the Guntur area. One day a Catholic friend came bursting into my office to announce, "Mother Teresa will be here in five minutes."

I phoned Ruth and said, "Put on the tea pot and find some biscuits, I'm bringing Mother Teresa home in a few minutes." I also phoned Kugler Hospital and asked for Dr. Sarala Elisha, the medical superintendent, to come as quickly as possible.

Mother Teresa arrived with Sister Georgina and several others including the local priest and our photographer, an ardent Catholic. After introductions and greetings, Mother Teresa came right to the point, "We would like to start work here right away. Do you have any unused buildings you could let us have until we can find our own place and build a missionary center?"

By this time Dr. Sarala had arrived. She had an immediate answer that gave joy to all of us. "Yes, the tuberculosis ward of the hospital has been closed for several years, because we now give domiciliary treatment to our patients with modern drugs and no longer keep them in a separate ward. We will have the whole place whitewashed tomorrow and your Missionaries of Charity can move in."

By this time Ruth had also joined us. Then Mother Teresa looked me in the eye and said, "I understand that you Lutherans have plenty of land here in Guntur City and that much of it is not used. We are hoping that you can give us a site of more than an acre in this part of town, near the slums, where we can put up a new center and minister to the poorest of the poor, who are Christ in our midst coming to us in the distressing disguise of the lowly poor. I hope and pray you can help us." I explained to her that we were a constitutional church and that I did not have power to make such decisions. We also had a policy that land could be sold or leased only at market value upon approval of the Executive Council. She reminded me that theirs was the work of Christ's compassion and mission to the poor. When I gently answered that our church was also on that same mission she gave me a look with her clear blue eyes that burned my heart. She was probably less than five feet tall, yet had gigantic spirit, vision, and will.

Ruth suggested that it was time for tea, and so we walked together the few yards to our house. There, with tea or limejuice and cookies, we continued the discussion. Sister Georgina even had an idea of which property they needed and had already showed it to Mother Teresa. After tea we walked over to Becker compound, where there was a vacant site ideally located for their purposes. I vowed to do my best.

After Mother Teresa left, I called our property officer and drafted proposals for our next meeting. The site was worth six lakhs, or 600,000 rupees (at that time over 50,000 dollars.) We finally decided to sell it to the Missionaries of Charity for 125,000 rupees, as a special case. Some of our members, still fighting the Reformation battles of the sixteenth century, were appalled at my plan to bring the Catholics into our midst, but in this matter I was Spirit-driven. When I made that offer she wrote me a short but beautiful letter. However, while studying the matter further we discovered that we would have to pay a huge capital gains tax on the sale. Father Heyer had bought this site from his friend, Collector Stokes, in 1845 for 300 rupees. The only way to avoid the capital gains tax was to sell it for less than 50,000 rupees. So we agreed that this was the will of God and sold it to the Missionaries of Charity for 49,000 rupees. I am certain that the Catholics of Guntur raised this fund. Thus the prayers of Mother Teresa and Sister Georgina were fulfilled.

Mother Teresa visited us two more times, first to finalize and sign the sale deed and to visit the work of the sisters at Kugler hospital, then for the groundbreaking service at the old Becker Compound site. We had a public meeting in her honor and rejoiced to have her opening this ministry of compassion in our city. During the meeting I asked her, "Mother Teresa, you and the Missionaries of Charity we have met, work hard and spend endless hours pouring out compassion as you minister to the poor and dying. You take no vacations, the work is strenuous. You are physically small people. How do you keep going?" Her answer was unforgettable.

"Every morning," she said, "we rise very early before dawn and pray. The priest comes and gives us the host before 6 a.m. Receiving the body of Christ makes us strong. Then, as we minister and touch the sick and dying we know we are touching the body of our Lord as he taught in Matthew 25, 'as you do it to one of the least of these you are doing it unto me.' This fills us with joy. We have strength and joy as we serve each day."

* * *

Cyclone relief aid poured in from many parts of the world and from many churches in India. I could someday write a book just about this period, detailing the superb response of the devastated Christian congregations, the flood of compassion, and the love shown from other parts of the church, the nation, and the world. This outpouring of God's grace and Spirit brought strength, comfort, and guidance for rebuilding. New ministries were established as a response to the challenges the major cyclonic disaster had forced upon us.

It was soon time for me to finish my work as president of the Andhra Evangelical Lutheran Church, as my third term was drawing to a close. In January 1981, I wrote a letter to all pastors of our church and published it in the *Andhra Lutheran*, our church paper, that Ruth and I had decided prayerfully that after my term ended on May 31, 1981, I would refuse to be on the panel for further election. I believed that the church needed a fresh, energetic, dedicated Indian Christian to be the Moses to lead his people. I was the last of the missionary presidents and bishops in South India. Bishop Leslie Newbigin of the Church of South India and Bishop Diehl, from the Swedish Lutheran Church, serving the Tamil Evangelical Lutheran Church had both retired and left the country. I was worn out from the incredible burdens that had absorbed Ruth's and my life for the twelve years I had served as president. I wrote that I planned to take a whole year of furlough in the United States doing promotional work for Missions and the Andhra Evangelical Lutheran Church, and would then be ready to take any assignment to work in the Andhra Evangelical Lutheran Church.

After conducting the convention of the church in Guntur in the middle of May, I installed the new president, Rev. K. Nathaniel, who had served well as president of East Guntur Synod and before that had served as evangelistic pastor for that synod. I packed up the books and things we wanted to take with us, and stored some of the things, including all our kitchen and household items expecting we would be called back to India. Then we had a grand yard sale and a special book sale for pastors. Any pastor could buy up to four books for one rupee each (40 cents for four books). On June 1, 1981, I handed over the office, files, house and furniture, and the president's car, now a jeep station wagon, to the new president.

Ruth, meanwhile, had gone to Kodai and packed our things there. We met in Madras and flew to America, looking forward to seeing our children again, to a long summer of rest in Bella Sylva, and to the renewal of our contact with our church in America. We thanked God for giving us health, patience, and for being with us in every time of difficulty and every time of joy during our thirty years of service to the church and people of India and to the mission of the Lutheran Church in America and in India.

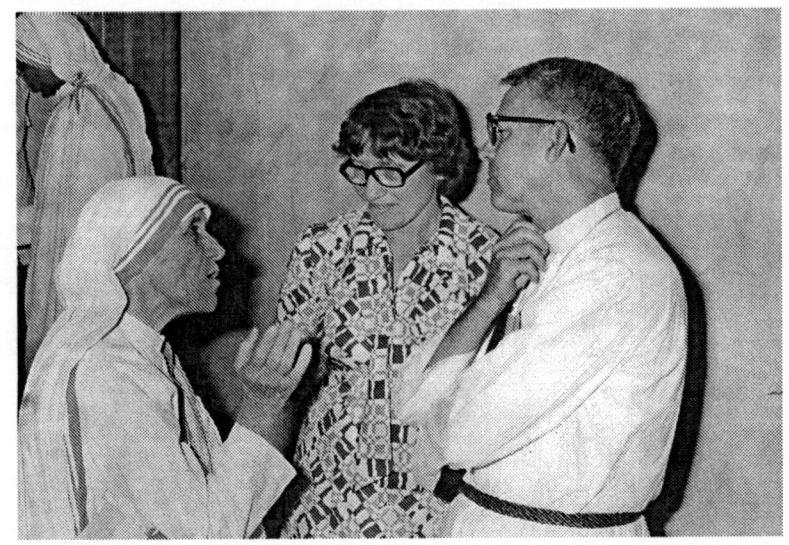

Mother Teresa vists us in Guntur

*Mother Teresa asks for a site in Guntur for the
Missionaries of Charity home*

Missionaries of Charity
54A, Lower Circular Road
Calcutta-16

54cc.

26/11/78

To the President,
Andhra Evangelical Lutheran Church

Dear Dr. Sw. Schmithenner.

Many thanks for your letter and the decision of your Ex. Council to sale the land at Rs. 1, 25,000/- We, the Missionaries of Charity - accept to take the land —

The legal formalities etc. we shall start immediately & get the land registered in the name of Missionaries of Charity.

As the place will be used for the Poorest of the Poor - kindly pray that it all be for the glory of God. — Let us pray. God bless you

M. Teresa M.C.

Letter of Mother Teresa

CHAPTER 19

BACK IN THE STATES: HANA, BELLA SYLVA, NEW JERSEY, AND NEW ENGLAND

Returning to the States we stopped first in Hawaii to see Aunt Rebecca at Hana, on Maui. Hana was still unspoiled by commercialization. We stayed in an apartment close to Rebecca and spent golden days with her. To us she seemed like the queen mother of Hana. Everyone knew her. When we went to the Hana Hotel for evening dinner the waitresses, who had been her students, couldn't do enough for her and brought her dishes they knew she liked without her having to order. Three evenings in a row we went with her to *puu puu* parties. Most who attended would bring wine or beer or small trays of lovely snacks. Such an abundance was brought in that the host and guests would decide there was enough left over for another party and persuade someone to host it the following evening. Guests and the host would then bring still more, and often there would be enough for another party the next night.

As Rebecca found it too strenuous to run around with us, we drove to our favorite places in our rented car. One day her friend from the Hana Museum across the street took us to an ancient prayer temple, or *heiau*, recently excavated but still off-limits for tourists. On the way we drove through a large plantation of macadamia trees that belonged to Jim Nabors. We saw his country mansion built on telephone pole stilts on a nearby hillside. The locals refer to this dwelling as "Gomer's Pile." The *heiau* was a massive platform built of lava rock overlooking a beautiful, silent, and desolate section of coast. Probably in the days of its use there were many thatch rooms and porches for the various activities. It made us sad to view the emptiness of what was once a place of worship filled with people. Inter-island wars and cruel exploitation by whalers and traders had obliterated a way of life that we can only imagine.

After visiting Rebecca we flew to Tucson to be with Ruth's parents for a few days, then journeyed to Gettysburg where we had booked the Mission Furlough House at 108 Springs Avenue. We went to Chambersburg to see our aunts Elizabeth and Dot. We missed Aunt Katherine who had passed away while we were in India. Now Aunt Elizabeth lived in a retirement home in Chambersburg, and Dorothy in a smaller apartment. We spent much precious time with each of them.

Next we moved to Bella Sylva for several months. Our children Hans and his girlfriend Joan, Pete and his fiancée Pam, Chris, and Bill came for a grand family get-together. Chris and the two girlfriends got along famously. We had a project repairing the porch, and I was the *maistry* (supervisor) since I had hurt my arm. The three girls were my obedient "slaves." We did a great job. We took many rambles to Mehoopany Falls, the Gorge, and High Cobble Lake (above our lake inlet and one of the sources of the Loyalsock Creek). We found and cleared out another trail to Mehoopany Creek following Carol Creek with its seven picturesque waterfalls. Swimming, fishing, and the preparation of sambar and rice and curry meals took up our days.

In the fall Ruth and I moved to Hamilton Square near Trenton, New Jersey, to serve as missionaries-in-residence. For four months we visited the Lutheran Churches of New Jersey, giving talks and showing displays and slides of our work in India. We presented a skit that Ruth had written about congregational life. I played the part of a new village pastor surveying his parish. Ruth, wearing a *sari*, was a woman of the congregation who told the pastor all about their village and congregation and asked many probing questions. Ruth's superb acting and all her lines were great; she carried the day! We were busy and gone from our apartment two or three evenings a week and on Sundays. We had programs in senior citizen homes and schools as well as at churches.

We returned to Bella Sylva on Columbus Day for the marriage of Peter and Pam on October 10, 1981. They were married in Old Zion Church near Dushore, in Sullivan County, Pennsylvania, just ten miles from Bella Sylva. What a happy wedding! The reception was at our picnic place in Bella Sylva. The weather was cool but sunny and beautiful, and the leaves in full color. The combination of their college and Kodai friends, family friends, and mountain neighbors made the gathering a great mix of people and a most joyful celebration. Ruth wore a lovely red silk sari. Peter dressed in a silk Indian shirt (*kurta*), and Pam wore a Kashmir silk dress which she had bought in New Delhi. Ruth was totally happy! We said, "One down, three to go!"

As we were finishing our time in New Jersey we heard from Ruth Sigmon, our last Lutheran missionary in India, that the church in Andhra had made a decision *not* to call us back. I took this very hard! We were in the midst of packing and we moved on January 1, 1982, to be missionaries-in-residence for the New England Synod, with residence at Millbury, outside Worcester, Massachusetts. Peter and Pam were working in Boston, and living in a small apartment on Beacon Hill. They were waiting for us and helped us move into our third floor apartment. We were happy to have good visits with them and went together to the fabulous South Indian Anna Purna Udipi veggie restaurant in Worcester.

My health had deteriorated with the stress of the Andhra Church rejection on my mind. I had trouble getting my breath going up three flights of stairs and was depressed. The road-bridge between our house and Millbury had been closed to traffic. This necessitated a four-mile roundabout drive, so we decided to walk to town. We did so every day we were home, for groceries, the post office, the drug store, and other shopping. This daily morning mile-and-a-half ramble gave us good exercise, fresh air, a time for discussions, and the chance to work out our plans, and my health improved remarkably.

We had been missionaries of the Lutheran Church in America serving in India for thirty years, since June of 1951, and wanted to remain in missionary service. We went to the headquarters in New York and volunteered to go to any country in the world where they might need us. The response of each of the three executives we talked with was cool and negative, "Have you considered parish service in America? Of course you may apply for the country of your choice. There may be a place for you in Tanzania. But don't you think you are too old to adjust to another language and culture?" We were fifty-four. Even so we sent in our application to go to Tanzania, but were not called to go anywhere. I wrote to Central

Pennsylvania Synod, which had supported me during my seminary years.

"Welcome to Central Pennsylvania!" said Bishop Howard McCarney over the phone. He invited Ruth and me to come and see him in Harrisburg after Easter. When we visited he spent several hours with us going over the profiles of vacant parishes in the synod. Finally we mutually agreed that Claysburg-East Freedom (a two-church charge) would be the best place. We were interviewed by both congregations, I preached in each church, and then I was called by the Synod to serve there for a three year term. This parish had been beset with problems and was then under synod administration. The actual call came from the synod, not the parish. We moved there by U-haul on October 1, 1982. Now we would be adjusting to a new culture, Appalachia, and the strange language spoken by the church youth.

Bella Sylva Lake

*Visiting stump of cherry tree lumbered back in 1949
when Ruth was camp cook*

Shaving on back porch at Bella Sylva on Peter's wedding day

*Sharing the story of Missions and our work with
Lutheran congregations in New Jersey*

CHAPTER 20

ALLEGHENY WALKS AND CLIMBS AROUND CLAYSBURG

When we came to live and work in Claysburg I was excited to be entering my first American parish, at age fifty-four, after more than thirty years in the ministry. Ruth and I quickly settled into our three-bedroom ranch-style parsonage. Fortunately we had our share of the furniture of the Eyster aunts. By then both Aunt Elizabeth and Aunt Dot had moved into senior citizen homes. Ruth and I were happy that Claysburg was only seventy-five miles from Chambersburg. Now we could see Elizabeth and Dot more often.

Claysburg lies in a valley of the Allegheny Mountains. Our parsonage was near the Little Juniata River at the base of the 1000-foot ridge of Dunnings Mountain. Because of this ridge the sun rises an hour later in Claysburg than it does in the wider valleys and plains of Pennsylvania. Because the Little Juniata River flows north the people of Claysburg spoke of going "down to Altoona," which was north of us, and "up to Bedford" which was due south. We made a few inquiries about trails up the mountain, knowing we would have to climb it soon before the cold weather set in. Monday was "Pastor's day off." The joint council, with true concern, had been very insistent that I take a day off each week. The last Monday in October, after a sourdough pancake breakfast, we crossed Old Route 220 and walked down a farm road crossing the Little Juniata on a homemade wooden bridge. Going through the Dodson farm and passing the original but now deserted log farmhouse, we climbed first through a stand of hemlocks, then more steeply through hardwoods on a track used by hunters. Near the trail were several tree stands put up by hunters. About three quarters of the way up we came to the gash in the mountain made by the brickyard miners, who had quarried ganister rock there from 1880 until sometime in the 1970s. The hard rock had been hauled by "dinky cars" over rails going south for about a mile. From there it had been taken down the mountain to the brickyard to be crushed, mixed and baked in kilns into the finest silica brick which was used for molds in the steel mills of Pittsburgh.

The rails had long since been taken up, but some old buildings were still there, including the shed and old scales where loaded ore cars had been weighed before being shipped. Above the old rail line is the huge mined rock face going the whole length of the rail line, nearly to the top of the mountain. Millions of tons of the rock had been blasted and hauled away from the mountain.

"Sam, this is so ugly. I've never seen a mountain so torn up. Will it ever be green again?" Ruth said in a hushed voice. As we walked up the floor of the gash a bunch of ruffed grouse exploded off the ground in front of us. Later many doves flew up. These had been pecking gannister gravel for their gizzards to help grind up the seeds that they feed on. Around us on the floor of the wounded mountain were groves of small black birch trees that had taken root in the crushed silica roadbed. With my knife I skinned some bark off a low branch. Immediately the air was filled with the fragrance of wintergreen.

"Look, Ruth," I said, "the land is already beginning to heal. Nature has a way of healing itself in its own time. Black birch thrives here where other trees can't yet take root, just as do white birch trees that grow all over the strip-mined rock near Bella Sylva." There's something totally marvelous about the power of the birch family to restore the land. After a few years leaf mold and the rotten wood of these trees produce topsoil for other trees to grow and the wonderful forest cycle continues. We chewed on the bark, enjoying a taste of birch beer, which is flavored by essence extracted from black birch root and bark.

I remembered and shared with Ruth one of my Dad's letters about climbing the cross-crowned hill behind Yeleswaram (a hill also scarred by stone quarrying). He had written, "From up there in the early morning light I could see the mission compound, church, school, the whole of Yeleswaram town, the Yeleru River, and many of the villages where we had congregations. This is the land the

Lord has given to me, and I prayed, asking God to bless the whole valley and to work through me his servant to bring His love and grace to the people of this place." It gave Dad the feeling that Moses must have had as he viewed the promised land he was never allowed to enter. Both my father and I had been blessed to live there with our families and to work among the people of the Yeleru valley. I believe Dad's prayers were answered and fulfilled in his and my lifetime and in the ongoing life of the churches there.

On Dunnings Mountain Ruth and I prayed for the people of the valley, its churches, and our two congregations as we viewed the lovely valley blessed with ever-flowing springs and streams. Our prayers also were answered. We were blessed in Claysburg beyond description and we saw God's people there grow in grace. We sat on a rock, and we looked into each other's eyes—hazel and brown—seeing love, joy, and contentment. We loved our new home, our two congregations, and each other. We talked about our children. Now we could see them more often and could accommodate all of them for Thanksgiving, Christmas, Easter, and other days in our spacious parsonage.

That first time we climbed Dunnings Mountain we did not try to make it all the way to the top. After a time we retraced our steps and coasted down the hill for home, passing again through the oak, tulip tree, maple, and hickory forest and noticing where squirrels had been gathering and eating the plentiful hickory nuts. I gathered some nuts and cracked them open when we got home.

It was good to be back in parish work again. As president of the AELC in India, I had been pastor to 225 pastors, ministering to the larger church of two thousand congregations in five synods. I preached often in Telugu, but each sermon was for a different congregation. Most sermons in India were for special occasions like cornerstone layings, church dedications, festival days, or dispute settlements. I worked mostly with leaders. Now at Claysburg I preached again and again to the same people, delivering a new sermon each Sunday on the lessons for the day. This discipline of the Word with a set periscope for each Sunday was good for me. I could preach series of sermons and see the long-run effect of the ministry of the Word and Sacrament in the lives of the people. Leading Bible study classes and a two-year intensive "Word and Witness" course held every Wednesday evening was very fulfilling. I came to know each parishioner personally, feeling as I called my sheep by name that I loved and enjoyed working with them in kingdom-building. This was a much more joyful and meaningful ministry than the administrative work as president of the AELC had been.

In our household were two fireplaces, one in the living room and one in the basement. While visiting parish members, Clyde and Ginny Feather, I noted the insert stove in their fireplace. "It's much more efficient, and will give more heat using less wood," Clyde said. So we bought an insert stove, putting it in the basement. In order to heat the whole house more efficiently, we installed two heat ducts from the basement to our living room and kitchen. One of our parishioners, "Boots" Zeiler, an ex-marine, helped me cut, haul, and store firewood. Occasionally I'd buy wood to split from our neighbor, Jake. We kept the insert stove going all winter, saving on the oil bill. We could go barefoot in the house and feel the warm oak floor. Wood heat was so cozy. Our bedrooms were cold, but we liked them that way. Having a woodpile was good for my work and my marriage. When I was upset with Ruth, had a parish problem, or when tense or tired from too much office work, a half hour of splitting oak or hard maple with a maul was great therapy.

Ruth continued to amaze me with her patience, perception, and understanding of what love was all about. One evening at bedtime I made what I thought were good romantic suggestions. Ruth frowned and looked at me with her honest eyes. "Now you think of love?" she asked. "All day you have ignored me and have been unkind. When are you going to understand that loving is something that should take place throughout the day? That's what makes physical love meaningful." She said this very quietly, but it had a powerful effect on me.

Ruth, in a way, was the family chaplain. It was she who would say, "We can't go to bed angry or upset. Come on, let's pray together." Could I say I didn't feel like praying? I found that even when I didn't feel like it, prayer was always healing and brought peace. Thank God Ruth was always calm and very frank with me, consistently providing me with balance, peace, and love.

On Mondays Ruth and I would head for Chambersburg to see Dot and Elizabeth. Elizabeth, at age 90, had been in the county home for five or six years. She was quite happily settled there, and

shared a room with a lady in her 80s. She was greatly loved by the
workers who helped her.

Elizabeth had been an English professor at Mariyan College, Virginia, and had inspired many students to excel in her courses. She
enjoyed reading, especially her favorite author, T. S. Elliot. When
her eyes deteriorated, she listened to book tapes from the library.
Talking with her was always stimulating. One day she said, "I can't
abide these evangelists who promise people prosperity, health and
social blessing if they will just believe in Christ and join their fellowship. Christianity should be doxological, not therapeutic." Her
comment caught me off guard.

"What do you mean doxological?" I asked.

"You know, Samuel, doxology—praise," she explained. "Our
work is just to serve and praise him with our whole heart, not to
seek therapy."

We had quite a discussion about that, because Jesus does promise
healing, rest, comfort, and the care of a shepherd. To this she replied, "But we must seek His love and praise Him, not seek Him
for selfish reasons. Praise is the main purpose of life!"

Dot had just entered Mennohaven and was having a harder time
adjusting to life in a home. She had been a physical education
teacher and coach and very independent. She liked to sun bathe
wearing only the minimum, and sometimes shocked the Mennonite
staff and residents. She also had to have her evening ration of wine,
which her doctor had prescribed for her before she entered the
home. The Mennohaven staff wouldn't purchase it, so we would
buy it every two weeks and give it to the nursing station. Dot had a
car and enjoyed driving around town, but gradually she became too
weak to drive safely. The day of reckoning finally came when her
car went way over the centerline and forced a van filled with children, driven by the wife of the Mennohaven director, into a ditch.
Ruth and I were summoned to Chambersburg 'at once!' and asked
to persuade Dot to give up her 1958 pushbutton gearshift Plymouth. Jerry, Fritz, Molly, and I had a fund with which to help our
aunts created by the value of their furniture which we had divided.
We promised to pay for Dot's taxi anytime she wanted to go anywhere. That made her angry. She said, "I'll never use a taxi!" And
she never did. Dot reminded us that she had taught me and my
brother how to drive. It was Ruth who calmed her and persuaded
her to give up her car. Dot made me take her car and wouldn't take

a cent for it. Thus the Matador became Ruth's car, and I had our Plymouth classic.

When both aunts felt up to it we would take Dot to visit Elizabeth, and sometimes take them both for a drive or out to eat. But when she grew older, Elizabeth could no longer go out. Still, her mind remained sharp. Once during a discussion she said, "The reason the Church is so divided about the meaning of Holy Communion is because most people can't understand the difference between a simile and a metaphor. If Jesus had said, 'I am *like* the bread of life,' there would have been no problem. But he used a metaphor, 'I *am* the bread of life.' Most people do not understand metaphors." I thought that was profound.

Ruth and I climbed Dunnings Mountain many times on our days off. We continued to find interesting treasures such as an old cedar log over two feet in diameter. The wood was still in good condition. No other cedars were known to have grown on this mountain. We found a few huge nineteenth century maples and patches of sassafras. We dug up some roots, dried them, and used them to make tea. We occasionally saw flocks of turkey and often would surprise deer. On one occasion a bear went ahead of us on the path. One chilly afternoon we saw a copperhead sunning itself on a rock. Walking on the mountain always brought us a feeling of peace and lifted our spirits.

The children and youth of the parish meant so much to me. First Communion and confirmation classes were held in the parsonage basement classroom where we had two long tables. Our sessions would end with ping-pong. I told the kids that one of the requirements of confirmation training was that they each had to beat the pastor in this sport. Eventually nearly all of them did; I played left-handed with the weaker players.

Each year I would use various shades of leftover paint to freshly paint two joining cement block walls in our classroom. Our confirmands would then depict how they were part of the living church, illustrating Ephesians 2:19-22 with magic markers. The four lowest corner cement blocks represented Christ, the chief cornerstone. The other blocks on the lowest level were given the names of the prophets and apostles, our faith foundation, with appropriate symbols and designs. The next two rows of blocks represented grandparents, parents, elders, and older siblings of the class members. On the highest rows of bricks came the students' names.

As the confirmands became part of the wall built on such foundations, they realized that they, too, as members of Christ's Church, were touching, supporting, and depending on others. Their parents and many others came to see the wall each year.

One day, after we had been in Claysburg for a year and a half, I received a phone call from the Asia Secretary of the Board of World Missions, saying, "Sam, there is a need for you and Ruth to go to Oman to minister to hundreds of Indian and Pakistani Christians. The Reformed Church in America missionaries of Oman know you and are asking us to send you there." The RCA was Ruth's parents' church and mission, and Joyce and Jim Dunham, Ruth's Central College friends, had served in Oman for many years, so the call was very appealing.

I explained to the secretary that the synod had called me to serve in Claysburg-East Freedom for three years and had pointedly asked us if we were willing to stay that long and we had promised we would. When he asked, "Can't you get out of it?" I felt anger starting to burn but tried to keep calm.

"By the rules of the Lutheran Church in America," I said firmly, "we were made to resign from Mission service in order to receive a call from the synod. Remember, I asked that our services be loaned to the synod, and asked for a 'lien on my post' but was told I must resign. We intend to keep our promise and stay in Claysburg for the full three years of our call. After that, if you need and call us we will consider it." He never called again. This turned out to be a blessing for us since we were soon called by the revived Christ-St. Paul's joint council and both congregations to serve them for a regular long-term call, and we became deeply bonded in our Faith United Lutheran Parish, FULP.

I took our FULP youth group up the mountain several times. Scott Sollenberger and Ross Helsel of the Boy Scout troop showed me the best way to get to the highest point, Indian Peak. Climbing up with the youth was always fun. Several times I took the confirmation class on a picnic hike up the mountain. We would sit around on rocks as I would read to them the whole Sermon on the Mount. Then we'd go to Indian Peak and have prayers together. Members of the class would pray, thanking God for the beauty and wonder of nature and for his love, asking Him to help us keep the environment clean. We prayed for the town and the church as we looked down upon them. Those were "cool," joyful, sessions.

Ruth and I walked the mountain even in the wintertime. If there was snow we'd drive our Matador to the top of Sproul Mountain and walk in three or four inches of snow along the dinky railroad bed. We could see mice, squirrel, porcupine, rabbit, raccoon, and deer tracks and trails.

One Christmas vacation there was no snow on the mountain. The day after Christmas, Ruth's birthday, was always the day for our family Christmas celebration and exchange of gifts. After our turkey feast, we all hiked up the mountain and across on the old dinky roadbed. On the mined slope above us new white pines were growing and would gradually restore that slope. One part of the trail was thick and spongy with moss, trailing pine moss and princess pine moss. We talked about how nature restores itself, and how beautiful the mountain now was to us. We knew it looked out over our home, and that it was a place of restoration, healing, peace and joy.

Then came disaster. The Route 220 bypass from Bedford to Altoona had been completed only as far as Sproul. Finally funding was found for the Claysburg to East Freedom section. For a couple of years we heard the noise of heavy machines removing stumps, blasting, and moving huge amounts of earth. Claysburg became dusty, and our car hoods were being pockmarked by the tiny bits of stone flung from the ever-present gravel trucks. Above the hemlock grove, the gully we had used to ascend the mountain was now filled by a 80-foot high pile of rubble. We had to find a new way up our mountain. We explored and followed Dodson Road on the other side of our creek as far as the sewage plant. We passed an old flatbed truck that had been rusting away for years. Wild roses and other wildflowers were growing in the accumulated dirt of the floorboards and through the cracks and open parts of the cab and engine. "Ruth, look at this truck garden," I said. She answered with a groan.

We ascended a gentle ridge to the cleared roadbed of crushed ganister, then hiked up the service road constructed for trucks to haul crushed rock for the new highway from the old gash-mine far above our house. Yes, eventually in that one newly torn-up area as well, more black birch trees would come in, and slowly work their way into and up the sides of the mine. Birch would continue patiently to bring fragrant green life, beauty and healing back to what man had spoiled in order to save a few minutes of driving time. We used the newfound way up Dunnings Mountain until the bypass, now Interstate 99, was opened.

Once traffic began to roll we could no longer climb from our home. Consequently we went around by the Sproul road and walked on the more level dinky rail-trail past Indian Peak. We missed the challenge of our old climb. For our eight Claysburg years this mountain was our favorite ramble.

* * *

Camp Sequanota, near Jennerstown, along route 30 in western Pennsylvania, was another one of our favorite places during the Claysburg years. In Tuscarora, Sequanota means "land of many springs." Camp Sequanota had seven springs, including the big spring that supplies water to the camp. Each year our church children went to Camp Sequanota for a special week of summer camping. We always chose the week when there would be confirmation camp shared by youth and pastors of other churches in our district. We had four hours of confirmation classes a day, totaling twenty hours for the week. The classes were taught by the pastors and several lay catechists. We divided up our church groups, mixing them for the classes. For the entire week we taught a special course on the Bible called The Whole Story, which showed the plan, pattern and continuity of God's Word. While going through the course we also helped our students learn the books of the Bible by heart.

After two morning classes, followed by "confir" campers' devotions, the youth would take camp courses in crafts, nature study, dancing and other electives. Following the first afternoon *confir* class they again would take camp courses, then, at 3:30 p.m. we all ended up in the pool. Our night class was usually a creative Bible game like Bible Feet or Bible Baseball, or a Bible scavenger hunt. On Friday afternoon the entire camp participated in Sequanota Olympics, and in the evening there was a serious hide-and-seek adventure. Other evenings we had campfires, sing-alongs, stories, and a counselors' night variety show.

During these common camp activity hours I would be with our younger Faith United campers, swimming, telling stories and sharing in their fun. During the week I made time to have an hour of personal talk with each of my FULP confir campers. It was a time of bonding and sharing.

Usually we had enough pastors and confir teachers for each of us to take a day off. On my day off, Ruth would drive from Claysburg with a picnic lunch and we would go hiking. Usually we hiked the Laurel Highlands trail that goes from Johnstown to West Virginia. We would begin from near the camp entrance on an old historic trace called Forbes Road. Parts of this historic trail running from Bedford to Pittsburgh are still intact. This road had been laid out and constructed by John Forbes during the days of the French and Indian War. Pioneers later traveled west on this trace in their Conestoga Wagons. About halfway up the hill in one cut there were eight-inch-deep grooves where the bedrock had been worn down by thousands of iron-rimmed wagon wheels. Forbes had laid out his road very carefully, keeping to the crests of ridges wherever possible to thwart ambushes. We were told that Washington led the British and American troops along this road after their defeat at Fort Duquesne and the death of General Braddock.

One summer, when confir camp was early in June, our daughter Chris was visiting us in Claysburg. On my day off Ruth and Chris came with a special lunch to hike with me on the Forbes Road and the Laurel Highlands Trail. From the junction of the trails we walked and climbed south, hiking to Route 30. The mountain laurel in mid-June was in unusually abundant and gorgeous bloom. Mountain laurel is the state flower of Pennsylvania, and the trail and the Highlands are aptly named. At one point we walked for more than half a mile nearly drowning in the ocean of scented blossoms surrounding us. We returned the way we had come and crossed the Forbes Road, hiking toward Johnstown for several miles. After enjoying a baked chicken lunch and rest we returned to the Forbes Road again and followed it to our camp, ending one of our most beautiful rambles ever. How good to experience this with Chris!

In 1989 the Laurel Highlands Trail was trying to tell me something. That week of confir camping I did not have a day off, as I was covering for one of the pastors who had to go for a funeral. But after the last confirmation class I had planned to have a good ramble. The camp nurse, a chaplain, and I hiked up Forbes Road and had just climbed to the highest point of the Laurel Trail when I felt dizzy and had lots of pressure in my back between the shoulders. Lately I had experienced this seven or eight times. My theory was that I was out of shape. So early each morning I had gone for a brisk walk, thinking exercise would set things right. I sat down and told the nurse I wasn't feeling well. She took my pulse. It was 58 beats per minute, and she was alarmed until I told her my normal pulse was 60. After a ten-minute rest I felt fine. The way back was all downhill. The nurse told me to see my doctor as soon as I got home and that I should have some tests. That Saturday evening after I had returned home I called Jerry, my cardiologist brother, and he said, "Sounds like you have atypical angina. See a cardiologist!"

The next morning after church, Clydene, a parishioner who was a nurse, said to me, "Pastor Sam, you look so tired!" I told her what had happened on the Laurel Trail. She said, "Tomorrow come see Doc Bulger at 9 a.m. Knock on the back door and I will let you in." Sunday night at midnight I was awakened with the feeling that an elephant was standing on my back. I had no pain, but felt such pressure that I had trouble breathing. I woke Ruth. She drove me to Nason Hospital. It turned out to be a mild heart attack; fortunately God had given me an early warning!

Thanks to the grace of our Lord Jesus Christ, good medical treatment, Ruth's loving care and a totally understanding and supporting parish and synod, I fully recovered. I received tremendous help and love from my new intern, Dan Breda, who took over all pastoral duties for three months. The visits and prayers of my family, friends, faithful church members, and Bishop Gerry Miller brought strength and healing. A change in diet and more regular exercise helped me so that now, fourteen years later, I am healthier than I was before the attack. How thankful I am to God, and to all who helped me!

Near Camp Sequanota, north of Somerset, is the village of Friedens. Father Heyer, founder of the Lutheran Church in Andhra Pradesh, had served there as pastor before he became a missionary to India in 1842. He and his wife were buried there in the churchyard. In the Lutheran Church at Friedens he is featured in a stained-glass window. He is one of the great saints and missionaries of the Lutheran Church, and was the first Lutheran missionary from America to serve overseas. He also served as pastor in Somerset, Pennsylvania, and in Newry, north of Claysburg.

On several occasions Ruth and I took visitors from India to see his grave. Pastor K. Nathaniel, President of the Andhra Evangelical Lutheran Church, Dr. G. Sampurna Rao, professor of Andhra

Christian Theological College, and Raja Kumari of the Guntur Ashrams Ministry all asked to visit his grave.

We had many visitors while in Claysburg: Ruth's parents, Christina and George, came several times for a few weeks; our children came often with their friends and families; other Kodai kids would call up and drop in; my brother Jerry and Shurlee, my brother Fritz and Alice, and my sister Molly and Alan; cousins, nephews, and nieces, and good friends, including many from India, stopped by. Among them were Rajeswari Matthew and Lily Agnes (two of the most capable Girl's High School headmistresses of the Andhra Church in India), and several pastors from Andhra Pradesh. Our home was open to parish members, fellow pastors, and their families. Ruth was again a wonderful hostess, gracefully taking all this in her stride. We were happy and content at home in our Claysburg years. It was our Bethany.

Climbing up Dunnings Mountain was a great ramble for my day off, but too long for a daily walk. One of our friends said, "Just walk up to the end of Hileman's Hollow—the road beyond our church." Thus we found a convenient place for our frequent regular rambles. Sometimes it would be an early morning walk. More often an evening stroll. We needed this to ease the tensions of the day, and to have a time of healing when we were in a disagreeable mood (as I was more frequently than was Ruth). Ruth was the calmest, most patient person I have ever known, a good listener, and by nature a reconciler. She had an inner strength and way of being totally truthful with me in private, and sometimes in public, sometimes with devastating effect.

One morning when I was very busy in the parsonage office going through records, writing sermon notes, and writing "urgent letters," Ruth came in wanting to discuss a number of "important things" with me.

"Look," I said, "can't you see how busy I am with all this urgent stuff? Maybe we can talk about it tonight." Hearing me, she just turned and left the room without saying a word. Then the phone rang. It was Tilly Deckerhoff, the most talkative woman in the congregation. I talked with Tilly patiently for forty minutes. When she finally hung up, the phone rang again. It was Reba, choir member, music and worship leader, and hymn selector. Again, we talked for at least half an hour. I was patient, kind, and polite, and took time to explain things, listening carefully to everything she said.

Then Ruth came into the office, her hazel eyes blazing. "Sam," she said, "I heard you talking on the phone from the kitchen. You were so patient and kind and took all that time with Tilly and Reba because they are members of your parish. I want you to realize I am also a member of this parish and I demand the same kind of thoughtful consideration and time you give to your other parishioners. If you can't treat me kindly as a wife, please treat me as you would a member of the congregation." I felt like I had been kicked hard in the stomach. I took the phone off the hook, went into the kitchen, and the two of us sat down over coffee and talked until lunchtime. After eating we went for a ramble up Hileman's Hollow. The rest of that day I treated her as a member of the parish and also as the loving wife and friend she had always been.

Hileman's Hollow began at New Route 220 beside our church. The road first passed the overgrown foundations of the shanty town where African American workers, imported from the South for work in the brickyard, used to live. At the top of the first hill is the small "colored" cemetery and nearby a few houses. No black people live in Claysburg anymore. When the brickyard began to shut down they all moved to work in Altoona. To the right of the road is the huge old brickyard dump. Any batch of silica brick that did not pass inspection was brought and dumped here. The dump is several hundred feet long, thirty yards across, and more than fifty feet high. Anyone in town who needed old bricks for landscaping, a patio, or to prop up an old shed could come with a pickup truck to load up what they needed. The rotten silica bricks are slowly turning back into sand in which wild strawberries thrive.

We proceeded up the hollow, passing a small farm with a few sheep and guinea foul. Hay fields were on both sides of the road. Near the end of the hollow were two farmhouses, each with a barn. Both farms and the five or six residences we passed were occupied by members of the Hileman clan. The barns were about eighty years old and in good condition, used to store hay and to shelter beef cattle. The first farm on the road had a good spring, and piped spring water was gushing into a large water trough beside the road. How picturesque, antique, and peaceful a setting!

As we walked, we talked about being more considerate of each other. I knew I needed to learn to listen more carefully and patiently. Ruth was concerned with how critical she was. She promised to think first and to be more positive in suggestions. We both vowed to work harder to be "subject to one another out of reverence for Christ" (Ephesians 5:21, RSV).

George and Pansy Hileman lived at the end of the hollow, where the road ends. One afternoon they were sitting on the porch and called to us, "Come over and set awhile." We gratefully accepted their friendly invitation. Pansy offered us baked goods and cold spring water. It was so good! Our parsonage water tasted of sulfur, as does much of Pennsylvania coal region water, but the Hileman Hollow springs were very good. George told us the history of the place. We asked him, "What's the difference between a valley and a hollow?"

"Around here," he was quick to answer, "a valley will have a road following a stream so you can drive from one end to another and out to other roads. But a hollow is a dead end. The road ends here up against the mountains rising up to Blue Knob. Actually, you can hike up over that ridge, and eventually come out on Bulls Creek Road, but you might get lost, too." Ruth was interested in the small two-story outbuilding on the hillside, a little above their home.

"What do you use that for?" she asked.

"The ground floor, built into the hillside is the spring house," Pansy replied. "That's where we used to keep the milk and butter long ago. But I still do my canning in the upstairs summer kitchen. George pointed out the grove of pine and spruce trees he had planted nearly fifty years back. We decided to take the long way home, going up through the pinewoods to his hilltop field, then walking down the center ridge of the field until it met the road.

"Be careful. Don't step in woodchuck holes and turn an ankle, " he warned us. After this good visit we headed through the pines to the hilltop. There we had the best view ever of the whole of Dunnings Mountain. The field was bordered by a line of wild cherry trees. Five bluebirds flew off as we walked by. They had been eating the ripe wild cherries. Walking through the knee-high thick grass was difficult. We walked carefully, but I still stepped in several woodchuck holes. We came out near the sheep pen.

Another good aspect of the Hileman Hollow ramble was that there was no traffic. Besides a very occasional Hileman car, no one else used the road. We walked freely. Speed walking, it took less than 15 minutes from the parsonage to the end of the hollow. The round trip was a little less than a mile and a half. The hollow was pleasant, a balm for our souls, and good for our health. While recovering from my heart attack this was my first longer ramble and it became our daily walk.

Once in late September the whole clan had gathered at George's brother's farm opposite the water trough. They were cutting cabbages on wooden tables and producing gallons of sauerkraut. They wanted us to stop and help and share in this goodness. We couldn't stay for long, as I had a meeting that evening. The whole event was a wonderful reminder of how family and neighbors used to do so many things together, canning, berry picking, making jam, butchering, and making kraut, that healthy green food that got them through the winter.

Springtime was special in the hollow. A little way up the hollow was the home of Nelson and Ellen Sell, members of our congregation. The Sells had a row of marvelous lilac bushes. The small stream running from the Hileman springs flowed through a meadow at the lowest point of their property. In early spring the old weeping willow tree there would turn green as the buds swelled. It was beautiful when its leaves unfurled. Near it was a large and many-branched ancient oak. I had never coveted a tree before, but this one was so magnificent that I more than admired it. I wanted it on my property. Further on, the stream became a marsh on the lower Hileman field. Mallard ducks nested there even through there was no pond nearby. We celebrated the new burst of life as we walked through God's miracle of spring in Hileman Hollow.

One day I received a call from the Lutheran Youth Encounter office in Minneapolis. They asked if Ruth and I would give orientation to the new Rainbow of Promise singing team that was preparing to go to India. We readily agreed, and in a few days eight college kids with joyful hearts and a mission to share their vibrant faith came to be with us for three days. The first evening, a Wednesday, they gave a concert at Christ Church for the youth of the parish and community. They sang good old songs like Ephesians 4:32 and *Lead Me to the Rock That Is Higher Than I* from Psalm 61. They also presented an amusing but meaningful puppet show and led our youth in action songs. Each member of the team introduced him or herself and gave a brief witness. Two stayed in our home and the other six in three other homes.

We had sessions with them about Indian culture and the life and challenges of the Church in India. We discussed the conflict young people in India face between traditional family values, including parent-arranged marriages, and modern ways, including choosing one's own spouse. The girls helped Ruth prepare rice and curry, which we ate with our hands, sitting on mats on the floor, Indian-village style. One afternoon we took the team up Hileman Hollow and returned via the pine forest and high field. They sang as we climbed.

In the morning of the third day I joined them for their prayer and planning session in our church. At their prayer circle we stretched out our arms with our hands meeting in the middle and prayed for a long time. These youngsters were an inspiration to me. Our last afternoon with them was a beautiful fall day. We climbed up Dunnings Mountain, and, on the way we talked to them about Kodaikanal and the school. We knew they were to spend a week leading a retreat at Kodai School. We gave them orientation about that as well, and, on the mountaintop, shared with them our prayers for our church and community.

The following year, after their India and Nepal tour, they visited us again. They showed slides, sang songs in Telugu and Hindi, as well as English, and shared their great experiences.

When the last India missionary, Ruthie Sigmon, was about to retire, my Ruth went back to India for six weeks to pack up or give away the things we had left, to visit, to help Ruthie settle matters of mission articles and furniture, and to see old friends. It was February of 1987. I missed her a lot, and since I felt closer to her when walking, I daily went up Hileman Hollow and wrote her romantic letters. Ruth was kept very busy. She had great meetings with friends, with the women leaders of the church, and was a good help and gave much encouragement to Ruthie. One of my friends, Raja Manoharam, wrote about her visit and said, "She came. She saw. She conquered." Her visit meant so much to her and to all who met her. With frequent letters she shared much of what she did and whom she had seen in Guntur and Kodai. But she did not say anything about missing me or express her feelings, and that was a disappointment to me.

Before Ruth's return, Brenda Marriner, chairperson of the Christ Church Women came and said with a twinkle in her eye, "Pastor Sam, we know Ruth is coming back soon. Don't feel insulted if I make this offer. The women of Christ Church think it would be nice if we could give the house a thorough cleaning before Ruth gets back." I liked the idea, so we set a date. The day before they were to come, however, I looked around and was horrified. "I can't let the women see our house like this!" So I worked for three hours just clearing stuff off the floor, putting things away and straightening up. The next day they came in and did floors, carpets, windows, and dusting, cleaning the entire house spick-and-span. As I returned to the house in the evening several of them said sternly, but with smiles, "Pastor Sam, Ruth doesn't come for two more days. Don't mess the house up before she gets back!"

She was due to arrive after 10 p.m. on Saturday night in Harrisburg. Being unable to find a substitute preacher, I had arranged for our old friends Marge and Clarence Lomperis to meet her and take her to their home in Mannheim. I said I'd be down Sunday afternoon to get Ruth and I had written to Ruth about the arrangement. However, the day before Ruth was to arrive, I repented of that stupid decision, called Lompie and said I'd meet the plane. I completed my preparation for sermon, prayers, and service. Saturday evening I drove to Harrisburg.

When Ruth came through the downstairs gate from the small commuter plane, for some reason I was at the top of the stairs. As she looked around for Marge and Lompie I hollered my Indian hill-tribal yodel. Her face lit up in a thrilled, loving smile that totally uplifted me. Wow! Never mind that she hadn't expressed herself in letters. As we met the look she gave me with shining hazel eyes was an unforgettable, great moment. Ruth was not the romantic type, but her love ran deep and true.

After Sunday dinner Ruth said, "Though I'm sleepy and have jet lag, I need to go for a walk. I haven't had proper exercise for days." By then it was the mid-March. We had a delightful spring walk up Hileman's Hollow, climbed through the pines, and came home by way of the high meadow. We had much to tell each other.

After the walk we made a fire in the upstairs fireplace and just kept talking. I told her, "Ruth, don't take a nap now or you'll nap for hours. Stay up. We'll have a light supper, watch PBS, and then you can go to bed early." The walk, cozy fire, and being in her own bed at home helped Ruth to have the soundest sleep she'd had for years.

Joyce Dunham, Ruth's room mate from Kodai and Central College

*Lily Agnes, our friend from Shade School, Rajahmundry,
visits us in Claysburg*

Our 40th wedding anniversary: Bill and Terry, Russell and Jenna, Sam and Ruth, Chris, Pete and Pam, Hans and Joan, Joseph

Ruth and her brothers with spouses: Sam and Ruth, Jean and Jim, Chuck and Char

CHAPTER 21

RETIREMENT RAMBLES AROUND PENNSDALE, BELLA SYLVA, AND TUCSON

We lived and served in Claysburg for nearly nine years and retired on June 30, 1991. In May the congregation honored me by celebrating my fortieth anniversary of ordination. Ruth had made many secret arrangements, including a slide show of my life set to some of my favorite music. She had sent invitations to college and seminary friends, my interns and, of course, our children and my brothers and sister. We had a great service, at which Bill Slee preached. He had kept all of our annual letters and followed our work in India since 1951. That night we had a magnificent banquet, "roast," and party. How loving and good this congregation was to me!

We had found a three-bedroom ranch house with hardwood floors, fireplace upstairs, and a wood stove in the full basement. It was in Pennsdale near Hughesville, Pennsylvania, in a valley with a good climate, just forty-two miles south of Bella Sylva. We loved the location. Across the road was a beautiful farm with a red farmhouse and barn. A stream, Carpenter's Run, flowed by our back yard. Two edible chestnut trees and three apple trees gave us hope of having our own fruit and nuts. We applied for and received a Pennsylvania State First Home Owner's Mortgage. Yes, besides our share in ancestral Bella Sylva, this would be the first house we had ever owned in our forty-one years of married life.

The day we moved in, our neighbors, Fred and June Harris, came to see us with Muncy Bakery goodies. We were out, so they left a note introducing themselves and inviting us to come to their Methodist Church. What wonderful neighbors they proved to be! They were always available for advice or help. Both were knowledgeable, hospitable, and friendly. Fred gardened the plot right next to us and, although we had our own garden, he kept us supplied with many vegetables, zucchini, corn, large potatoes, and melons. June was an expert at income tax and helped us with our tax forms. (I called her my favorite "taxidermist.") Fred became one of my hunting buddies. Our other neighbors were Paul and Bonnie Beaver. We did lawns together. Paul and I went trout fishing and hunted at Bella Sylva together. We were blessed to have such good neighbors.

We joined the Trinity Evangelical Lutheran Church in Hughesville. I had been driving past this church on the way to Bella Sylva for years, and we knew the pastor, George Doran, and his wife Ruth. We were warmly welcomed. I joined the choir, and occasionally filled in for Pastor George when he was away, and, when needed, taught Sunday School. We felt at home and treasured the good fellowship and love of the church family.

For evening and early morning walks Ruth and I rambled up Hunterstown Road. Going slightly uphill parallel to Carpenter's Run, we passed Bill and Mary Rall's log cabin and several farms. After a mile we came to Griggs Road going left over Carpenter's Run. Sometimes we kept straight on, going as far as we wanted, past a wild pond where kingfishers would hang out. In the spring we would find black raspberries to munch along the way. Occasionally we would go to the left on Griggs Road, up a steep half-mile-long hill. That was a good place for me to have full cardiovascular exercise. Going up the hill fast and nonstop I could double my pulse from 60 to 120. Before a stress test or medical checkup I prepared by climbing this hill.

Sometimes in the spring Ruth and I would leave the road at the bridge and follow the stream for a few hundred yards past patches of skunk cabbage, abundant purple trillium, jack-in-the-pulpits, and marsh marigolds. On these walks we occasionally saw turkeys and deer, and once, a bear.

How good it was to live so close to Bella Sylva! We could commute in an hour and ten minutes. We spent a lot of time there during our first summer of retirement, seeing more of our children than usual. In late September we stayed in Bella Sylva for a few days to enjoy the lake, woods and beauty of the fall leaves.

It had been raining for the past two days. In the stillness of the night from the upstairs bedroom windows we could hear the roar of Mehoopany Falls. The next morning, over a sourdough pancake breakfast cooked on the big, old wood-burning range, we decided to hike there. We knew we could not follow the stream; it would be in spate. I'd never heard the falls roaring so loudly. We made sandwiches and brought along a thermos of tea, but no swimsuits. Today it would be too dangerous to swim.

We started out on the trail going past Kaercher's Lake. Paul Feil and his brother Andrew, sons of Wilhemina Bella Sylva Kaercher Feil, had dammed the outlet to encourage beavers to return to the lake. But the dam leaked badly and, in spite of the rains, it held only a little water. We had perfect fall weather, a cool breeze and very warm and bright sun. The trees were turning to their glorious multicolor fall garments. Blueberry bushes with some leaves turning red but still laden with old blueberries gave us a special scenic feast. Arriving at the high point overlooking Mehoopany Valley, we followed the ridge instead of descending to the stream. Coming to the first small feeder brook flowing into Mehoopany, we decided to follow it up to Ghost Beaver Lake. It took about half an hour to find the lake, the headwaters of that brook. A series of old dams along the stream had all broken through and partly rotted away, leaving only shallow ponds and beautiful meadows with knee-high grass. The uppermost dam had contained the biggest lake. Now this lake was less than one third full. An old partly caved-in beaver house was on the shore. We could look into the center of it through the roof sticks and examine its once underwater entrance, now high and dry. How silent it was! Why did the beavers move? Did they run out of feed? Were they all trapped? Were there other deserted beaver houses on the lower ponds, now surrounded by hardtack and blueberry thickets? We were seeing the beaver equivalent of a ghost town.

We hiked toward the main stream through a beautiful grove of spruce trees high above Mehoopany Falls. We picked out a good campsite for the future and then went toward the roar of the falls. From the north bank of the stream, clinging to some old birches, we had a wonderful view of the waterfall in all its glory. It was full and powerful. The whole basin below the falls, where we normally picnicked with our kids, was flooded.

"Look, there's a raccoon fishing!" Ruth had spotted the raccoon right below us at the southern edge of the flood, digging under rocks and flipping up stones. We saw it catch and eat three crawfish. It was so close! Yet because we were partly screened by trees, and our voices were drowned by the roar of the falls, it was oblivious to our presence. We just watched with delight, then ate our sandwiches and drank hot tea. What fun!

We started on our way home going at a new angle, climbing toward the ridge. A deer trail took us through a wide slope of blueberry bushes loaded with very ripe, tasty berries. We had nothing to put them in so we just grazed until we felt full—like bears packing it in before hibernating. We found a lovely, sunny, grassy spot and it was time for us to hibernate. We lay in the warm grass talking gently about our life together, our children, and the refreshing beauty of Bella Sylva in the fall. We dozed off. There we were again, alone with each other in the Garden of Eden, and surrounded by the beauty of the hardwood forest in fall colors. We shared time rejoicing in our love and the good years and blessings we had. What a delightful ramble!

* * *

One month later, in the third week of October 1991, Ruth and I went on safari in our new Honda to be with Ruth's mother in Tucson. We drove by way of the Carolinas and Florida, visiting our daughter Chris and some missionary friends in North Carolina, and our son Bill and his wife Terry, and George's brother Bob in Leesburg, Florida. We also saw Molly and Alan in Miami, Ruth's brother Jim and his wife Jean in Louisiana, and more missionary friends in Arkansas and Texas. To keep our long journey pleasant we followed careful plans to have walks and exercise each day, picking out a state park where we could have a lunch or tea stop and go for a ramble on one of the trails. Finally after three weeks, we made it to Tucson. Ruth's mother had been living alone there for almost a year since Ruth's father had passed on to eternal life.

Christina and George had loved their retirement home in Tucson. We had fond memories of great visits together. When in college our children had visited them for holidays. One summer Peter stayed in their home and worked at a job they had arranged for him. Chris spent six months studying in University of Arizona, Tucson. Later, while serving at the Navaho Nation hospital in Fort Defiance, Arizona, she went to see them quite often. Hans and Joan took their first child, Joseph, to see them and stayed for a few happy days. While we were in India, Bill represented our family when George and Christina celebrated their 50th wedding anniversary in 1976. We had sent them a cablegram, saying, "We are sending you the same gift we presented to you at your 25th anniversary in Basrah." The gift was Bill, this time 25 years old.

We came to know a number of our parents' church friends and missionaries who had retired there. Their fellow missionaries, the DeJongs, had retired there, and their son Dave with his wife, Mary, had moved there, too. Christina's cousin, Gary Scholten, and his wife Lou lived nearby. With these friends and family members we had many good times—desert picnics, rambles, visits and dinners. By the time Ruth and I came to live with Christina, Carl and Jenny Phelps had both passed away, as had Emily and Spencer Hatch.

In November of 1989, after recovering from my heart attack, Ruth and I had spent a week with her parents. George and I had worked together trimming a tree in their side yard that had many dead and misshapen branches. He insisted on taking his turn going up the ladder and cutting a limb. At age 89 he had seemed to be in good health.

In their backyard were an apricot tree, a night-blooming cereus, a small garden, pots of lettuce and spinach, a pyracantha bush growing all over the sidewall, a good fruitful grapevine, and a mission-fig tree that in season produced abundantly. Christina would preserve and pickle the figs and grapes, and she and dad would share tedious work of curing and preserving the olives from their front-yard tree. When I would see Mr. George standing under the fig tree or beside the grapevine, I recalled that this was the Biblical image of *shalom*. To me George's life and nature were the embodiment of peace. Micah 4:3-4 reads in part:

> And they shall beat their swords into plowshares
> And their spears into pruning hooks
> Nation shall not lift up sword against nation
> Neither shall they learn war any more;
> But they shall sit every man under his vine and under his fig tree
> And none of them shall be afraid (RSV).

* * *

Just a month after our return to Claysburg, George had tripped and fallen, breaking his hip while going for the morning paper. Recovery was not going well. After Christmas we talked to Ruth's mother. George was now home taking therapy, but was getting worse each day. "Ruth, this doesn't sound good," I suggested. "He needs you. I feel you should go right away."

Ruth flew out the next day and was with her dad for six days. She called me each day. One evening her dad said to her, "I never knew there could be so much pain and so little air." The next day he died while she was helping him brush his teeth and comb his hair. That brought us all to Tucson for a simple burial service followed by a most meaningful memorial service at the church. It was January 1990. The day of the burial it snowed several inches; we took it as a sign of blessing upon the ground as it received God's servant, George Gosselink. The snow covered his favorite palm tree.

George had been a father to me also. I had lost my dad in 1946, and since marrying Ruth in 1950, Mr. George had been to me both father and close friend.

Ruth's mother had decided to stay in Tucson for another year. Now, eleven months later, we were back in Tucson to spend the winter with her and to invite her to move the following spring to live with us in Pennsdale. We settled into the small guest bedroom and soon felt quite at home. Her friends immediately began to encourage us to make our retirement home in Tucson. We loved it there, but with our children all back East and Bella Sylva so much a part of our life, we knew that it would never work.

During our six-month stay we had many picnics with Christine's friends, with Ed and Mary DeJong and their girls, and sometimes just the three of us. Winter days were so delightful. Ruth and I would go on a ramble together almost every week, and many of those were in the Sabino Canyon area. First we took the sightseeing bus tour to learn more about the canyon and plant life. Next we walked the six mile round trip along the road. As we learned more about the area we began taking longer hikes.

The Telegraph Trail started at the highest end of the Sabino Canyon road. It followed the contours of the hillside for over four miles and then descended to cross the stream near the beginning of the canyon. We hiked from the visitor's center to the trailhead and climbed further up to the trail. There were still telegraph poles and occasional sections of the old copper wire. From the trail we had many great views of the deep canyon. Far below we could see tourist buses, people hiking and biking, those exploring the stream, and others sunbathing and swimming in some of the deep holes. Each time the trail looped around a ravine or valley between two ridges, the shrubs and trees would change due to the increase of moisture in those drainage areas. In some spots in the shade of great slabs of rock and boulders we would see moss and flowers though it had not rained for a long time. This hike reminded us a bit of Priest's Walk, as it is about the same distance and followed the hillside contours.

The hike was most pleasant. We met only a handful of hikers. We talked about Ruth's Mother—would she be able to leave all her Tucson friends? Could she adjust to this move and a new home at the age of ninety-two? Ruth was greatly concerned about how things would work out, yet was determined to make a home for Mother and care for her for the rest of her life. We stopped for our picnic lunch of sandwiches, iced tea, juice, and water. In this dry desert air we needed lots of liquid. As lunch settled we spent time close together. Several hikers passed by as we sat holding hands. They'd smile and say "hi," or ask, "are we half-way there yet?" The bird life here was much different from that back East. We had our bird book along and made notes about the birds we could identify.

Going back to Christina's place after each ramble, we'd have a full dress tea with Mother pouring, just like old times in Kodai and Basrah. Then we'd tell her about the hike.

Ruth and I took the Telegraph Trail twice. The second time Ruth and I followed a branch trail out by a different way, discovering another trail which ascended a different stream flowing down another valley descending from Mount Lemon. Later in the spring we followed that stream up and greatly enjoyed the wild flowers in that valley—white chicory, mallows, poppies, and blue lupines.

Next on our list was the challenging Esperero (Hope) Trail. Starting at 2850 feet elevation, this trail climbs through the valleys and ridges of Mt. Lemon to the "Window" at 7000 feet. We knew we lacked the stamina or time to climb that high, but were determined to climb as far as we could. We started on a beautiful crisp February morning, making good time. Coming across a giant dead saguaro cactus, I cut several narrow but strong dried ribs of the plant, so we each had a light but sturdy walking stick. We saw varieties of prickly pear, cholla, and what they call beaver-tail cactus. I remember identifying the cactus wren, some hawks, gambol quail, and we saw a few roadrunners. From a higher ridge we had a good view of Tucson. Then, as we climbed the narrow trail traversing a rather steep hillside we noticed horse dung on the path. "Ruth," I said, "this is amazing. How could any rider dare bring a horse up this narrow trail? This is like Zane Grey country!"

Crossing a wash, we came out in a beautiful, narrow, but green flower-filled meadow. Across the way were some cliffs from which a small delicate lace curtain waterfall was flowing. We climbed the steep trail for perhaps half a mile and came to the top of a ridge. We were starting to tire and needed a drink, a snack, and a rest. We enjoyed the accomplishment and the view. Below us we could see a good stream going down Esperero Canyon, and lower down a full waterfall.

"Had enough Ruth, or shall we go further?" I asked.

"I feel O.K., Sam," she replied. "Let's keep going to the big stream." We continued, first through another blossoming meadow, and then we descended steeply to the stream. Finding a pleasant spot for a picnic, we ate our lunch, and then rested.

Ruth and I hiked the return journey, climbing the first steep hill from the stream, the hardest part of the day's hike. After that it was pleasant and gradually downhill most of the way. We had to be careful though. Several times I was so awed by the views and scenery that I failed to watch the path, tripped, and tumbled. "Slow and steady" was a good motto also for downhill rambling. On our high desert rambles we had much to share and always grew closer in heart and mind.

After the "monsoon" caused the desert to blossom abundantly with flowers, especially Western Poppies, we went with Mother and the DeJongs and some friends for a picnic to Picacho Peak, about thirty-five miles northwest of Tucson. We had a beautiful day with them. Millions of poppies painted the desert like the golden streets of heaven. Before our picnic some of us climbed up the mountain for a panoramic golden view. The scene reminded us of Isaiah 35:1-2.

The wilderness and the dry land shall be glad
The desert shall rejoice and blossom;
Like the crocus it shall blossom abundantly
And rejoice with joy and singing (RSV).

That winter we took many rambles. We went to California for ten days to visit the California Gosselink cousins Ruth had not seen since college days. I have never seen her so filled with laughter and happiness. How she enjoyed getting to know her cousins again! Then we visited my cousin, Cynthia, near San Francisco. She took us for a ramble through a monarch butterfly winter sanctuary, and to a redwood grove. Then we visited the sanctuary where elephant seals have their breeding assemblies. The fat, snorting, bellowing alpha male seals were astounding, totally selfish, and hilarious to watch.

Next we spent a day in Yosemite National Park taking a ramble around Mirror Lake Trail in six inches of snow. Along the way we heard and saw seven or eight avalanches. Snow dams on the heights would suddenly give way, releasing huge amounts of snowmelt and making large instant waterfalls down the nearby steep cliffs. When I saw the first one I yelled, "Ruth, look!" But by the time she did it was gone. So we took turns keeping our eyes on the cliffs and were rewarded seeing a number more. Usually, by the time the sound would reach us, the avalanche was over. The huge trees, waterfalls, cliffs, and roaring snowmelts made our day most memorable!

On the way home we visited Grand Canyon National Park for a day. We hiked down the Bright Angel Trail for one and a half miles. Next we visited the Kaibob trail which Bill, Hans, Pete, and I had taken to the Colorado River and Bright Angel Ranch in 1970. The wintery scenes at the Grand Canyon were so special! We stopped to view the canyon from every possible place, as the colors of cliffs and sky kept changing with the sunset's blessing.

When our daughter Chris came to visit in Tucson, at her suggestion we explored a dirt road going into Madera Canyon, then entered a bird sanctuary where we parked and climbed part way up an 8000 feet peak. While descending, we followed deer tracks much of the way and finally saw a deer.

Another day, with Ruth's cousin Dorothy and Dalton McClellan, an old Kodai friend, we climbed a peak near Old Tucson where cowboy movies are made. The climb, the view of Tucson, and the fellowship along the way was very special. Dot was one of Ruth's very special cousins.

The final hike we planned was to Douglas Springs in the Rincon Mountains. From the extension of a Tucson street named Speedway we drove to the trail parking lot. From there we walked a mile on the level through desert scrub forest to the trailhead. Signing in the trail register, we began our climb, following a full flowing stream. We climbed through valleys, across ridges, and past varieties of wildflowers. In one valley we saw six mule deer grazing nearby.

From a higher ridge we spied a party of ten mounted dude-ranch guests taking a horse trail up a nearby valley. We talked about trying that some day. "Yes, Ruth, I should learn to ride and get a couple of horses of my own—it's time to put this old pastor out to horses." Her groan of agony was my reward for a worse-horse pun.

The whole time we climbed we had a clear view of snowcapped Helen's Dome, the highest peak of the Rincons. A few years previously Christina had painted this peak of the Rincon Mountains with mountain ridges descending to a small stand of cedar trees and an old house in the foreground. It was her best painting, and one of the reasons Ruth and I were now hiking this trail together.

We noticed that the trees had been burned and were dead. In July of 1989 a lightning storm had ignited a huge brush fire that burned for days. Now there was beautiful green grass, abundant brittle bush, and many flowers, but still no trees except the black skeletons of the former forest. I picked some wildflowers, giving them to Ruth as I had so often done in the past.

Finally, after climbing from 2800 to 4800 feet, we arrived at Douglas Springs. We had expected to see springs coming out of rock or sand. However, this campground was beside a live, fast-flowing, full stream. After washing up we enjoyed our lunch as we sunned ourselves on the rocks while viewing the snow on the peak. From here on the trail would be more challenging with views more magnificent. We had seen no hikers but noticed there was a tent in the campground. As we were talking, two hikers came down the trail from the peak and crossed the stream toward us looking very tired. They were the tent owners. "Did you climb Helen's Dome?" I asked.

"Yes, we sure did!" one of the hikers said. "But it was tough going. A foot of snow on the peak made it difficult for us to slush our way to the top. Our feet were freezing." Leaving their tent after an early breakfast they had climbed to the top and back by 1 p.m. At our age we decided to be satisfied with their experience.

On our way back we talked about our plans for returning to Pennsdale and what we still had to do to help Mother sell the house, pack, and move. Christina planned to fly to Iowa, spend a month with her sister Mina, and then join us in Pennsdale. With that agenda we sensed that this would be our last Arizona ramble, and so we savored and treasured the walk home together.

Our hikes and rambles during our five months' stay in Tucson and the West gave us much enjoyment and kept us in condition. This gave us confidence that we were in good health and would have many more rambling years together. Little did we realize that this confidence would soon be shattered.

At Pennsdale, our retirment home, with Christina and Aunt Mina

Retired, enjoying Bella Sylva cabin and woods

Ruth and Sam at Bella Sylva picnic place grill

Grandma Ruth

Picnic on Mount Lemon above Tucson

Hiking in the Rincons

Christina serving tea the "proper" way

CHAPTER 22

WALKING THROUGH DIVINE PROVIDENCE—WHERE ALL NATURE SINGS—AND SAVORING HEAVENLY HANA

Ruth's cousin Gary and his wife Lou, who lived in Tucson, had been Mother's greatest help during her year without George. They helped us celebrate when we found a buyer for Mother's house. How hard we had worked for that! Getting the house and grounds ready for showing was quite a challenge. Nature helped by giving good rains that had brought forth a most luxurious bed of marigolds and daisies in the front lawn. There were also roses and jasmine blooming in time for the showing. Gary and Lou assured me that Christina and Ruth would get well at Pennsdale. If two women can share a kitchen amicably that is a good sign. "Chrissy and Ruth work together in the kitchen so well!" they said. "We know they'll be fine together."

Ruth's brothers, Jim and Chuck, came and helped mother make decisions, sort and pack. We found that she had sewed a patch on the back of each rug stating what type it was, and who should receive it. Most of these she gave away before moving. Then we packed her up and off she flew to be with Aunt Mina in Iowa. Ruth and I worked on categories—things for the moving van, items for the Rescue Mission and Salvation Army, and unneeded furniture and equipment to be sold. Then, with the help of a Tucson friend, we "mined" the kitchen. We took out everything, scrubbed the shelves, and gave supplies to friends. Finally, we swept the house "broom clean," and we were soon on the road, taking the long way home to Pennsdale.

We traveled home by way of Colorado, visiting my niece Heidi and her family near Colorado Springs and driving through a section of the snowcapped Shining Mountains. After leaving them we drove past herds of antelope, crossed Kansas, and went through Nebraska, where we spent a day with the Kochers. Shirley Kocher was one of the Wood girls who had been a sister to Molly, and so kind and comforting to her when our mother had died in Kodaikanal. Next, several very joyful days were spent in western Iowa with Ruth's Scholten cousins, aunts, and Christina in Sheldon, Rock Valley, and Boyden.

In Madison, Wisconsin, we met with Kasturi Elizabeth and her family. The Saturday before Easter we had a memorial service for her husband Cheeranjeevi, who had been a professor of History in Andhra Christian College in Guntur. They had been dear friends. This memorial time of thanksgiving, held a year after his death according to Indian custom, was attended by Telugu friends from all over the States, as well as their Wisconsin community friends. Easter morning we worshiped in Telugu at the motel. I preached the sermon in Telegu. More Indian curries and Telugu fellowship were enjoyed. Then we continued on our way home, visiting two missionary families along the way.

We reached Pennsdale two days after Easter, 1992. How good it was to be home after that long safari!

On our first night home I detected a lump on one of Ruth's breasts. What's this? Suddenly all our joy about being home and being in such great health was marred by uncertainty. We were in a new place with no personal doctor. With the help of Pastor Doran and his wife, however, we managed to get an appointment in two days. Ruth's new physician said the lump was only an inverted pimple and would drain in a couple of days. But then, doing a thorough exam, she found a mass in Ruth's abdomen. Then the tests began. If it hadn't been for the false lump in the breast, her illness would not have been known until our scheduled checkup in July.

Within a week Ruth was admitted in Divine Providence Hospital, Williamsport, for serious surgery. During the eight-hour surgery I was alone the entire time. After six hours the verses of the Nunc Dimittus started going through my mind:

Lord, now lettest thou thy servant depart in peace
According to Thy Word
For mine eyes have seen thy salvation
Which thou hast prepared before the face of all people.
Luke 2:29-31 (KJV)

I thought in despair, "I'm going to lose her."

Finally the surgeon came out looking tired, sad and sick, and said, "Ruth has third stage ovarian cancer, and we could not get it all. I'll talk to you tomorrow." Ruth had survived the massive operation, but the news was fearful.

Ruth recovered fairly rapidly from this first operation. By June we were going on walks together again, as her strength returned. We wondered how it was possible for one so healthy, who had never been in the hospital except for the birthing of our four children, to have ovarian cancer? She had always maintained a healthy diet, exercised and walked regularly, often for long distances. She had enjoyed such abundant health over the past six months! How could this happen?

One month after Ruth's operation, her mother Christina came to live with us. We had fixed a room with her Persian rugs and furniture, a sewing cabinet, the rose wood rocker made in Katpadi, India, her favorite easy chair, and her books. This was her home! Christina took over most of the cooking, and at ninety-two years was very active and most eager to help.

In July we went to Bella Sylva and went on some short rambles. Ruth wanted to walk every day. I remember vividly going with her to Kaercher's Lake. "Ruth," I said, "you go ahead and take your time setting the pace." So she did. Every now and then she'd bend down, take a branch off the path and continue. This was my Ruth, business as usual.

"Always leave the path better than you found it," she'd say. When she came to a large branch across the path she turned to me and asked for help. "It's my turn to lead," I said, and I removed the branch. I am sure she did this path clearing unconsciously, but for me it was an epiphany of her nature and character.

Back in Pennsdale, three months after her operation, Ruth began a course of chemotherapy, which she went through pretty well. However, by December, in the area they had not been able to deal with in the first operation, a small tumor near her liver was increasing in size in spite of the chemotherapy. The best option seemed to be surgery again.

Meanwhile, we both had been educated about how difficult it is to have a permanent cure for ovarian cancer, especially when it is so advanced. It's like a forest fire—stamp it out in one place and it flares up from a spark somewhere else. After one frank session with the doctor Ruth wept for a long time. I held her, and we talked about life and eternal life, about God's purposes for us. We also pondered the mystery of disease, especially cancer, and how faith and love sustain us. During this period Ruth had difficulty praying and often felt her prayers and mine did not help. I cannot say that she went through the anger stage, but she did experience a period of great disappointment and doubt. She shared her real thoughts with me in her straightforward way. All I could say was, "Hold on to your faith. God loves you and suffered for you. I love you, and will suffer with you, and will be with you every minute of the way."

In January 1993 there was a second operation by the same surgeon. Peter and our pastor, George Doran, were with me most of the time. The doctors were able to take out the tumor before it invaded the liver, and they explored the whole area of the first operation. This was another long operation—more than eight hours—impeded by adhesions.

A week after the operation Ruth had radioactive phosphorous fluid injected into her abdomen. She was then tilted at many different angles so that the fluid would flush the whole area. The purpose of this painful procedure was to knock out cancer cells that might still be there. Within a few days Ruth developed a serious systemic infection from the injection, and again was admitted to Divine Providence Hospital. The lab messed up her work. She began sinking. An infectious diseases specialist, Dr. Latimer, was called in. A wise and thorough scientist and caring physician, he had led in solving the Legionnaires' disease problem. He personally checked the lab samples, found the lab reports to be in error, and quickly started a different medication that no doubt prolonged Ruth's life.

From all this I found that a patient, to get the proper treatment, needs a strong persistent advocate, one who will ask questions, bug the medical staff, get second opinions, seek advice from other medical personnel (including those in the family like Dr. Jerry and Chris), go to bat for the patient, contact the lab and the dietary department, and insist that concerned doctors reveal the whole truth. I worked long and hard at this. Meanwhile the stress of the systemic infection, massive doses of antibiotics, and all the rest of what she had been going through sent Ruth into severe depression. But her oncologist did not seem to notice. As her advocate I talked it over with the nurses, Jerry, and others. One of the nurses suddenly said, "She is in flattened effect." Ruth would just stare at me, wouldn't talk, answer questions, or show any kind of emotion. Finally I persuaded her doctor she needed some medication for this.

"Yes," he said, "I think she's in depression." Medication for depression didn't seem to have any effect. She wouldn't eat. It looked as if she would not last long.

Sister Carol, assistant to the chaplain, came in every day for prayer, as did a number of our pastor friends. One day Sister Carol just held Ruth's hands for about five minutes, looking into her eyes. Then she asked, "Ruth, what is your favorite Bible verse?" I thought that Ruth would not answer. After all, she wouldn't answer my questions. A minute dragged by. Then Ruth spoke slowly, softly, and clearly.

"We know that all things work together for good for those who love the Lord and are called according to his purpose. Romans 8:28," Ruth recited. Then Ruth gave a little smile. Wow! Sister Carol's love, concern, and her question, helped Ruth to reach way down into her heart's memory for her favorite verse. She came up with the Word that would break her long depression. From that moment she responded, laughed, cried, talked, and got better.

"Thank you Lord," I said, "and thank you Sister Carol!"

The nursing staff at Divine Providence was superb. The nurses included several nuns and several who had been nuns. Their spirit and concern were a great influence on all the staff. They were all part of Ruth's healing and became like family members to us. When Ruth would go in overnight for her monthly two-day chemo treatment she was always cared for by friends. We were thankful for them, for their dedication and superb training and work.

Ruth came home after forty-one days in the hospital. She again recovered and by summertime was almost back to normal. Another course of chemotherapy was begun, which lasted for nearly a year. Ruth began to cook, help with the housework, go for walks around

Pennsdale, and occasionally accompany me to Bella Sylva for short one or two-day visits. She joined the Bible study group at Church every Wednesday morning and made new friends. The task of being the family treasurer became hers again. After she took over the books she referred to me as her "no-account husband." She patiently worked her way through Medicare and ELCA Pension medical insurance reports and claims, becoming quite an expert. I learned to make up daily 'do-it' lists with her. She would identify the things she wanted to do, and the things I might help her with. She wanted and needed to do as much as she could by herself.

Life for us was filled with thanksgiving. Ruth had come through two massive operations and the systemic infection that nearly ended her life. Now she had quality of life once again, and each day was precious.

* * *

Ruth said, "Sam, after we vote tomorrow morning why don't we drive up to Bella Sylva just for the day? I'm feeling much better. Our overnight-stay there last month to see the leaves was so quiet, refreshing, and beautiful. Let's take some apples and see if the deer have been using the path down by the lake. My answer was a simple "yes!" The next morning, November 8, 1994, I picked up two buckets of apples with defects from the boxes where we had stored our Macintosh harvest. After a leisurely breakfast of Bella Sylva blueberry sourdough pancakes and morning-prayer we voted at the Pennsdale Fire Hall, then drove the forty two miles to Bella Sylva.

As we entered our private road below cousin John Schmitthenner's house, the clean air, fragrant with pine and hemlock, lifted our spirits. A glimpse of the lake through the pinewoods gave us a flood of joy and energy. Crossing the lake outlet culvert, we came around the curve by Fritz's woods, and were amazed to see a big coyote standing broadside to us in the middle of the road. For a period when time seemed to stand still the coyote showed no fear. We'd often seen coyotes in Arizona, but this was a first for us at Bella Sylva. We knew they were here, though, and sometimes heard them howling at night. Two winters before, I had shot a buck down by the lake outlet. Several days later we saw signs in the snow that a coyote had been there, feeding on the viscera. To actually see one so close for so long a time was a great thrill!

"Sam," Ruth said, "you go ahead, open the house and get water. I'm going down to the lake alone. I'll be really quiet." I unlocked the house, opened the doors to air it out, lit the stove, and went down to the springhouse for two buckets of water. As I approached the spring three ruffed grouse blasted off into the air.

"Ah, too bad Ruth couldn't hear and see that," I thought. Meanwhile as Ruth entered the spruce stand bordering the lake, a large covey of ruffed grouse flew off the ground right in front of her with an explosive booming of wing beats that often startles and give the unwary an adrenaline jolt. As Ruth came to the lake and went out on the dock, a nearby flock of wood ducks took off with their peculiar sound, like the squealing of an old rusty pump. Ruth came back to our already warm kitchen with excitement and happiness to tell me what she had seen and heard. Then while eating our soup, bread, and cheese lunch, Ruth said, "What's that moving through the woods?" Looking toward the outhouse, we saw a turkey tom coming down the path. It checked out our house, went down to look over the spring, circled our house again, and then headed up to cousin Keith's log cabin. By the time the tom had left we had to reheat our soup.

After a gentle togetherness nap Ruth and I enjoyed a cup of tea, then I took a bucket of apples and we went down to check out the path going part way round the lake. Deer tracks, scraping, and droppings were everywhere. I scattered the apples along the trail. We noticed down near our favorite two pine trees that the beaver had been active. They had chewed all the bark off the trunk and roots of the last cucumber tree on the mountain. That mighty tree had fallen years ago, during Hurricane Hazel. A branch had grown up near the base of the trunk that was now thirty feet high, a new tree.

We walked to the dock by way of the 'deer' spring and through the spruces, passing the place where otters liked to hang out. On the bank beside the lake were piles of fish scales and otter droppings. The otters would catch fish and swim here, jump up on the bank to eat, and then do their business.

We rowed about the lake in the warm afternoon sun, crossing through the "floating islands" to explore the far end of the swamp. Dirt, mud, and grass had accumulated on some old fallen and rotting hemlock logs over the past 100 years. This has created spongy islands where various sedges, shrubs, and plants grow. This particular spot had the last surviving pitcher plants on our lake, and several sundew plants. Pitcher plants and sundews are carnivorous plants. Attracted to the fragrant fluid in the rose and green colored pitchers of the pitcher plant, insects fall in and are digested. Insects stick to the sundew's tentacle-like sticky leaves, providing the plants with nourishment. Next we explored the three to four-foot deep channel the beavers had dug along the bottom of the lake, from the beaver house entrance to the shore and up into the swamp. It was more than seventy feet in length. Beavers do this so that they can drag and float larger logs from their cutting grounds right to the beaver house without the obstruction of old tree trunks, branches, and rocks.

As we rounded the beaver house, I heard a sound behind me like an animal clearing its throat, "Kghaah, kghaah." Ruth pointed with delight, saying, "Look, it's an otter!" Then we heard and saw another otter just thirty feet off to the side of the first. Both otters were standing straight up treading water with their hind paws, with their chests, shoulders, paws, and heads clearly visible. They seemed to be curious and hung around us for quite a while. This was Ruth's first sighting of otters.

Soon after that we noticed some deer moving through the blueberry bushes beyond the beaver house. We rowed quietly at an angle in the direction they were going, very gradually drawing closer and silently watched them as they grazed one third of the way around the lake—six doe and one big buck. The stag came toward us to drink at the lake, so we could see his impressive sweeping horns. It had only four points, but a great wide rack.

After checking out the swimming place and beaver dam, we headed back to our dock and viewed the sunset from the love seat Wendy and Steve had built for Wendy's parents, my brother Jerry and his wife Shurlee, to enjoy. The rich coloring of the sunset, contrasted with the pines and hemlocks around the lake and reflected in the still water, made this the most beautiful time of the day. We sang together a favorite song from Kodai days:

> This is my Father's world.
> And to my list'ning ears
> All nature sings and round me rings
> The music of the spheres.

As I reflected on the sunset of Ruth's life, I realized that in spite of her suffering and constant struggle with cancer, this was the most beautiful time of our life and love together. During this sunset time we could see colors of life not usually visible. We drew closer together than ever before, and our relationship grew to be more inspiring and peaceful. At this sunset time we shared all our thoughts and could discuss the deepest matters of life. Yes, this was the time of rich coloring between Ruth's full life of love and grace and her gentle slipping away from this world to be born into heaven, where she would know perfect love and be fulfilled in a place more beautiful even than Bella Sylva. Even as the sun sets in glory, we know it continues to exist, touching the rest of the world with life. We know it will rise again. Even so, I knew that Ruth's life would continue and that she would rise again to life in the joy and presence of our Lord.

We put the old aluminum boat up on the dock, turned it upside down, and took the oars up to the tool room. We had high tea, Gosselink style, with bread, cheese, and jam. Then as we headed for home on the "mud road," a bear crossed the road in our lights. That completed Bella Sylva's *most generous day* in which nature sang for us showing us a coyote, grouse, wood duck, turkey, otter, deer, and bear. All this besides the beauty of the lake, forest, and sunset! On the way home we had dinner at Hotel-Motel Laporte, where we had hosted Pete and Pam's pre-wedding dinner over Columbus Day in 1981. The Lord had given us so much happiness. That night as we prayed, we thanked him for sharing with us so much of his love and the beauty of his creation on this special day.

* * *

Aunt Rebecca Eyster, resident of Hana on the island of Maui was soon going to be ninety-four years old. Two years previously, when I visited Hana with my brother Jerry, we had enjoyed her company so much! She said as we left, "Now don't come to my funeral, because I won't be there. Death (she used the Hawaiian word for death) will not be difficult for one who has lived in heavenly Hana. It will be going from one paradise to another. People in Hana are so gentle and loving, and the sea, mountains, and flowers are all so beautiful. Now, if you can come again, come visit me while I am alive. I'd like that!"

"Ruth, do you feel up to a visit to Aunt Rebecca in Hana?" I asked. Her eyes sparkled!

"Wow, that would be great," she said. "My second course in chemotherapy will be over by the middle of January. I would love that! But I won't be able to hike much with this swollen right leg. We'll have to ask the doctor if I can go."

Her oncologist, Dr. Ed Wyshock, was most supportive. "Go for it Ruth. You need this. We'll schedule a checkup one week before you are to go." So we made our plans for a ten-day trip, January 31 to February 9, 1995, and reserved a suite with a kitchen at Hana Kai, where we had stayed in 1988.

On the flight to Hawaii Ruth wore a facemask for protection against infection, because her white blood cell count was so very low. Dr. Wyshock had given her a shot of Nupygen and had shown me how to give the daily injection. This brought her white blood cell count up high enough to make the trip.

We arrived in Kahului Airport at 6:00 in the evening, and picked up our rental car. Then we went shopping at a supermarket, and then to Maui Seaside, the only motel on the island owned and operated by native Hawaiians. We phoned Rebecca and told her of our arrival. She said, "Aloha, I'm delighted that you have arrived. See me in the morning after ten o'clock."

The next morning we drove the about forty miles to Hana, stopping from time to time at our favorite places. Some of these were views of hidden beaches, waterfalls, an irrigation ditch tunneled through the hill, a garden of various fruit trees and our favorite stand of eucalyptus trees. The very curvy road follows the contour of the hilly coast. Each mile crosses five to ten streams which flow from the high rain forest on the slopes of Mt. Haleakala, the huge extinct volcano that dominates the island. People from the Midwest are terrified by the road, but we Pennsylvanians love it. We arrived at our condo to find flowers and a bunch of bananas arranged by one of Rebecca's friends on the table. Aloha is the spirit of the island and of Rebecca.

Rebecca was a graduate of Wilson College in Chambersburg, Pennsylvania, her hometown. She had a degree in classical studies with a minor in teaching. During the depression she worked for the Federal Emergency Relief Administration as a social worker. She enlisted in the Red Cross during World War II and ended up in Hawaii. There she was asked to be director of the Fernhurst

YWCA, a residence for 80 young single women working for government agencies. For five years she mothered, protected, counseled and was a role model for hundreds of young women, many of whom still continue to keep in touch with her in later years.

While at Fernhurst during the war Rebecca had taken an R and R (rest and relaxation) holiday tour to Hana and stayed at the Hana-Maui Hotel. She was so taken by the beauty of the people and the place that she decided right then to spend the rest of her life in Hana. Before leaving Hana she made inquiries and found that they always needed teachers. Most teachers assigned there sought for a transfer to the "big" island. As soon as the war was over, Rebecca took courses at the University of Hawaii, and then applied for a teaching position. She was assigned to Hana in 1952. Except for occasional summer vacation trips to see her sisters in Pennsylvania, she had been in Hana ever since.

Rebecca laid the ground rules for our visit, "Come to see me every morning at 10:00. Then leave me, for I have my own lunch of blended stuff every noon. You have your lunch at one of the many places around here, then come back and visit at 3:30 because my nap will be over by that time. Then at 6:00 in the evening you go have dinner somewhere and spend the evening as you please. Friday night you must have dinner at the Hana-Maui Hotel. Stay for the entertainment because the staff and their families put on a show of Hawaiian music and dancing that is superb."

We brought Rebecca up-to-date on family news. Then Ruth read to her while I browsed through books about Maui and the old days of cattle ranching. We played tapes of messages from Jerry and Molly, and piano music by Molly.

That afternoon we visited the Hana Museum, right across the road from Rebecca's home. She was one of the founders of the museum and had volunteered hundreds of hours of work there, until two years previously when she had fallen and cracked her hip, and could no longer walk up the hill. We met her best friend, Coila Eade, a beautiful person and superb woodcarver. In the museum there were many kinds of native Hawaiian artifacts and old photos of the sugarcane industry. Coila's carvings were also there. Her late husband, Leslie, a photographer had taken marvelous portraits of Hawaiian people which were also on display. Coila took care of all of Rebecca's bookkeeping, helped her plan, and was her general manager. She told us that Rebecca's health was failing and that her greatest fear was that Rebecca might have to leave Hana if she couldn't manage with her present help. There was no retirement home in Hana. She told us the museum people all loved Rebecca and had asked her to be the keeper of the museum keys. So every evening the key was dropped at her house and every morning at 9:00 picked up from her. "This is how they check on her without her knowing it," she explained.

On one of our evening visits Rebecca told us that all her funeral plans had been arranged. She had a plot in the cemetery close to her beloved Wahanalula Congregational Church, where she had been a faithful serving member. She told us about the congregation and her many Hawaiian friends who worshiped there.

That evening Ruth and I cooked a simple supper and sat on the porch overlooking the moonlit Pacific, listening to the rhythm of gentle waves coming ashore in Hana Bay. We could smell plumeria (frangipani) blossoms. It was very romantic. I began to give Ruth a massage with sesame oil, like I often did at home. She dozed off. About halfway through the massage she woke up and asked, "What's that smell?"

"Nothing," I replied, "it's just sesame oil, the same as I always use in Pennsdale."

"No, Sam," she said. "You bought a new small bottle yesterday at the store. Let me see it." It turned out to be toasted spiced sesame oil for stir-fry cooking. "Oh, great! Now I'll smell like stir-fry for a week." Well, I finished the massage—what to do? Then Ruth took a long bath. We went to bed, snuggled up like stir-fry, giggled for about an hour, and finally fell asleep.

Early in the morning as Ruth still slept, I climbed the hill above the Hana-Maui Hotel up to the cross looking over the village. In a nearby valley I found and picked as many ripe wild guavas as I could carry. They were pretty good, but very seedy. Back in the condo, I cut out the seeds and cooked them with sugar. We had stewed guavas and guava juice for breakfast every morning along with our toast and eggs.

Then we had a happy morning visit with Rebecca. She told us the story of an escapade back in 1919 during her senior year at Chambersburg High. She and her friend, Dorothy Bitner, had walked toward school with roller skates in their bags instead of books. They went out to Route 30 that had just been paved for the first time, and skated ten miles to Caledonia Park. From there they hitched a ride over the mountain to Cashtown. Then they skated nine more miles to Gettysburg, walked out Seminary Ridge (Confederate Avenue) to the place where Pickett and Pettigrew made the famous charge, ate lunch by a cannon, then skated back. In Cashtown a "very interesting and nice man" picked them up and drove them to the top of the South Mountain. He asked them all about their exploit and seemed to be very amused. He also warned them that they were lucky, and said they could have been picked up by some unscrupulous person and *"ravished."*

"Good heavens, we had never thought of that. We were so innocent back then, and the country was innocent," said Becky. They skated home and no one knew the difference. The next day when the Harrisburg newspapers came to town, everyone knew about their great exploit. The "nice" driver had been a reporter for the Harrisburg paper and had written a lead article under the headline, "For *This* We Build New Roads."

That afternoon Ruth and I drove to Waianapanapa State Park and walked to the secluded volcanic black sands beach. We'd been there in 1970, after Bill and Hans had graduated from Kodai. We visited it again in 1981 and 1988. I swam a bit while Ruth soaked up some sunshine. We met a honeymoon couple. The wife talked with Ruth while her husband went spear fishing. Very few people were there. It was peaceful and beautiful.

From there we walked a little distance along the trail that follows the coast to Hana. There are a number of "blow holes" at the beginning of the trail. When high waves pound against the rocky cliff, the sea surges up old hollow lava tubes and is jettisoned high into the air. As we walked, we found several little clefts in the rocky hillside. In niches in the rock wall there were curious bundles of flat stone wrapped in *tei* leaves that have significance to native Hawaiians. On a previous trip we had hiked that rough rocky trail all the way to Hana. The views from the trail were breathtaking as the surf pounded away at the cliffs, sending spray flying higher than the cliff tops. After each wave would recede, waterfalls created by the surf flowed back into the sea.

Each evening we'd report our day's activities to Rebecca. The first time we had seen these places, she had been our guide, the best on the island. She had carefully planned every excursion and picnic, anticipating what we would enjoy the most. She knew much about the island and had countless friends. As we now took very short walks with her, her old students of all ages would greet us. The waitresses in the Hana-Maui Hotel were her former students. In her younger days, when she could get around, she had a circle of bridge-playing friends, including Frayne Utley, mother of commentator Garrick Utley. We enjoyed having tea with Rebecca.

Another day we went to see the restored Congregational church where Charles Lindbergh is buried. A huge spreading banyan tree is in front of the small church. From the ocean viewing side of the church we could look out over the graveyard with its coconut trees, flowering shrubs, crotons and Java plum trees, with the Pacific Ocean in the background. What a beautiful spot! We found Lindbergh's tomb. Nearby were the tombs of Major Pryor and his wife (friends of Lindbergh) and the tombs of the Pryor chimps. Ruth paused by the grave of Lindbergh, her hero. With pride she reminded me that she was born the year he flew across the Atlantic. In a way, visiting this beautiful spot meant more to Ruth than any of the other places. The Lindberghs loved their Hana home. During his final illness Charles chose to return from the New York area to die and be buried on this beautiful island.

One morning in Rebecca's kitchen Ruth found a large box of dried fruit, which Rebecca had received as a Christmas present. Rebecca said, "You take it, I can't eat that stuff anymore. Everything I eat has to be blended, as I can only have liquids." Ruth and I shared a few dates and apricots. Then Ruth remembered how much both Elizabeth and Rebecca had loved dried apricot pie. "I can't bake her a pie, but apricots she will have." Ruth cooked some apricots, blended them, and served ice cream with apricot sauce. Rebecca loved that. Then Ruth boiled and pureed all the dried fruit, making several kinds of sauce. She and Rebecca loved each other very much, and it was a joy to see them sharing time and thoughts in many tender ways.

Friday evening we dined in style at the Hana-Maui Hotel, and for two hours enjoyed the beautiful Hawaiian dancing. Some of the *howli* staff kids danced the hula to perfection with their native Hawaiian friends. The music was delightful. We were sad that Rebecca couldn't join us as she had on previous visits.

Saturday we went to the Seven Pools in the Haleakala National Park which stretches from the volcano peak down through the desert crater and then rain forest to the coast. Ruth felt like walking

so we went down the path past each of the falls until we could see
the last one flowing into the sea. What a pretty sight!

Returning to our apartment from Seven Pools, we stopped at the
Church of St. Mary on the hillside above the road. We stood in the
beautiful sanctuary and worshiped quietly, joyfully thanking God
for the beauty of the earth and for his love. Behind the church was
a mango tree that Rebecca had showed us in 1988, during mango
season. Now the tree blossomed with sweet promise-laden fragrance.

On Sunday we walked to Rebecca's church. She was too weak to
come with us. A guest preacher had a great sermon about *shalom*
and *aloha*. Henry and Marie Kahula, the resident lay ministers, and
Annie Rahl, with her beautiful voice, led the worship. We sang
hymns in English and in Hawaiian. When visitors were introduced
they remembered Ruth and me. I thanked them all for the love and
care they had given Aunt Rebecca through the years, and they
thanked our family for her.

We visited Rebecca for the last time. She and Ruth understood
that it would be a short visit without too much emotion expressed.
We knew we'd never see each other again. I knew that Ruth would
see Rebecca before I would, as she went from *heavenly* Hana to
heaven. "*Aloha! Shalom!* Peace! God be with you 'till we meet
again."

That afternoon we drove to Mt. Haleaka through the village of
Pukalani. The more than twenty-mile *ghat* road ascended to 10,000
feet. We stopped at the Kalahaku overlook. Just as we ascended to
the top of the viewpoint, the slanting sun gave us the treat of a
brockenspecter visible on the cloud rising from below the crater.
Directly behind and above us was a little peak. The shadow of the
whole peak on the cloud was surrounded by a rainbow. Wow, a
brockenspector even in Maui! We had often seen our own shadows
surrounded by a rainbow on the clouds when we viewed brocken-
spectors in Kodai. Here the peak hid our figures, but what a sight!
We then drove to the top of the mountain and from there enjoyed
the crater view and a classic sunset over the Pacific.

We had a good fish dinner at the Maui Seaside. Later, I gave Ruth
a massage, with non-stir-fry lotion, and we talked about our week
with Aunt Rebecca. We also gave thanks that we had been able to
have this ten-day period together without phones, deadlines, or

duties, and with much leisure to share in many small but wonderful experiences.

On the long flight home I looked at my happy, peacefully sleeping beauty. Our Hana ramble was our last flight. Our forty-fifth wedding anniversary would be the next big event for us.

Ruth with grandchildren, Joseph, Davey, and Hillary
in cousin John's ancient jeep

Walking to Hana along the coast of Maui, Hawaii

Aunt Rebecca, queen mother of Hana, Maui

CHAPTER 23

JOYFUL CELEBRATION AND LAST GENTLE RAMBLES

"Our forty-fifth wedding anniversary is coming up on July twelfth," I said. "I'm going to call Chris and arrange for the whole family to be with us to celebrate. Do you think we could have the bash at Bella Sylva?"

"Of course," said Ruth, "where else? All our relatives will be there and we can be reminded of our Bella Sylva honeymoon and all the great times we've had there over the years." Chris made the arrangements. Actually it worked out best for all concerned that we have the reunion over the 4th of July weekend. That would turn out to be providential.

I had prepared our anniversary present months ahead of time. The Quilting Ladies of Clarkstown (near Pennsdale) had begun working on a log cabin-pattern quilt for our queen-size bed. The log squares were done in various shades of blue, and some Calico logs made it look old fashioned and pretty. In each of the larger log squares was a bright red patch representing the fire or hearth of the log cabin. Before the reunion I took it directly to Bella Sylva alone, so that Ruth wouldn't find it.

She always knew where everything was in the house and often inadvertently found the Christmas, birthday, or anniversary presents I had bought for her and put away where I thought they were safely hidden. Sometimes forgetting where I had hidden one, I'd have to ask her where I'd stashed it, and she could always tell me where it was. This anniversary present had to be a real surprise!

Chris did a fantastic job of planning our family reunion and celebration. Ruth's brother Chuck came to stay with Christina in

Pennsdale for the four-day period. He was to bring Mother to Bella Sylva for the day of celebration.

The morning before the day of our anniversary party, Bill and his wife Terry had gone hiking in Ricketts Glen State Park. Terry had slipped and fallen, injuring her back. She was in such terrible pain she couldn't walk. A full-scale rescue operation was launched by a local fire department and park rangers. Chris and I had had to leave Ruth with the others to help in the rescue. Terry was taken to Divine Providence Hospital in Williamsport for X-rays and treatment. Bill, Terry, and I spent the night of July 3rd in Pennsdale and then drove up on the 4th for our celebration. Terry was still in quite a bit of pain but managed to join in our festivities.

All our families and the Bella Sylva neighbors, cousin John Schmitthenner's family, the Kuhls, Adolf Otten, the Conants, the Plessingers, our four children and their families, my brothers, and their children, Chuck and Christina. We had varieties of food at the picnic place as everyone brought something to eat, along with presents. Ruth delighted in talking with everyone.

Then came the picture-taking session with our Bella Sylva home in the background. It was hard to get the grandchildren in the right mood and the dogs to be still, but we managed. We had lots of fun posing in American Gothic type serious poses with garden forks and shovels. What a joy it was for Ruth and me to have so many loved ones take part, and to be surrounded with so much love! Then I took Ruth upstairs with the children following, and there on our bed was the log-cabin quilt, perfect for Bella Sylva.

That evening we spent time boating on the lake. Going near the beaver house, we saw our furry friends swimming; then we enjoyed the sunset. I think both of us sensed that this might be our last anniversary, but our mood was not sad. Rather it was one of thanksgiving for all the Lord had brought us in our married life. It was a time of tranquility and peace.

It was good that we had celebrated on July 4th when we did. A week later, July 11th, at 1 a.m. when Ruth went to the bathroom, I heard her call. Jumping up, I ran to the bathroom to find her fainting and caught her just as she was falling off the seat. She vomited great amounts of blood. I was sure she was gone. Laying her on the bathmat, I put a towel under her head and turned her head so the blood would drain. I could not find a pulse. Then I called 911, gave them our address, and told them "Hurry, my wife is dying."

"Sam, what's going on?" I heard her say softly, as I hung up the phone. "Why am I on the floor?" The sweet sound of her voice overwhelmed me with the great surge of joy, for I really had thought she had died. I said, "Ruth, don't move at all. God is so good; you are alive! Help is on the way." Then I called my neighbor Fred. He came within three minutes. We moved furniture so the medics would have room to maneuver in the hallway. The ambulance came within five minutes, as did an emergency medic, Klein De Wire from Muncy Hospital. Meanwhile I had mopped up the blood with some towels and thrown them down into the basement. As Ruth's blood pressure had dropped, the bleeding had stopped. Within 30 minutes Ruth was in the emergency room. She was conscious and I held her hand and then massaged her cold, cold feet. The medics gave Ruth two units of warmed blood, and then packed her off to ICU.

I stayed with her until 6:00 in the morning, then thought of Ruth's mother, who had slept through all this. She would wonder what on earth had happened when she woke up. I had a prayer of thanksgiving with Ruth, and then told her I was going home to be there when Christina woke up. The nurse was in the room. As I turned to go, Ruth gave me instructions, "Sam, now, to get out those blood stains. First soak the things in cold water, then rinse, and wash in cold water. Just to make sure, in my Better Homes and Gardens Cookbook, page 3, it gives directions on how to take out different stains. Read that first. The book is in the bottom drawer of the cabinet in the kitchen to the right of the door going to the garage."

I was totally amazed! The nurse and I howled with laughter. The nurse said, "Well, I guess there's no brain damage at all." Ruth could go through the worst kind of crisis and as soon as she began recovering get right down to the practical, everyday side of life. What a woman!

When I arrived home I had breakfast with Christina, calmly telling her what had happened. Next, carefully following instructions, I washed out the towels—no stains. Then I went back to spent much of the day with Ruth. The sweetness and wonder of just being together was unimaginably precious. I told her stories and she slept. A gastroenterologist scoped her, found out where an ulcer had caused a small blood vessel to burst, and cauterized it. Then Ruth was given more blood. She recovered rapidly.

By the next morning Ruth looked more like her old self. As we talked, we realized it was July 12, the actual day of our wedding forty-five years earlier. We shared memories of our wedding and honeymoon, and were delighted to still be together. So our hospital anniversary was actually a rather private, joyful celebration of how precious life is, but the food was not special.

Ruth was finished with chemotherapy for good, but the doctor wanted her to have radiation. We agreed to a course of radiation with hope that the only tumor showing could be destroyed. Ruth didn't seem to mind the therapy or have any severe reactions. But ultimately it did not accomplish the desired objective and only weakened all her innards. As a result, Ruth was subsequently in the hospital frequently with blockages and general bowel problems.

Early in November we decided to go to Bella Sylva for a couple of days. I asked my hunting buddy Dick Harner to help for one day to make ready the cabin for hunting season. Ruth looked forward to this. So Ruth's last visit to Bella Sylva with me was November 6 and 7, the Monday and Tuesday after All Saint's Sunday. She wrote about that visit and the 4th of July wedding anniversary in our Bella Sylva journal.

Dick and I first cleaned each stovepipe and then lit the stoves. We checked out our hunting stands, moved several beds and mattresses into the middle room, and split wood for the stoves. It was cold and crisp, but we stayed warm with beech wood in the kitchen stove, cherry wood fires in the middle room stove, and a kerosene heater in the dining room. Warm air flowed up the steps to heat our bedroom as well.

Ruth didn't have much energy but did want to go to the lake. After lunch and a nap we put on jackets and we went fishing in the boat with Dick and caught a few perch. After returning to the cabin, Dick had to go home.

We had fresh perch for supper, and then Ruth and I walked to the lake again, sat on the love seat, and watched the stars, always extra brilliant at Bella Sylva. Ruth reminded me of that late-fall night several years previously when we had seen the Northern Lights in all their glory. I set out nightlines for catfish. We then returned to our toasty warm living room and finally to the cozy log cabin-quilted bed. As I did every night, I held Ruth close for our evening prayer, "God bless this good woman, put your hand of healing upon her. Give her comfort, peace, and healing. Thank you for being with us and for your love. Amen."

I got up early and harvested two catfish on the nightline. We had fish and toast for breakfast, Ruth's favorite. Ruth wrote in the Bella Sylva journal, "This morning we saw a beautiful six-point buck right by the house. Now it is raining and Sam is doing a few chores, wood, dishes, etc., before we leave. He also treated the outhouse. Try to write up your visits in this journal. It has been somewhat neglected, except by Molly."

Just before leaving we went down to get the rest of the fishing poles and saw a whole flock of migrating geese on one of the floating islands of the lake. Then we paused to say goodbye to Bella Sylva. It was especially hard for Ruth to leave. This was a place where she had always felt at peace and in harmony with the world, with the Creator of all beauty, and with our family and neighbors.

Ruth's two favorite places had always been Kodai and Bella Sylva, and so they are to me.

Our 45th wedding anniversary at Bella Sylva

Bella Sylva American Gothic

My, how our children have grown and grown up

CHAPTER 24

THE STORY OF RUTH WHO WOULD NOT LEAVE US

For many months one of Ruth's kidneys had not been not functioning properly. Her left leg did not have proper lymph drainage and had been swollen for some time. Through it all she kept her composure, wrote letters, and tried to do what she could on her do-it list. In late November our daughter Chris decided to leave her job and stay with us as long as we would need her.

Once Chris joined us I had to live with these three generations of strong women. Often in discussions of household matters the three of them would outvote me. One day I said, "Jesus taught, 'No man can serve two masters,' but I have to serve three mistresses." We kept in good humor, enjoying each other's company and support.

From mid-summer of 1995 I had accepted the position of interim pastor at St. Marks Lutheran Church, Williamsport. With me was Reverend Charlie Heaps, retired pastor from Chambersburg. We shared pastoral duties and preaching, and also invited other pastors to preach. I conducted one service a month, visited hospitals, and worked about twenty hours a week, as did Pastor Charlie. I felt I needed this, and Ruth didn't seem to mind. Yet, looking back, I wonder how I could have accepted and stayed with that call.

By the end of November a distressing fistula had developed, involving Ruth's bowel and bladder. By this time she was almost too weak to undergo the necessary surgery. Yet living with the fistula was intolerable. On December 12th surgeons operated to repair her bladder, remove much of the colon, and perform a colostomy. This took eleven hours. At first she seemed to be recovering well, but then she began to bleed from the bladder and her small intestines. I spent many nights at the hospital, and Chris and I spelled each other. The bladder bleeding cleared up on December 20th. But her bowel bleeding increased. The situation again looked very grim. Ruth had been receiving four units of blood a day. She was on morphine but in deep pain, and hardly knew what was going on. Nurses we had known for the past three years came around to comfort me, talking and looking at me in a certain way that made it clear they thought she soon would go. "Maybe she'll celebrate Christmas with Jesus," whispered one of her dear nurse friends.

On the evening of December 20th I wrote in my diary, sitting by her bed while she slept:

> Who is this woman who has made my life so good for the past fifty-three years, as my girl of choice from age fourteen and wife since 1950? Various names remind me of her love and faithfulness: *Aneesa* (her Arabic name meaning *the beloved*), *Sateemani* (Telugu, meaning *jewel of a wife*), and *Hepzibah* (Hebrew for *My delight is in her*). Now she lives close to the edge, bleeding and on a morphine pump. Will she be able to go home and spend her last days surrounded by her family and her grieving mother and pass into life eternal from her own home? Or will that great birthday into heaven take place here?"

My devotions included Psalms 37:23-29, Psalms 38, 40, and 94, and 2 Corinthians 4:7-5:8. God's Word and the prayers of our family, friends, staff members, and many church members across the United States, Canada, India, and Great Britain upheld us. Cards of encouragement, phone calls, and the visits of Pastor George and other pastors all gave us hope and strength.

On December 21st permission was asked by her physician to scope her upper gastrointestinal portion—for a person in her condition a very dangerous and possibly fatal procedure. At that time I was reading Isaiah 7, "Ask for a sign —the sign is Emmanuel, God with us." I needed a sign! Ruth Sigmon, a close friend from India, wrote of "making bold decisions." While they scoped Ruth, I wrote, "Oh give thanks to the Lord for He is good, and His mercy endures forever." Tests, safely done, revealed nothing.

Our children rallied round. Bill came from Florida for several days, and Hans from Rochester. Chris, of course, was there each day helping me make decisions and spending time with Christina and Ruth. Ruth's brother came. These visits lifted Ruth's spirits. She knew how deeply she was loved. The visits were also good for Christina, Chris, and me.

On the 23rd Dr. Beltz indicated that the bleeding would probably get worse. Chris, the doctor, and I agreed that we should not go above four units of blood a day. She was in the Lord's hands, "The life of the flesh is in the blood" (Lev. 17:11).

That night I told Ruth, "It's all right to go. We want you to be perfectly healthy and whole again, glorious and fulfilled. You often used to go ahead of me to Kodai or to the States to get our new home ready, remember? It's all right!"

Then I thought, "What is God's plan?" So I tried imagining. "Ruth," I said, "you know how the beavers fix every leak in the Bella Sylva dam. There are hardworking beaver in your blood stream trying to stop this leak so that the lake of your life will be safe once again. We'll pray for the beavers to work." Then I prayed with her saying, "Lord, either way is all right. You know best. 'For to me, to live is Christ, and to die is gain' (Phil. 1:21)."

I repeated these messages and verses, as well as Psalms 23 and 121, John 14:1-6 and the Lord's Prayer, close to her ear many times. Then I'd sing her favorite hymns like *O Love That Will Not Let Me Go*, and ended with *All Praise to Thee My God This Night*, the Tallis' Canon.

When she lived through December 23rd, I was sure she would go on Christmas Eve. Many visited and prayed with us that day. While Hans was there on Christmas Eve, our friend and nearby pastor, Cathy Shuck, came in and gave a short simple prayer, "Come, Lord Jesus!" Ruth was out of it, sleeping soundly. I attended the 11 p.m. service at St. Mark's in Williamsport, hoping she'd live until I got back. During the service of praise I cried as I sang. My friend and co-pastor Charlie Heaps preached in my place that night. He had special prayers and a wonderful sermon. Many of the congregation spoke to me, giving comfort and love, assuring me of their prayers.

Then I hurried back to Ruth's side. The nurse arranged a reclining chair so I could nap as I held Ruth's hand. Twice she sat up struggling with great agitation, then calmed down and lay back, but she never spoke. About 2:30 a.m. we both fell asleep holding hands. Dr. Beltz woke us at 7:30 on Christmas morning. The naso-gastric tube was full of bile, not blood. The bleeding had stopped at

2:30 a.m., as marked by the nurse when she had emptied the drainage container. The Christ Child had once again brought "healing on his wings." Our Christmas gift was Ruth's life. Christmas is a miracle. So was Ruth's life!

Peter, Pam, and Hillary, meanwhile, had been on their way from Blacksburg, Virginia to see Ruth before Christmas, during the time of her dangerous bleeding. By the time they reached Winchester, Virginia, Peter was in agony from complications caused by a previous botched hernia operation. He had to have an emergency operation in Winchester to repair the damage on Christmas Day. Peter has expressed his belief that somehow his own experience of pain and critical situation helped to alleviate his mother's pain and bleeding. I believe the Lord was working in love for both mother and son as the whole world focused on the Mother and Child, Mary and Jesus.

By noon of Christmas Day Ruth was talking, and she asked Chris, who had replaced her exhausted father, "Where's Sam?" On the 26th, her birthday, she was sent back to progressive care. That night during prayers as I sang, *All Praise to Thee My God this Night*, Ruth joined in the singing—what a precious moment!

Being part of Ruth's three miracles has changed me. She had come back from the systemic infection, from the severe bleeding on our 45th anniversary eve, and now from this. Having shared in these wonders I now view life and death differently, and have gained a much sharper sense of what is important. Life was now richer, my faith firmer, and my days more full of joy and praise.

By mid-January Ruth came back home for good. Chris and I promised her we would give her all the nursing care she needed and would never again let her go back for radiation, chemotherapy or another operation. Caring for her included emptying and cleaning her colostomy, keeping up her fluids, giving pain medication when she needed it, and making her as comfortable as possible.

During this time Ruth prepared me for life without her. She handed over to me the Bella Sylva account books and the family finances. She wrote a beautiful newsletter and helped me put notes on the copies we mailed to nearly 300 friends and family. Then she taught me how to cook some of my favorite dishes. She'd enjoy coming to sit in an easy chair in the dining room to guide me through recipes and the steps of preparing certain favorite dishes. Together we reviewed the cookbook she had edited with Jean

Reble with the improvements she had written in the margins. Our kitchen sharing was fun.

We put a waffle foam mattress under her side of the double bed. I joked about our split-level sleeping arrangement. During those last months she wanted me by her side at night. We were thankful she never needed a hospital bed. At night I was always there beside her whenever she needed me. For care of the colostomy, going to the bathroom and medication, Chris, the professional, was the day nurse, and I the night nurse. Ruth kept an Indian dining room brass bell to summon us when needed. I would answer, "Yes, coming Madame," as had our cook in India.

Many friends came for visits to encourage Christina and to be with Ruth: her brothers, Chuck and Jim, cousins from Iowa, fellow missionaries, people from Hughesville, our Pastor George Doran and Pastor Cathy, our children, and grandchildren. Days passed gently, and were filled with love. Florence and Rajamanoharam, our best friends from Guntur days, drove down from Worcester, Massachusetts, where they were had been visiting their daughter. Their whole family came, bringing dishes and taking over the kitchen. They comforted and upheld us with scripture and most meaningful Telugu and English prayers, showing their faith and love for Ruth. Anne Fichthorn, a missionary friend, came with her friends from her home near Reading, Pennsylvania, and with enthusiasm led us in a service of thanksgiving and hope with hymns, prayers, and Bible readings. These visits brought us comfort, assurance of love, joy, and hope.

CHAPTER 25

RUTH'S WALK INTO GLORY

Ruth began hospice care late in March. One of her hospice nurses had previously been her nurse in Divine Providence. Another, whose child I had baptized, was a member of St. Mark's. The nurses said they would not need to come often because Chris and I were doing everything, but promised they'd come whenever we called. Their concern and ministry was so caring!

Ruth's body began to shut down. She wasn't getting much nourishment from what little was left of her gastrointestinal system. She had lost interest in food. Even feeding her favorite foods that she would ask for became a most frustrating experience. Slowly life was ebbing away. Each night I would put my arms around her and ask for God's blessing, that His will be done in her life. Our prayers and God's presence sustained us. Most of all I asked for God's love to surround us as Ruth walked "through the Valley of the Shadow of Death." His goodness and mercy followed her. During all this time her mind remained focused. We talked a lot, about our children, our life, and eternal life. I told her stories.

"Sam," she said, "tell me stories of Kodai and things we used to do in India ... Tell me stories of Bella Sylva ... Let's share memories about Claysburg." Hearing these things gave her joy.

We discussed funeral and burial arrangements and were completely open with each other.

On the evening of May 27, Memorial Day, Ruth's breathing changed and she no longer tried to talk. Christina, Chris, and I gathered around her, held her hands and touched her head. Together we said the 23rd Psalm, the Creed, and the Lord's Prayer. We prayed, committing her to the Lord as she walked into glory.

Four days later, on the afternoon of June 1, we buried Ruth's mortal remains in our newly acquired family plot at the Bella Sylva Cemetery, on a high hill top looking across to the ridge above our lake. With all of our siblings, nephews, nieces, children, and grandchildren taking part, we placed pine branches in the open grave, lowered the casket by ropes the old-fashioned way, and then placed flowers and evergreen branches, signifying eternal life on the coffin. According to an old German custom, one still faithfully followed by the churches in India, I gently tossed three handfuls of dirt into the grave in the name of the Father, Son, and Holy Spirit. With a sense of great loss seasoned with hope, thanksgiving, and joy, I watched the dirt falling on the flowers and pine branches, the earth mingling with beauty to begin reclaiming the pines, flowers, casket, and Ruth's body, even as the Lord had reclaimed the life of Ruth, giving her the gift of a resurrected body. The others all followed, sharing in this act of farewell and closure. We felt comforted and close together as we laid her body to rest. Now I could picture Ruth going on rambles along the riverbank, lined with fruitful trees of life and healing, with her dad, other family members, and old friends in the most beautiful place of all, heaven.

The day after the family burial service at Bella Sylva Cemetery a stirring memorial service was held in Trinity Lutheran Church in Hughesville on Sunday afternoon, June 2nd. The combined choirs of Trinity and St. Mark's in Williamsport and Clarkstown provided led us in wonderful singing. *Great is Thy Faithfulness, O Love That Will Not Let Me Go, He Will Raise You Up on Eagle's Wings, A Clean Heart*, and, of course, all verses of *For All the Saints* made it a joyful celebration of life. A number of people spoke, witnessing to Ruth's meaningful, peaceful and loving life of ministry. Several of our children also spoke and Bill thanked everyone. Afterward we had a comforting and joyful fellowship dinner.

On her memorial stone a map of India with a cross set in Andhra Pradesh witnesses to where Ruth had served the Lord and his people so faithfully. The symbol of Kodaikanal School, Mt. Perumal, with the lake in the foreground and a eucalyptus tree to the right of her name indicates the place that meant the most to her. Her favorite verse, Romans 8:28, is carved in the stone, "All things work together for good for those who love the Lord who are called according to his purpose." (RSV)

Praise be to God Who is great and good, Who has fulfilled His purpose for His servant, my beloved and my lifelong most faithful friend, Ruth. Thanks be to God for His great gift!

EPILOGUE

MY MEMORIAL PILGRIMAGE TO SHARE GRIEF, HOPE, AND PURPOSE

Several days after Ruth's burial, my daughter Chris offered to help me go through Ruth's things. First, we looked at her clothing, found a friend about her size who gratefully took most of it, and gave the rest to the Rescue Mission. The following day we divided her jewelry between three daughters-in-law and Chris. Finally, we sorted her table linens, lace, and Indian fabrics, making five portions—one for me as Chris suggested. Doing this we were comforted and grateful as we shared joyful memories of holidays, anniversaries and birthdays.

Chris then went through Ruth's files: talks, letters and articles she had written, including a drama for the Women of the Lutheran Church in America to celebrate the Centennial of Dr. Anna Kugler's ministry in Guntur. Chris found Ruth's baby book and a bill for twelve dollars from Holland Michigan Hospital for Ruth's delivery and care, dated December 26, 1927.

Chuck came after a few weeks to help mother Christina pack and move to a home in Rochester, NY to be near him. It was hard saying goodbye because we had been through so much together and had shared a deep love for Ruth for over half a century. My son, Hans, and family lived near Rochester and visited her often, and I came when I could. Christina stayed in Rochester until she passed away at age ninety-eight in 1998.

In mid-July many of our retired and in-service missionary friends attended the Global Mission Event of the Evangelical Lutheran Church in America at Susquehanna University, Selinsgrove, Pennsylvania. I arranged for a special re-union luncheon at which time we shared memories of Ruth and experienced most comforting and joyful fellowship.

Later that summer I joined my Kodai classmate Elinor Potee Nichols and Joyce DeBruin Dunham (Ruth's college roommate) at Elinor's home near Scituate, Massachusetts. We spent four enjoyable days together sharing Ruth stories, going on long walks, and visiting historic places in and around Boston with Elinor as our guide. I was greatly comforted and encouraged by the caring friendship of these two good friends. Before we parted Joyce invited us to visit her and Jim in Pella, Iowa, in the spring of 1997 at "Tulip Time." We readily accepted.

Meanwhile I helped Chris move to her new home, the Woodburn Hill Farm Community in Southern Maryland. It was good to see her settle in that rustic, beautiful place with good people. Now I was alone.

I went to Bella Sylva to find healing and peace from God's Word, and the calm beauty of the lake, forest, and hills at one of Ruth's favorite places. Alone I hiked to Mehoopany Falls, the Gorge, and walked around the lake, remembering rambles of long ago. I visited the cemetery and planted mint and wild iris at Ruth's grave.

While at Bella Sylva I thought of making a memorial pilgrimage back to India to visit Andhra Pradesh and Kodai and made travel plans.

Next, I went to Barnsville, Ohio, to visit brother Jerry and his wife, Shurlee. She had been struggling with a re-occurrence of cancer. She passed away on December 6, just six and a half months after Ruth. The whole extended family gathered at her church near Barnsville, on December 29, 1996, to participate in a most meaningful celebration of her life. What a remarkable wife, mother, friend, artist, and crafts person she was. She, too, was buried in the Bella Sylva Cemetery, close to Ruth's grave.

We had celebrated our family Christmas at Pennsdale, grieving, yet sharing hope, comfort, and love. On December 26, we shared memories of past Christmases and her birthday celebrations.

I said farewell to my sons and their families and after packing up drove to Chris's place. She took me to the airport the next day, and I began my oft-dreamed-of journey to the land of my birth, on January 4, 1997.

I landed in Madras, now called Chennai, (the ancient name of the original Telugu fishing village), to be met by friends with whom I

stayed for several days. On the second evening we visited the Lutheran congregation in Madras for a prayer meeting. To my delight,
even after sixteen years absence my Telugu came back to me like a
flowing stream.

For the next ten weeks I visited all the places where Ruth and I
had lived and worked for the thirty years of our India service, first
going to Guntur, then to Rajahmundry. Then I visited our first-
term home Yeleswaram, and some Agency villages where I had
been the pastor from 1952-1958. At dawn I climbed the cross
crowned hill behind our Yeleswaram house, and prayed there for
the continued ministry of that region. Next I went to Peddapuram,
place of our language study where Hans was born.

In East Godavari Synod, Bishop Kantha Kumar and his wife
Priscilla traveled with me graciously taking care to make transport,
lodging, food, and program arrangements. In other synods the pre-
siding bishop usually accompanied me. Sometimes I was with my
friend Navaneetha Raju, a social worker. What kindness!

Wherever I went old friends and co-workers would come to greet
me, burst into tears. Then at their request would share stories of
our life and ministry together in America, of Ruth's suffering and
hope and passing. I wept with them. Then we would comfort each
other.

I made a point of going to our favorite places: Nagarjunasagar
and the Palnad, where Ruth and I had done flood relief work, Srisailem and Tokapalle. On the way back from Tokapalle, we drove
to Narasaraopet, visited the high school and saw the homes where
we had spent our second term. While driving I had clear views of
Kondaveedu Hills and Kotappa Konda, I remembered rambles we
had with our family and friends.

One day I attended the annual convert's retreat at Vadarevu by
the sea. The guest house there had been badly damaged by a cyclone, but the casuarina grove was beautiful, and the sea most refreshing. During the retreat ten Hindus received holy baptism.
Some of them had waited for years. One whom I baptized was
Paapa, a girl Ruth and I had met on our very last Sunday together
in Andhra Pradesh, in May, 1981, at the ground breaking service
for a new church in the "Hindu" area of her village. Then she was
only 14 years old. Paapa had waited for sixteen years for her par-
ent's permission to receive baptism. What joy we shared! Now she
is a graduate and a social worker.

Returning from Vadarevu by way of Chirala I visited Ruth's friend, Dhanamma, who had lost her husband, my good friend, Pastor Adam. When we had first come to Guntur, he had been our parish pastor and neighbor. Dhanamma's grown-up married daughter with her baby were visiting, too. Dhanamma and I remembered that I had baptized her daughter, Evangeline Moonlight, twenty-four years previously. We shared our thoughts and memories and then prayed together giving thanks to God for our beloved spouses and our families. Of all my visits this was the most deeply moving.

On another occasion our friend Vijayamma, a Bible women's supervisor with whom Ruth had worked, came to me with a request: "Ruth's special friends here in Guntur want to have a meeting, just with you. We don't want pastors or big church people there, just us." On the appointed day, about forty of Ruth's special friends met with me. They told Ruth stories, and I shared events of our life together for the past sixteen years. Vijayamma then stood up and imitated Ruth speaking Telugu, sounding exactly like her as she used Ruth's favorite Telugu words and idioms. We howled with laughter and also wept as we shared that amazing moment. After a good curry and rice meal we ended with a prayer meeting.

That night I wrote in the diary I had begun during my Andhra tour, "What an unforgettable day!" As places and people reminded me of good times Ruth and I had shared, I wrote of these in my diary.

In every town and village I visited, friends requested me to speak at prayer meetings. Each Sunday I preached in Telugu at least three times. From Ash Wednesday, February 12, I was amazed to see daily evening Lenten devotions conducted with full churches. I was called upon to preach almost every day. A joyful but exhausting challenge!

Particularly inspiring were my visits with our large dynamic congregations in Hyderabad, the State capitol, and Vishakhapatnam, India's premier naval base. In both cities the number of Lutheran congregations had tripled since I left in 1981, and magnificent churches had been built by these new growing congregations.

Visiting Bhimavaram was most heart warming. Our old spacious bungalow, (the Bishop's House), had been remodeled as a dormitory to house fifty college women. The great *nidraganerru*, sleeping iron wood tree, that had shaded our upstairs bedroom was still there, as were successive generations of parakeets. I had breakfast with the residents and Mrs. Rayapatti John, housemother. The college girls thanked me for arranging for our old residence to be their dormitory. What a story this would make. "Bishops house filled with college girls!"

In each place, meeting with friends I hadn't seen for sixteen years was healing, and filled me with thankfulness for the abundant life and work Ruth and I had shared together.

The state of the Andhra Evangelical Lutheran Church was a puzzling contradiction. Congregational growth was astounding, new churches were being built, Bible study and evangelism greatly increased. But the church administration was ruined: beset with massive corruption, vicious politics, endless court cases, and betrayal. From my notes I later wrote a paper for friends and the Division for Global Mission of the ELCA called "The Ecstasy and the Agony."

After saying goodbye to my Telugu friends, I journeyed to Kodaikanal, arriving before Palm Sunday. Old friends, Gerry and Rocky Nichol, who had served in Kodai School for many years, welcomed me into their home. Principal Paul Wiebe and the staff accepted me as part of the Kodai International School (KIS) family. I was invited to preach and help with foot washing at the Maundy Thursday evening service. Later I was asked to speak in assemblies and classes, and taught four sessions of "story telling" to the fifth grade.

On Good Friday we had "The Stations of the Cross" service. We started at the Chapel and went to various places in the campus. At each station there was a batik painting depicting the stage of Jesus' passion journey. There we would pause, sing a hymn, listen to scripture, pray and then move on. At one station by the stone steps at Kennedy Hall, as we were singing, it dawned on me that Mother had fallen down these very steps and been mortally injured. Although forty-nine years had passed, I began to weep. I was crying for Ruth, too. What a powerful moment of realizing love and loss.

Easter in Kodaikanal was a powerful, hope-filled, comforting experience. We gathered in the dark outside St. Peter's Church on the ledge overlooking the plains 6,000 feet below. We saw first the lights of Periyakulam Town, then distant dawn spreading color and light from the Bay of Bengal across the plains. As the sun slowly rose up, we welcomed the Day of Resurrection with trumpets and joyful Easter hymns of triumph. The age-old Easter texts and hymns renewed our faith and hope. Singing Easter hymns with tears of joy and hope, my heart was lifted up, and I knew where Ruth was singing in celebration. At the 9 a.m. service at the school chapel, we had a great celebration of music, song, and the Living Word. A number of students were baptized by immersion in the pool in front of the chapel. This grave-like cement-lined pit normally covered with stone slabs, became a baptism pool giving new life on this glorious day!

While in Kodai I walked three miles around the lake every day. After Easter I began walking longer distances. One day I went around Priest's Walk with, a friend. We collected flowers, lemon grass, and thirteen varieties of fern. That night I began writing about my ramble with Ruth around Priest's Walk. The following day I went by myself part way to Vellagavi, as far as Dolphin's Nose. Crossing Pambar Stream and I wanted to follow it through the wild shola down to Snake Falls, but wisely did not try it alone However, my memories of that ramble were renewed, and recorded.

Then I started serious hiking, taking with me a friend, Muniyandi. On one exploration near Green Hut we had a unique view of Vembadi Peak and the whole Gundar drainage basin, and came close to six bison.

Betty Swavely, a member of my class of 1944 had been teaching in Kodai for seven years after retiring as a teacher near Cleveland, Ohio. Her dad and mine had been seminary classmates and best men for each other's weddings. Betty and I spent a lot of time talking together about old times and how best to build up Lutheran support for Kodai School.

Betty arranged a "jeep hike" expedition to Vanderavu with the Nichols, and a number of staff members. Driving three jeeps on the badly rutted road past Berijam Lake we were thrilled to see herds of bison, close to the road, and numbers of jungle fowl. From the road's highest point it starts to descend into Kerala State we hiked to the top of the 8302 Vanderavu ridge. From there, at 8302 feet elevation, we could see the whole Palni Range to the East, and to the West the valleys and some tea estates and a dam in Kerala. On the way home some swam in Berijam Lake, near where our family used to camp. These experiences refreshed my memory and heightened my desire to write of more adventures I had shared with Ruth and our family.

The two most difficult hikes I deliberately saved until the last week to be in the best possible shape. First, I went to Gundar Valley all the way to the falls with Rocky Nichol and Barbara Block. We saw one bison in the wild, lots of animal signs, rock orchids, swam in Gundar Pool, and enjoyed a "mist-ical" experience looking out over the falls.

Finally, I went with Muniyandi to Vellagavi to find out more about their changing deity. That was the last ramble for me in memory of Ruth before returning to the States.

Now that I had finished my Ruth-memorial-journey, I was ready for life to go on. While in India I had been exchanging letters with Barbara Kolumban, an old friend from missionary days in India. Her husband, Steve had died of a heart attack in 1993. Her four children and mine had all studied at Kodai School. Would Ruth want me to continue walking alone? I think not. She certainly would not want all of the "training" she had given me, since tenth grade, for 54 years go to waste!

I said "goodbye" to my Kodai friends thanking them for their many expressions of love and the extraordinary care they had given to me, and promised to return some day.

Barbara and I were engaged soon after my return to America. We set the date for September 7, 1997. I went to Rochester to tell the good news to my Mother-in-law, Christina. She beamed with delight and said, "Wonderful, you know, Sam, you're no good by yourself!"

In June of 1977 I went to Pella, Iowa, to meet with Elinor, Joyce and Jim Dunham in their home at Tulip Time. Each evening as Joyce read from her diaries I took notes. We walked together around the quaint old Dutch town, ate Dutch letters, enjoyed the Tulip Festival, and visited the college and dorm where Ruth and Joyce had roomed together. We ate curry and rice, and talked more about Ruth. With their encouragement and blessing, I was now ready to begin writing "Ramblings with Ruth."

Quiet Waters Publications
P.O. Box 34, Bolivar MO 65613-0034
http://www.quietwaterspub.com
Email: QWP@usa.net

Touched by the African Soul

Compiled by Gloria Cunningham & Lois Okerstrom
A collection of short stories, written by 62 missionary women
who recall their adventuresome years in Tanzania. The stories tell
of personal experiences of the writers and give insight into the culture and Christian faith of the Tanzanian people among whom they
lived and worked.
ISBN 0-9663966-9-3

On Our Way Rejoicing

By Ingrid Trobisch
Ingrid Trobisch, tells the story of what happens when God takes
away the father of ten children. A whole family is called to service
and sent into the world. The story surges with movement, partings
and reunion, sorrows and joys, adventure and romance, shining
courage, and above all, the warm love that knits together a large
Christian family.
ISBN 0-9663966-2-6

Miracle At Sea

By Eleanor Anderson
In 1941, before America was at war with Germany, a German
raider sunk the Egyptian liner Zamzam in the South Atlantic. On
board of the vessel were more than 120 American missionaries,
among them Mrs. Lillian Danielson and her six children. Eleanor,
who was then only nine years old, presents a detailed account of
the family's departure from America, the catastrophe, and the distressing and arduous back to safety.
ISBN 1-931475-05-9

Singing I Go

By Beryl Ramsey Sand

She heard the Spirit's call to serve as a missionary at the age of fifteen. Ten years later, in May of 1944 and in the midst of World War II, Beryl arrived in Africa. She worked as a nurse, as a literacy teacher and she assisted in writing the first Bible teaching material in the Gbaya language. In this book Beryl chronicles her life through her memories and her letters.

ISBN 1-931475-02-4

Daktari Yohana

By John Hult

This book is a compilation of stories, which grew out of the author's four years as a medical missionary to Tanzania from 1957-1961. If you love Africa, you will enjoy this book.

Passport to Borneo

By Adeline Lundquist Hult

In 1951 the author was called as a missionary teacher to work with a Chinese church in Britisch North Borneo. Her experiences of living abroad, the joys, frustrations, and adaptations necessary to cope with life in a multi-cultural colony, are all graphically portrayed.

ISBN 1-931475-03-2

I Loved A Girl

By Walter Trobisch

'Last Friday, I loved a girl—or as you would put it, I committed adultery.' This deeply moving story of a young African couple is Walter Trobisch's first book. It has become a classic with its frank answers to frank questions about sex and love. Its tremendous worldwide success led Walter and Ingrid Trobisch to leave their missionary post in Cameroun and start an international ministry as marriage and family counselors.

ISBN 1-931475-01-6

I Married You

By Walter Trobisch
Set in a large African city, this story covers only four days in the
life of Walter and Ingrid Trobisch. Nothing in this book is fiction.
All the stories have really happened. The people involved are still
living today. The direct, sensitive, and compassionate narrative presents Christian marriage as a dynamic triangle.
ISBN 0-9663966-6-9

The Adventures Of Pumpelhoober

By David Trobisch, illustrated by Eva Bruchmann
"In Austria they call someone who has a lot of bad luck, 'Pum-
pelhoober.' I, too, often have bad luck," Walter and Ingrid
Trobisch's nine year old son David explains his nickname. This
humorous children's book tells the story of the Trobisch family in
Africa from the perspective of a child.
ISBN 0-9663966-4-2

LaVergne, TN USA
11 September 2009
157572LV00003B/4/A